THE JEWS OF THE UNITED STATES

LIBRARY OF JEWISH KNOWLEDGE
Geoffrey Wigoder, General Editor of the Series

The Jews of the United States
What Does Judaism Say About . . . ?
Bible and Civilization
Biblical Archaeology
Kabbalah

The New York Times
Library of Jewish Knowledge

THE JEWS OF THE UNITED STATES

Edited by PRISCILLA FISHMAN
Introduction by ARTHUR HERTZBERG

QUADRANGLE/THE NEW YORK TIMES BOOK CO.

6/27/74

973
F536?

Published in the Western Hemisphere by
QUADRANGLE/THE NEW YORK TIMES BOOK CO.
10 East 53 Street, New York, N.Y. 10022.
Distributed in Canada by Fitzhenry & Whiteside, Ltd., Toronto.

ISBN 0-8129-0350-1
Library of Congress Catalog Card Number 73-77033

Manufactured in the United States of America

PREFACE

The arrival of Jews in America predated the creation of the United States, but their history as a community is to be associated most closely with the development and expansion of the republic.

Although recent research has corrected earlier exaggerated statements regarding the number of persons of Jewish ancestry who accompanied Christopher Columbus on his first voyage of discovery to the New World, it has been established that Columbus' interpreter, Luis de Torres, the first European to set foot on American soil, was a former Jew who had been baptized the day before the expedition set sail. Jews of Spain and Portugal whom the Inquisition had forced to convert, realized the potentialities of the new lands and sought a new life there. They turned first to the Spanish and Portuguese colonies in South America, but in 1654 a small band of refugees from the Inquisition in Brazil sought a home in New Amsterdam (later New York). The early years of settlement of North America saw the sporadic appearance of individual Jews all along the eastern sea coast.

In this new land of expanding frontiers and fluid society, Jewish settlers enjoyed a degree of social freedom and civic emancipation greater than in their countries of origin. 1776 is a date not only in United States history, but also in Jewish history. It marks the first emancipation of the Jew as a matter of public policy. The new states (with few exceptions), unburdened by traditions of oppressive practices toward Jews, accepted the equality of people of all religions, in principle and in fact. The Virginia Bill for Establishing Religious Freedom (1785) was the earliest law in history to grant full equality to all citizens regardless of religion. The Constitution of the United States, ratified in 1789, stipulated that no religious test should be required as qualification for any federal office. Thus, as a by-product of the social and religious history of the United States, with its guarantees of religious freedom and its emphasis on the separation of church and state, American Jewry was assured a legal security unprecedented in Western history.

The American Jewish community was created by three main waves of immigration: the relatively small group of adventurous souls who arrived in colonial times and during the early years of the republic; the several tens of thousands of Jews who fled hunger and revolution in Central Europe in the mid-19th century; and the mass of almost three million, mostly Eastern European, Jews who came in the last two decades of the 19th century and in the years preceding World War I. In addition, smaller immigrations came after both World Wars, and during the Hitler era. Each wave of immigrants encountered a historic and economic reality that influenced its acculturation into its country of adoption. In turn, each wave left an indelible imprint on an expanding, pluralistic society.

The domestic history of the United States was profoundly affected by the mass migration to its shores of Eastern European Jewry. Their arrival created the largest and most diverse Jewish community in history, a community which has grown to number almost one-half of the total Jewish population of the world. Living in sizable concentrations in urban areas, Jews were able to preserve their sense of self-identity and certain patterns of communal organization and religious practices against the assimilatory influences of the general society. At the same time, they came to possess great influence, disproportionate to their numbers, in several areas of cultural and economic life. In New York City, the area of greatest Jewish concentration, this "cultural fall-out" has been highly pervasive.

As a happy accident of history, Judaism and American democracy have found themselves in a complementary relationship. Both civilizations promote (indeed, their existence depends to a substantial degree on) the individual's sense of participation. Thus the Jew in America never felt awkward about his participation in the broad spectrum of American life.

This book is based on comprehensive research in the history of the American Jewish community, conducted by a staff of scholars in various areas of specialization, under the supervision of the Americana Divisional Editor of the *Encyclopaedia Judaica,* Lloyd P. Gartner, Professor of Modern Jewish History at Tel-Aviv University (formerly Associate Professor of History at the City College of New York).

INTRODUCTION

Who is this new man, this American? Is the society created by emigrants to the new Western frontier a recreation, with some inevitable changes, of the world they left behind, or is it indeed a fresh beginning?

Such questions have been asked almost from the very beginning of American history. To this day the answers remain in doubt. Some of the immigrants did come to devise a new heaven and a new earth; others fled hunger or persecution, and they dreamt of recreating their native world on happier shores. Oscar Handlin has said in a by now famous sentence that American history is immigration. To this I would add that the American society which these immigrants have fashioned is an interweaving of their dreams of the utterly new and of their longing for a more loving and generous old.

We are here concerned specifically with the Jewish element in America. Inevitably, even as one is fearful of clichés, two aspects of the history of over three centuries of Jewish presence in America come to mind. One must perforce ask what has the Jewish presence meant as an element in the formation of America as a whole? This question can be cheapened, as indeed it often has, with long lists of Jews, or people of Jewish origin, who "contributed" to various endeavors in America. In a more fundamental version this question has to be raised in at least two ways: what adjustments, if any, of its own image of itself has American society had to make because Jews have been present within it? What specifically Jewish ideals and experiences are present in America today that would be missing if Jews had been absent as a force of some consequence, at least in the last century, in America?

There is a second question, of great significance not only to the understanding of American history or the history of American Jews, but to our very conception of Jewish life worldwide in the twentieth century. Is this American Jewish community different from all other Jewish communities that have existed in the past? Are its relations to the Gentile majority therefore to be conceived in different terms? Is its relationship to its own tradition, and therefore its own continuity, and its sense of its own identity new and unprecedented?

These are not idle questions, to be indulged in for the sake of theory. The American Jewish community is about half the Jewish world population, and the assessment of its future and of the nature of the Jewish energies that it will create, or fail to create, is a matter of most fateful importance, not only for itself, but also for the rest of the world Jewish community. For that matter, it is certainly not unimportant to America as a whole. Clearly, there can be no definitive answers. All that historical description can give us is some more facts on which to base our judgments, but with so many of the facts laid out before us in the pages of this book, it would perhaps be useful to state one view, my own, on the meaning of the experience of the Jews in America.

The most obvious fact about America is that it has no medieval past. The feudal structure was not imported to any great effect into the thirteen colonies founded by English-speaking people. What was brought over was swept away by the American Revolution. This meant that Jews began in America under quite different relationships from those which prevailed for them anywhere else in the world.

Those who came from England and other countries to the American frontier in the colonizing centuries did bring with them a certain exclusion of Jews, and this remained in some of the states even after the American Revolution, into the first decades of the national history of the United States. Nonetheless, the situation on the frontier was radically different on several important levels. Economically, there were no guilds which restricted commerce and excluded Jews from certain pursuits. As a matter of actual fact, none of the colonies, even those that did not allow Jews real civic equality in the early days, excluded Jews from living among them.

A century and a half after the settlement in America began, on the eve of the American Revolution, the Jews numbered about 2,500 in a population approaching three million. This small handful of exotics, led by a few merchants with trade connections which were obviously of social benefit on the frontier, posed no threat to anyone and did not therefore evoke any serious consideration of a "Jewish issue." The religious question that faced the founders of America was to still the warfare among the various Protestant sects, for even Catholics were then a tiny minority. The American constitutional provision about the separation of church and state and the equality of believers before the law was really constructed on the presumption that the various forms of the dominant religion which had been at war with each other in the mother country, would here live and let live. The provisions applied also to Jews and Catholics, in part because reasonable men, some of whom were Deists, wrote the Constitution, and really believed these principles across the board for everybody, but at least in part because Jews were really too insignificant to matter and it was not imagined that they would ever be numerous.

In the formative era of its national life, the seven decades between the founding of the Republic and the Civil War, some tens of thousands of Jews came to the United States, and began a quite rapid economic ascent. Some of the descendants of the older settlers became individually very prominent indeed, and occasionally such a figure as the naval officer Uriah Levy ran into problems which were related to his Jewishness. Nonetheless, American society itself remained very largely open, in the era of expansion westward and the beginnings of industrialization. The Jews, indeed, played an economic role of some consequence as peddlers and then as storekeepers in the Western expansion, and in the spreading of goods and services to the South.

The Jews, however, were not a factor of any central significance in the fashioning of American society in the nineteenth century before the post-Civil War era. They were spectators to the critical battles, and whatever were the gains of freedom in America, these accrued to them precisely because they were not a central issue in American society, or a central force in this period. It was the emancipation of black slaves that was the big trauma of America's nineteenth century. The secondary battle was the relationship between the Protestant majority and a growing Catholic minority, mostly from Ireland. The very fact that as late as the 1870s the overwhelming majority, some 200 of the American synagogues, had turned Reform, and the Reform Judaism of that day was a quite conscious attempt to behave in the mode of respectable Protestantism, was indicative of what Jews were about at that time in America. They accepted the dominant notion that belonging to America meant to behave in the modalities of the dominant Anglo-Saxon images. Left to itself, the American Jewish community of 1840, in the persons of the descendants of those who had been present in America during the 18th century, showed a rate of intermarriage of 40% or more. This meant that the oldest Jewish element was in the process of disappearing as Jews.

The crucial turning of American Jewish history happened after 1881, the year of the great outbreak of pogroms in Russia. This is not to say that East European Jewish immigration did not begin earlier in a serious way. There was already Jewish immigration in the 1870s. In fact, many of the earliest Sephardim, or mid-century German Jews, turned out to be Polish-Russian Jews who had "assimilated" somewhere on their journey to these supposedly more prestigious identities. Nonetheless, the great rush came with the 1880s, and it was part of the great leap of European immigration as a whole to the United States. Between 1865 and 1914 a number approaching thirty million emigrated to the United States. Some ten percent of these were Jews, and it is they who become the visible and transforming presence, for good or for ill, on the American scene. Jews as a force in their own right, as a contending element within American society rather than one trying to adapt and become invisible, are thus less than a century old in the United States.

What did these hundreds of thousands bring with them that was different? Most fundamentally, it was their very foreignness, their very Jewishness. To be sure, they arrived as part of the great peaking of the wave of migration to the United States, and they can thus be conceived as a quite normal part of that migration—but it was not quite so. The reason for the arrival of all the rest was mostly poverty and the hope of greater possibilities in the new land. This was also the reason for the Jewish migration, but there was a crucial difference, the driving force of persecution. In the mind of America itself, precisely because there were protests and reactions throughout this era to attacks on Jews, those Jews who were arriving were not merely new hands for the American economy; they were an element with a particular set of problems which they had come to solve in the United States. There were, indeed, ideological tinges to other waves of immigration to America, for there were liberal and even Socialist elements among the immigrants from Germany in the middle of the nineteenth century, but the largest ideological ferment to be found in any group that came to American shores around the turn of the twentieth century was to be found among the Jews from the Russian empire. The richest Socialist press in America in the early decades of the twentieth century was in Yiddish and the greatest impact of such politics anywhere in the country was in the East Side of New York. The internal impact of this new migration on the American Jewish community was even more pronounced. In a very few years, the religion of the majority of the Jews was no longer American Reform. It was East European Orthodoxy. Their language was no longer German and English, but Yiddish. Their culture no longer presented itself as part of a Western tradition; it was ethnically itself. The Jewish community in America was thus transformed in a few short years from the prime example of successful integration into American norms into the prime example of scandalous otherness. Both America and the Jews thus had to wrestle with the Jewish element for the first time, in any serious way.

The very first and most obvious demand that America made of these new immigrants was that of the "melting pot," i.e., that they transform themselves culturally to conform to the dominant, largely Protestant-Gentile norms, not only in language but also in behavior. The older Jewish settlers indeed cast themselves for the role of teachers through agencies for Americanization that they created. This policy was conceived as the cure for foreignness, and the high road to preparing those masses for full acceptance in America. Such programs in Americanization were not resisted by the new immigrants. They knew that they would have to learn the dominant language and mores in order to make their way, in the most practical terms. Their children, who had been denied easy access to secular education in Russia, went as a matter of course to the public schools and, in remarkable number, to the institutions of higher learning. Before World War I, the children of Jewish immigrants already dominated the student body of the City College of New York. Nonetheless, the notion of almost complete assimilation never did succeed in conquering the East European Jews or even those of their children who left the Jewish community for radical politics. Zionists, Orthodox Jews, Socialists, anarchists and all the rest, in their myriad parties and factions, all proceeded on the assumption that they would have something to say about the America they had found and did not accept it as a given to which they were simply to conform.

Internally, within the Jewish community itself, the battle was joined on many fronts between "uptown," older, more established Jewish settlers, led by such men as Jacob Schiff and Louis Marshall, and the more recent, foreign, "downtown," younger representatives of the "Russian Jews." The split between the two communities was not absolute because such figures as Stephen Wise, Judah Magnes and Louis Brandeis identified with the "Russians," but the overwhelming majority of the followers of Brandeis and the rest were "downtown" Zionists, Socialists and Orthodox Jews, who might be battling each other on East Broadway but were united by certain notions: the Jews were an international community; the very deep ties of American Jews with world Jewry were not merely philanthropic, the concern for less fortunate people, but were emotional, historical and situational. These newest American Jews did think that they themselves were now better situated than any other Jewish community, but they did not imagine for a moment that they were "Americans of the Jewish persuasion." They were also not prepared to define themselves in radical Zionist ideological terms as "exiles in an alien land, waiting to rebuild their own homeland," because this would have called into question a deep American patriotism which was present from the very beginning, their sense that this was the "golden land," the country of fresh beginnings, where the tragedies of Europe had never happened and could not happen.

The public rhetoric about differences among Americans in the first part of the twentieth century was indeed the language of distinction as valid only on the basis of religion. Such language was revived briefly in the 1950s by Will Herberg, when he defined the differences within American suburbia, now involving the adult and successful children of the immigrants, as falling into the religious compartments of "Protestant-Catholic-Jew." Herberg added that America itself did not merely countenance such differences; it actually encouraged religious loyalties as proper differentiations and true American values. The truth, for the Jewish immigrants and their children who had been raised in the re-echo of their own culture and tradition, was other than the Herberg formulation. It was a deep and pervasive sense that American Jews belonged not only to America but also to the world Jewish community, and that these loyalties were not in impossible tension with each other. This sense of oneself validated the right for Jews to apply pressure in America for Jewish objectives, such as the recognition by the international community of the Balfour Declaration and of all the Zionist declarations that followed. It is now an accepted fact of the American and of the American Jewish landscape that the Jewish community lives in particular and uniquely close association with the state of Israel, and that association is a fact not only of the Jewish scene but of the American scene. If this was questioned in some Jewish circles in the 1930s and 1940s, it is no longer seriously challenged anywhere. One of the meanings of American Jewish experience is that between 1882 and the present, American Jews have succeeded in convincing America as a whole that those loyalties and connections which they regard as minimally necessary to the maintenance of what is their own unique character are valid and acceptable.

Anti-Semitism appeared as a serious phenomenon in America with the very arrival of the vast masses of Yiddish-speaking foreigners beginning with the mid-1870s. It was an inevitable concomitant of the sudden presence of this blatantly alien element, and it persisted. In the 1920s Jews were attacked for Bolshevism, on the ground that there were Jews both in the Soviet Union and even in America who were prominent leaders of Communism. More fundamentally, right-wing forces correctly perceived that the American Jewish community then belonged to those elements in society which wanted to bring about social change in order to make possible its own advancement.

The Second World War, and what followed after, made an end of the problem. Intellectually and ideologically, it became completely unrespectable, in the sight of Auschwitz, to be an anti-Semite. The booming post-war economy needed all the skills that were available, especially in such new industries as electronics. If on the frontier in the middle of the nineteenth century the handful of Jews who arrived could peddle in equality, it was now possible for the vast masses in their millions to enter the newer economic mainstream. The great achievement of Roosevelt's New Deal, within which political coalition the Jews had played a significant role, was to create the principle of careers, at least in the public bureaucracies, open to merit, and it was this principle that Jews fought out in many walks of life in the immediate post-war era. In economic terms, the Jews were translated within less than a generation from one of the poorest groups in America to one of the wealthiest, with particular involvement in such public and prestigious roles heretofore largely denied them as academicians, writers, artists and makers of opinion and decisions. Some social anti-Semitism remained, especially among the more traditional elements in the country, but it is, at the present, hardly of any serious consequence.

The most recent tensions involving Jews with other groups have come
not from above, but from below, from blacks, now battling for their
own social and economic advance. Here the Jews are often the group
that blacks encounter as immediately ahead of them in the socio-economic
stepladder, as landlords, shopkeepers, or bureaucrats. More important,
the very concept of a meritocracy, which is congenial to the Jewish notion of how to advance, is less congenial to blacks, at least in this
generation, who largely prefer access to the honorific and rewarding
roles of society according to some approximation of their numbers within the whole society. Though Jews have played, and are still playing,
an outsized role in this particular battle, as the whites most prominently
both pro-black and on the firing line, and there are even those who say
that the American establishment may be tempted to make peace with
black anger by letting the blacks assume the roles of the Jews, this, as
such, does not seem believable. Despite a few genuine anti-Semites among
the radical black leadership, the older alliance of Jews and blacks still
holds to a very large degree. All studies show that blacks are less anti-
Jewish, even at this moment of conflict, than whites on the average,
even at this moment of relatively insignificant anti-Semitism in America.
In the elections of 1972 the Jews were the only white group which joined
with blacks in remaining, in their majority, Democrats.

Most important, however, is the simple brute fact that Jews may
not quite be, even now, of the very essence of America's power structure,
though they are certainly not powerless in America. What might happen
in a large-scale depression, or any other substantial social turmoil brought
on by other causes, is unpredictable, but at the moment, any fair assessment of anti-Semitism in America must conclude that no Jewish group
in history has ever been as uninhibited in its actions and policies by the
threat of Jew-hatred as are American Jews, in all their varieties, at
this moment.

There is, however, a theoretical and historical point worth considering.
The hospitality of early America to Jews, to this handful of Jewish exotics
who came here in the first two centuries of its national life, had something
to do with the kind of Christianity that dominated, especially in New
England, and created the mainstream of the American intellectual
heritage. It was a Biblical kind of Protestantism that took its images
of what was a proper Commonwealth from the legislation of Moses,
and which took Hebrew quite seriously as God's own language. Within

this Hebraizing tradition, Jews belonged, at least as some kind of living link with the Bible itself. If in one aspect of this Protestant tradition it imposed assimilation on immigrants, Jews included, in another it took particular note of Jews as having something rather special to say.

Both as a secular and religious phenomenon, the twentieth century Jewish community has not behaved as the Jewish wing of the Boston Brahmins. The seriously religious among American Jews have transplanted to America institutions such as *yeshivot* and Jewish parochial schools, which are almost literal copies of European models. The thrust of American Jewry as an element on the scene of American society as a whole has been to help break down the older dominant forms, in the name of "cultural pluralism." This means that both the philo-Semitism and the anti-Semitism which descend from the Christian tradition, Protestant version, have been broken and replaced by a new American society within which the Jews operate as a group among groups. The conflicts, even though they sometimes still express themselves in the language of anti-Semitism, are now really to be understood as intergroup battles. This is no doubt ultimately "good for Jews" and for all America, because it takes both angelology and demonology out of the arena. It may also, at a moment of crisis, leave the Jews in the situation where an ill-defined, but ultimately protective, element, their specialness within the Christian tradition, will no longer be present.

In their socio-economic journey of the last generation, the politics of Jews are no longer as self-evident as they were in the 1930s. It was then an axiom, and remained one in the post-war years, that Jews were overwhelmingly part of the New Deal coalition. Even in the post-war decades in the 1950s and the 1960s, as children and grandchildren of the East European immigrants ascended to wealth and power, Jews continued to regard themselves as still sufficiently "outsiders," as still involved in trying to open American society for depressed groups, so that Jews played the major white role in the early stage, the integrationist one, of the Black Revolution. Several elements within the Jewish community are now no longer to be defined within this political outlook. Some of the rich have taken on the social and political conservatism of their peer Gentile group, and hope for a society of minimal social change. What remains of the Jewish lower middle class and poor in the big cities, especially in New York, has become "ethnic" in defense of its own neighborhoods and position against the rising numbers and demands of blacks.

Parts of the Jewish intelligentsia, especially some of the academicians, are now talking of the defense of the position of Jews as they feel threatened by black demands for an increased share of the action on the academic scene. On another level, that of the over-arching Jewish interest in Israel and in the safety of all Jewish communities all over the world, Jews used to find that their friends were liberal, and that the criticisms, the arguments that America should do "what is good for America," were traditionally expected from the men of the right. In recent years there has been some reversal: there is largely increased support for Jewish views and demands in the political, and even the religious, right; the most serious anti-Israel voices today come from some elements of the political and religious left.

In summary definition, the political situation for Jews in America today is that they are now almost as internally divided as any other white group in America, and the Jews have thus, to a considerable degree, "assimilated" to the American political mainstream, at least in domestic affairs, and yet they cannot be categorized, even domestically, as the normal ethnic politics of a self-interest group. In foreign affairs, there are some specific Jewish issues which are by now generally accepted as one of the inevitable concerns of the American mainstream. Jewish politics as a whole today are no longer the politics of automatic belongingness to one of the major elements in the American political spectrum. They are the politics that are made up issue by issue, element by element.

The most confident element, and the most universally shared, on the American Jewish scene is the involvement in Israel. Since the 1967 war this has increased at every level, in geometric proportions. By now, after one-quarter of a century of the existence of the state of Israel, the original structure of the activities on its behalf comes very close to being the basic matrix of the organized Jewish community. The emotions and concerns that this work engenders and the activities which it commands are, in my view, the lineal successors of the older Jewish religion, i.e., the involvement in Israel is the "social gospel" of American Jews, the frequent visits to Israel are their pilgrimages, and the fund-raising events are their communal feasts. In the realm of the education of the young, it has been increasingly agreed in almost all Jewish circles that some time spent in Israel is necessary to their contemporary Jewish commitment. Israel does still depend to a very substantial degree on American Jewish moral and economic support, but the labor for Israel has become the over-arching content of American Jewry, its contemporary verve.

Nonetheless, here too the situation is complicated by counter-themes. Within the American Jewish establishment itself, there are elements which retain a primary orientation on American domestic affairs, and especially on the preservation of American Jewish life as the primary good. There is some current Jewish opinion that American Jewish activity so largely Israel-oriented tends to downgrade the American Jewish community itself. This feeling exists despite the frequent reply that Israel is in itself now perhaps the main preservative of American Jewish distinctiveness. Of even greater concern than these tensions within the in group is the fact that parts of the younger generation, and not only the small handful directly affected by left-wing thinking, are now more interested in such "universal" problems as colonialism, racial justice in American society, or, for that matter, the very personal problems of their own careers, and that many are quite indifferent to all specifically Jewish concerns. This is coupled with a rate of intermarriage among those now getting married which is at the very least of the order of three in ten, and possibly higher. Even the most alive and contemporary element in American Jewish caring, the effort to help build Israel and the allied effort for the emigration of the Jews of the Soviet Union, is not at this moment a guarantee that the majority of the next generation will remain Jewish in any significant way.

By 1973, about one hundred years after the East Europeans began to come to America in significant numbers, and a generation after the murder of European Jewry by Hitler and the creation of the state of Israel, the American Jewish community has reached, or is perhaps even past, a watershed. It has gone as far as is conceivable for any community in the Diaspora in the achievement of nearly absolute freedom and an open society for itself. It has lasted into the third and fourth generation, so that it is now a community of the American-born children of American-born parents, and sometimes even of American-born grandparents. The generation now matured is really the first generation of "American Jews" out of the East European migration of the last century. For them the links to the tradition of their ancestors are tenuous, and the sense of Jewish otherness, of Jewish danger, is very much less, if not minimal, than that which plagued the generations before them.

In every previous situation, including that of the small earlier waves of migrations to the United States within a century, the descendants of the first arrivals were in a hundred years evaporating out of the Jewish community. In Europe, where comparable assimilatory processes were at work in various countries, these were often attacked by anti-Semitism, which forced Jews back into their own community. At this point in American time, one can only ask questions. Is America really proof against the kind of turmoil which turned Jew against Jew back in on themselves? For that matter, does some of the contemporary conversation about "good for Jews or bad for Jews" really mean that there is a turning within, or are those who use these slogans merely using ethnicity because it is fashionable to get exactly where they were going in the first place, i.e., to the making of their personal careers in the larger society? I, for one, sense no upsurge of Jewish cultural and spiritual commitment in those who now talk of the Jewish ethnic interest. The real thrust of this effort, despite its rhetoric, is outward.

More seriously, what will be the content of the inner Jewish experience of the generation that is now adult? In quite pragmatic American fashion, the American Jewish community has been living for a century on the tasks either of its own advance or of helping world Jewry. Will there always be such tasks—and will succeeding generations always adopt them as their own? Can the community live primarily on tasks?

The process of Jewish emancipation which began in Europe came to its fruition in America, in the creation of the only western state within which Jews have been in the last century a major and lasting co-maker of the total society. Jews have helped shape it in many respects into accommodating their own willed uniqueness. The question to be decided in this very generation is whether the achievement is the end of the community, or the foundation for an unprecedented kind of Jewish life. My own best guess is that it is neither. Jewish life in America in the next half century will have about it the not-quiteness of neither the option of large-scale assimilation nor of a renaissance of major Jewish creativity. I suspect that Jews will continue to operate in America as a quite important elite group, but probably one of lessening significance in America as a whole. I wish I heard the clanging cymbals of some Messianic future. What I do hear are the counter-themes of conflict and survival, now lessening, now increasing.

Arthur Hertzberg

CONTENTS

LIST OF ILLUSTRATIONS

2

1

STRIKING ROOTS

COLONIAL AMERICAN JEWRY

DUTCH PERIOD

The arrival of 23 Jews of Dutch origin in the harbor of New Amsterdam early in September 1654 marked the birth of the Jewish community on the North American mainland. Their journey had begun earlier in the year when they left Recife, Brazil, after helping in the unsuccessful defense of the Dutch possession from Portuguese attack. With the reconquest of Brazil by Portugal, the Jews fled the territory which had come under the jurisdiction of the Inquisition.

Although the new arrivals were Dutch subjects, the New Netherland governor, Peter Stuyvesant, and the dominie Johannes Megapolensis tried to refuse them haven. They protested to the Dutch West India Company against the possible settlement of a "deceitful race" who professed an "abominable religion" and whose worship at the "feet of Mammon" would threaten and limit the profit of loyal subjects of the company.

While Stuyvesant's protest was under consideration, other Jews arrived in the spring of 1655. Letters written by the new settlers to their coreligionists in the Dutch West India Company resulted in vigorous intercession by Amsterdam Jewry on their behalf. This pressure plus the imperatives of mercantilism and the need to compete with British traders induced the company to send instructions directing that the newcomers be permitted to live, trade, and travel in New Netherland and, in effect, enjoy the same privileges extended to Jews in the home country. The population of New Amsterdam, on the whole, accepted the Jewish settlers. However, despite the orders of the company, Stuyvesant continued to subject them to numerous and severe restrictions. The right to trade with some areas, to serve in the militia, to own land, and to engage in retail trades such as that of baker, were denied the Jews.

The settlers' response was twofold. The first took the form of a series of petitions addressed to the Dutch West India Company. The company's answers were affirmative, overruling Stuyvesant. Burgher right, the right to conduct retail and wholesale trade in New Amsterdam, was extended to Jews in 1657, and the right to own property was upheld. On the legal front, Asser Levy and Jacob Barsimson (the first Jew in New Amsterdam—he had arrived in August 1654, prior to the main body of settlers) began a successful court action to permit Jews to serve in the militia in lieu of the payment of a special derogatory tax. Thus, primary civil rights were gained within a few years of settlement. Still, the Jews in New Amsterdam were not allowed to hold honorific civic offices. They were permitted to maintain a burial ground, but could not hold public religious services.

Despite the economic and social gains, many of the New Amsterdam settlers were lured by the greater opportunities which beckoned in other parts of the New World, along the Atlantic seaboard and especially in the West Indies. The community dwindled in numbers. Asser Levy was one of the few pioneer Jews who remained and died in New York. A butcher and tanner by trade, Levy carried on his business just outside the city's wall. He later expanded his interests to real estate and commerce, and became a prominent merchant.

ENGLISH PERIOD (1664–1776)

In 1664 the English conquered the province of New Netherland and eliminated the Dutch presence on the North American mainland. Henceforth, New Amsterdam was known as New York. The surrender of the town to the British brought a number of changes to the Jewish settlers. Generally, civil and religious rights were broadened as the Jews struggled to obtain full citizenship. This was particularly important as it applied to commerce.

CITIZENSHIP RIGHTS

The Jew who wished to engage in overseas or wholesale trade had to establish his status. Was he an alien or a citizen? As a citizen, except for some ambiguity with respect to his right to vote or hold office, he was allowed most rights, including that of trade. The regulations facing aliens, however, were clearly set forth in the Trade and Navigation Acts passed between 1650 and 1663. This central body of British law applying to the colonies was intended not only to foster mercantilism, but also to prevent the encroachment upon trade by "Jews, French and other foreigners. . . ." Under these acts, aliens could not engage in British commerce, and flouting of these regulations was subject to severe penalty.

The necessity for some form of citizenship status for Jews was made manifest by the Rabba Couty affair. In November 1671 Couty's ship *Trial* was condemned by the Jamaica Vice-Admiralty Court on the ground that Couty, a Jew, was by definition a foreigner. Couty's successful appeal of the decision to the Council of Trade and Plantations in England was partly based on certificates from Governor Lovelace of New York indicating that Couty had been a free burgher of New York for several years. Thereafter, those Jews who could prove native birth did not need to bother with naturalization proceedings. However, the alien Jews, who were the majority of the Jews in the colonies, had to become citizens if they wished to engage in foreign trade.

In 1740, eager to further intercolonial trade, the British authorities, more liberal than the colonies, passed a naturalization law that conferred no political rights on colonial Jews, but did permit them to carry on trade anywhere in the British Empire. Ownership of property, inheritance rights, and freemanship, which granted the right to engage in retail trade and to practice crafts, were also relatively easy to obtain.

ECONOMIC ACTIVITIES

In 1700 there were, at most, 200 to 300 Jews in the colonies. The stability of Jewish settlement depended on its economic viability. For a variety of reasons, Jewish settlers were heavily involved in overseas trade. International commerce negated somewhat the onerous local controls and requirements and provided a measure of independence and protection. Investments that were varied and scattered were less vulnerable to inspection and control. A transient trader who carried his wealth with him was more difficult to investigate and tax.

Jewish merchants had built-in advantages and special skills. They had a knowledge of the international market and a network of kinsmen-business associates in the Caribbean, Italy, Spain, the Near East, and India. Knowledge of languages—Hebrew, Yiddish, German, Spanish, Portuguese, Dutch—was an additional asset. In commercial correspondence of the period, letters were written in three and sometimes four languages.

Certain markets were Jewish specialties. When, in 1699, Governor Bellomont of New York wanted to appraise a bag of jewels which had been seized from an accused pirate, he "ordered a Jew in town to be present, he understanding Jewells well."

Jews helped develop the country's colonial prosperity, largely as shopkeepers, traders, and merchants. The Trade and Navigation Acts limited colonial trade primarily to the British Empire, so the Jewish merchant exchanged local raw materials—lumber, grain, fish, furs, and whale oil—for English consumer wares, hardware, textiles, and commodities such as rum, wines, spices, tea, and sugar. He also sold American products to the West Indies in exchange for molasses and rum. Jewish traders were among the first to introduce cocoa and chocolate to England, and at times they had a virtual monopoly in the ginger trade. As members of the United Company of Spermaceti Candlers, the first American syndicate to attempt control of production and prices, they are said to have introduced spermaceti candles to the colonies.

The typical Jew of this period lived in tidewater commercial and shipping centers like New York, Newport, Philadelphia, Charleston, Savannah, and Montreal. He was a small shopkeeper, or a merchant or merchant shipper who engaged in retailing, wholesaling, commission sales, importing, and exporting. Some succumbed to the formidable hazards of the precarious American economy and became debtors, ending in jail.

A number of Jewish entrepreneurs were engaged in the slave trade on the North American mainland, participating in the infamous triangular trade which brought slaves from Africa to the West Indies, where they were exchanged for molasses, which was in turn taken to New England and converted to rum for sale in Africa. (Although Jews in Philadelphia and New York City were active in the early abolition movement, Jewish merchants, auctioneers and commission agents in the Southern states continued to buy and sell slaves until the end of the Civil War.)

Jewish settlers in New York and Pennsylvania were active in the fur trade. They rarely dealt directly with the Indians, but were wholesalers supplying goods to the traders who traveled to the army posts and Indian villages. It was an easy shift from fur trading to speculation in land, and Jewish businessmen helped open the new territories west of the Allegheny Mountains to American settlers.

The economic aristocrats among the Jews were the army purveyors who provisioned the British forces on the North American continent. During the frequent wars, Jews also engaged in privateering. Some few individuals were planters, or farmers, and in Georgia, some raised cattle in the pine barrens. Other colonial Jews were artisans, tailors, soapmakers, distillers, tobacconists, saddlers, bakers, and silversmiths.

Myer Myers, who became a freeman in 1746, was a noted silversmith whose ornamental and functional pieces are displayed today in many museums and private collections. A highly skilled and versatile master craftsman, Myers created the first American examples of Jewish ceremonial objects, and alms basins and baptismal bowls for colonial churches. Myers was active in the general community, in Freemasonry, and in the synagogue, serving as president of Congregation Shearith Israel in New York. (A staunch patriot during the American Revolution, he and his family left New York City during the British occupation. He used his skill to smelt down metal household goods and turn them into bullets. Myers returned to New York in 1783, and was a signatory of a letter to Governor George Clinton from the "congregation of Israelites lately returned from exile.")

Few Jews were found in the professions during the colonial period. Dr. Isaac Cohen was Pennsylvania's first physician, practicing in Lancaster in the mid-18th century, and a Dr. Elias Woolin lived in New York City in 1744. There were no Jewish members of the bar, though Jews represented about 10% of the litigants in the various courts. This may reflect both the difficulty of entering the legal profession, and the fact that lawyers were unpopular in the colonies until the period of the Revolutionary War. They were generally held in disrepute and were subject to suspicion as enforcers of inequitable and corrupt laws.

PUBLIC LIFE

During the period of British rule, Jewish merchants were able to hold many positions of public responsibility. Jacob Franks and his son David were provision agents for the Crown during the French and Indian War. In 1731 Rodrigo Pacheco was named colonial agent representing the interests of the colony of New York in the British Parliament. Sampson Simson was a member of the group which received the charter for the Chamber of Commerce in New York in 1770.

A number of Jews were elected to office in New York, generally to the position of constable or assessor, and the Christian oaths necessary for office, voting, and naturalization were often modified or eliminated for the Jewish citizen. It was, however, quite unusual for Jews to hold office in the other colonies—one exception is Moses Lindo who helped develop the important Carolina indigo trade and was named "Surveyor and Inspector-General of Indigo" for the province—and the fact that they did so in New York was an indication of the cosmopolitan nature of the colony and its general acceptance of the Jewish community. Most of the Jewish population in New York lived among non-Jews in mixed neighborhoods; in 1748 the Swedish naturalist Peter Kalm, then residing in New York, wrote that Jews "enjoyed all the privileges common to the other inhabitants of the town or the province."

In contrast, Jews avoided settling in Maryland during the first 150 years after its establishment because of the religious intolerance expressed there. (The first definitely identified Jew in Maryland, Jacob Lumbrozo, was arrested in 1658 under the Toleration Act of 1649, which imposed the death penalty for denial of Christianity; he was saved by an amnesty proclaimed while he was awaiting trial.) The Carolinas, however, welcomed Jews. The *Fundamental Constitution* for the Carolinas, composed by the philosopher John Locke in 1668, expressly stated that the colony was to be open to settlement by "Jews, heathens, and other dissenters," and that "any seven or more persons agreeing in any religion shall constitute a church or profession."

COMMUNITY ORGANIZATION

The average Jewish settler in the colonial towns was devoted to Judaism. The Jewish community (*kehillah*) he established was essentially voluntaristic, with a certain amount of compulsion built into it, especially in matters of dietary laws (*kashrut*). However, discipline was tempered by the desire to keep more negligent fellow-Jews within the framework of the religious community.

The typical colonial congregation had a lay leader (*parnas*), a board (*mahamad* or *junta*), and sometimes a treasurer (*gabbai*). The *kehillah* in New York had first-class (*yeḥidim*) and second-class members. No congregation in North America had a trained rabbi until 1840, but each employed a *ḥazzan* whose task it was to lead the congregation in prayer, a *shoḥet* (ritual slaughterer), and a *shammash* (beadle) charged with daily ritual needs. On occasion, the first two offices and that of *mohel* (ritual circumciser) were combined in one individual.

During the English colonial period, six synagogue communities were established in North America—New York (1706), Savannah (1735), Philadelphia (1742), Charleston (1749), Newport (1763), and Montreal (1768). The Touro Synagogue in Newport is the oldest extant synagogue on the continent and has been declared a national historic site. Congregation Shearith Israel of New York, probably organized in 1706, erected its first synagogue in a small building on Mill Lane—known also as Mud Lane—only in 1729. This event, occurring some 75 years after the original Jewish settlement, was an indication of the community's perma-

Lithograph of the present junction of Pearl and Chatham Streets, New York City, 1861. The letter D indicates the Jewish cemetery.

nence, as well as of the acceptance by English authority of the Jewish economic and social position.

Although education was not a community responsibility, except for the children of the poor, Shearith Israel and other congregations made provisions for their children's schooling, for there were no public schools in the colonies. Religious subjects as well as arithmetic and English were taught by itinerant teachers who were often brought from abroad to serve as *ḥazzan* as well as teacher. Education was largely limited to boys.

A sizable portion of the Jewish community's budget, at least in New York, went for "pious works" and charities. Itinerant Jews arriving from West Indies, Europe, and Palestine were usually received courteously and treated generously. Impoverished members of the congregation were granted loans to tide them over; the sick and dying were provided with medicine, nursing, and physicians; respectable elders who had come upon hard times were pensioned; and the community itself saw to all burials. Permanent cemeteries were established as early as 1678 at Newport, and 1682 at New York.

DEMOGRAPHY

Exact census figures are not easily available, but it appears that from a population of 200 to 300 in 1700, the number of Jewish settlers on the North American continent grew to about 2,500 by 1776. In New York City, the most populous center, Jews represented between 1% and 2% of the total population during most of the 17th and 18th centuries. As a group, the Jews in New York appeared to be slightly more affluent than their neighbors, as reflected in the assessment rolls of the early 18th century. In 1701 Jewish merchants accounted for 12% of those engaged in overseas trade in New York; in 1776, they numbered fewer than 1% of the overseas merchants. This decline indicated not only that they had become rooted, but also that they had found other means of earning a living.

Up to 1720 the majority of colonial Jews were Sephardim, of Spanish-Portuguese derivation. After that year, Ashkenazim, Central- and East-European Jews, predominated. Many of the latter came by way of England, where they had learned some English and had anglicized their names. A certain amount of hostility existed between the two groups.

JEWISH-CHRISTIAN RELATIONS

The number of Jews in the colonies was so small that they were regarded as exotics. Despite the fact that Jews were second-class citizens, physical anti-Jewish violence was very rare. A cemetery was desecrated now and then, "Jew" was a dirty word, and the press nearly always presented a distorted image of Jewish life both in the colonies and abroad.

American Protestants were Bible-oriented and enamored of the Hebrew language, but this love did not extend to contemporary Jews. Rather, they saw the church as the new Israel, and Christians as the new chosen people. Nonetheless, a spirit of tolerance prevailed. In essence, Jews were accepted in the settlements because they were needed. Men, money, and talent were at a premium in that mercantilistic age, and Jews were welcomed as business partners. Wealthy Jews were highly respected and were influential even in political circles.

ASSIMILATION

At one time or another, most Jewish merchants worked closely with Christians, which often led to the formation of firm friendships. Social intimacies frequently resulted in intermarriage. A study of Jewish marriage patterns in America before 1840 has shown that at least one in seven colonial Jews and their immediate descendants married unconverted Christians. After that year, in the fourth and fifth generations of colonial Jewish families, intermarriage was so dominant that most of these families disappeared from the Jewish community. Indeed, by the eve of the American Revolution, the pioneer Jewish citizens of New York City had all but disappeared from the New York scene. Practically every Jew who settled permanently in Connecticut married out of the faith and most of them assimilated completely.

This acculturation to the largely English majority population was the result of neither conscious assimilationist pressure nor ideological choice. Inevitably, so small a Jewish population, numbering fewer women than men, would intermarry, especially in a society almost totally open, at that point, to its handful of Jews.

The Jews identified easily with the larger community into which they were integrated. In 1711 the most prominent Jewish businessmen of New York City, including the *hazzan,* made contributions to help build

Trinity Church. In the days before the Revolution, the Union Society, a charity composed of Jews, Catholics, and Protestants, made provision for the poor of Savannah, Georgia.

The Jews dressed, looked, and acted like their gentile neighbors. Away from the community and its controls, many of the younger generation flouted traditional Jewish observance and dietary laws. A desire for low visibility prompted the *hazzan* Saul Pardo to change his name to its English equivalent, Brown.

The typical American Jew of the mid-18th century was of German origin, a shopkeeper, hardworking, enterprising, frequently uncouth and untutored, but with sufficient learning to keep his books and to write a simple business letter in English. He had brought with him from Europe to America a sense of Jewish community, and despite his absorption in business as he struggled for economic sufficiency, he supported his religious congregation. He seems to have felt that America was home for him, and was beginning to put down roots.

FROM REVOLUTION TO CIVIL WAR

THE REVOLUTIONARY WAR

When the Revolution broke out in 1775, most Jews were Whigs. They had few ties to England and were determined to become first-class citizens. Many of them had accepted the revolutionary propaganda that had already been aired for half a generation, and were fascinated by the "Great Promise" of July 4, 1776, the Declaration of Independence. Quite a number were in the militia—which was compulsory—and some served in the Continental line as soldiers and officers, three attaining relatively high rank. A few Jews were Tories, among them David Franks, who was expelled by the Continental authorities in 1780 for his pro-British sympathies.

Many Jews played military and financial roles in the Revolution. Some Jewish merchants ventured into privateering and blockade-running; but the Jew on "Front Street" was still a shopkeeper somehow or other finding the consumer goods so desperately needed in a non-industrial country whose ports were often blockaded by the British fleet.

notable Jewish rebel was the Polish immigrant, Haym
ardent patriot who, at great personal risk, served as an
nd agent for the American forces while working for the
When discovered, he fled to Philadelphia where he soon became
st known bill-broker in the country. He lent money without
rge to impecunious members of the Continental Congress, among
them James Madison. It was in his capacity as a chief bill-broker to
Robert Morris, the superintendent of finance, that Salomon helped
make funds available for the successful expedition against Cornwallis
which brought the war to an end.

Francis Salvador, the first Jew to represent the people in a legislative
body in America, and possibly the first Jew in the modern world to hold
such public office, was a delegate to the Revolutionary Provincial
Congresses of South Carolina (1775–76), which constituted itself as the
legislature of the newly independent state. When the British attacked
Charleston in 1776, Salvador joined the patriot forces. Shot and scalped
by Tory-led Indians on August 1, 1776, he was the first Jew to give his
life in the struggle for American independence.

CIVIL LIBERTIES

Independence from England did not immediately improve the political
status of the American Jew. In 1787 the Northwest Ordinance guaran-
teed that the Jew would be on the same footing as his fellow citizens in
all new states. The Constitution adopted a year later gave him equality
on the federal level. At the time, this was not a great victory, for most
rights were still resident in the states, and as late as 1820 only seven of
the 13 original states had recognized the Jew in a political sense.

The last significant traces of legal inequality disappeared early in the
19th century. The most significant episode was the public agitation and
debate in the State of Maryland over the disqualification of Jews for
public office, which was finally removed by the "Jew Bill" of 1826. The
deliberations concerned the alleged Christian basis of the state, rather
than a contest between pro-Jewish and anti-Jewish feeling. The states
of North Carolina and New Hampshire retained legal obstacles to
Jewish tenure of public office, but very few Jews resided there. The
prescribed Christian oaths for taking public office appear to have been
a dead letter.

Ultimately, men of talent were appointed or elected town councillors, judges of the lower courts, and members of the state legislatures. The national authorities appointed them marshals and consuls. Outstanding individuals made careers for themselves in the army and navy, though the latter branch of the service was particularly inhospitable to Jewish aspirants.

In general, opportunities were expanded and new fields were opened for American Jews. The first Jew to study law professionally was Moses Levy, who was admitted to the Philadelphia bar in 1778. (Though he was the first Jewish lawyer in the United States, he was not the first Jew to be made a judge. Isaac Miranda, a layman, was appointed deputy judge of the Vice-Admiralty of the Province of Pennsylvania in 1727. Georgia had appointed Jewish justices of the peace in 1766 and 1773.) Gershom Mendes Seixas, one of the 14 ministers who participated at George Washington's first inaugural, served as a trustee of Columbia College from 1784 to 1814.

MORDECAI M. NOAH

Probably the most influential Jew in post-Revolutionary America was Mordecai Manuel Noah. Born in Philadelphia in 1785, he entered public service as consul to Tunis in 1813. He became a member of the Democratic Party and was elected, successively, high sheriff of New York, surveyor of the port, and judge of the Court of Sessions. However, as editor of various newspapers he took an anti-Tammany stance and eventually became a founder of the Whig party.

In addition to his involvement with politics, Noah actively espoused

Foundation stone of Ararat, the proposed Jewish city founded by Mordecai Noah in 1825 near Buffalo, N.Y.

Jewish causes and, long interested in the idea of a Jewish territorial restoration, helped purchase a tract of land for Jewish colonization near Buffalo, New York, which he named Ararat. After the project's failure, Noah turned more strongly to the idea of Palestine as a national home for the Jews.

POST-REVOLUTIONARY EXPANSION

The affluence and expansion that followed national independence brought new economic fields into prominence in the United States. The Jewish citizens in turn adopted new patterns of livelihood. As cotton became "king," Jewish planters increased in number. Retail and whole-sale urban merchants turned away from overseas trade toward the expanding hinterland. Jews became involved in land speculation in the states and territories. Cohen and Isaacs of Richmond, Virginia, employed Daniel Boone to survey their holdings in Kentucky. Jews turned to shipping, garment manufacturing, mining, distilling, banking, insurance, and the stock exchange. Benjamin Seixas and Ephraim Hart were among the founders of the New York Stock Exchange in 1792. Jewish railroad directors prospered in South Carolina, and Jewish bank directors were active in that state, in New York, and in Rhode Island. By 1820 Jews were practicing law and medicine, and were involved in engineering, education, and journalism.

As the American economy burgeoned in the half-century following the Revolution, people skilled in trade, moneylending, the distribution of commodities, and the establishment of wholesale and retail outlets were needed with increasing frequency everywhere in the country. Jews took advantage of the expanding opportunities in a developing America to become well integrated into the country's economic life.

POPULATION GROWTH

The salient development in United States Jewry during the four decades before the Civil War was its growth from a small group estimated at 6,000 in 1826, to an important Jewish community numbering 15,000 in 1840 and 150,000 in 1860. This vast increase was largely due to immigration from German lands. In Bavaria, dozens of small, largely Jewish villages saw most of their inhabitants leave for the United States.

Total Jewish Population of the United States and Canada in 1800: **2,500**

Main centers of Jewish population in the United States, 1800, according to the state borders of today.

There was also emigration from Posen, Bohemia, and Hungary. Immigration attained a peak during the early 1850s, when economic depression and the repressive aftermath of the Continental revolutions of 1848–49 impelled the greatest movement to the prospering American republic.

During those years, Jewish settlement spread across the North American continent. New England did not participate in this growth, and old seacoast Jewish communities like Charleston, Newport, and Norfolk declined. But the Jewish communities of Baltimore and Philadelphia assumed new importance, and dozens of towns in the southern Cotton Belt sheltered small groups of German Jews who traded in cotton and kept general stores.

The most important expansion took place along the route of the Erie Canal which crossed upstate New York after 1825, and on the shores of the Great Lakes. The Jewish population of some major cities such as Albany, Syracuse, Rochester, Buffalo, Cleveland, Chicago, Detroit, and Milwaukee quickly rose into the thousands. On the banks of the Ohio and Mississippi rivers, scores of smaller towns had Jewish settlements. Jews played a prominent role in the commercial and industrial

Main Street of Salt Lake City, Utah, 1869, with the shop of Nicholas Siegfried Ransohoff, one of the early German-Jewish merchants in the West.

development of Cincinnati, Louisville, St. Louis, Minneapolis, and New Orleans, and in the establishment of a continent-wide commercial network.

A striking growth in Jewish population occurred in northern California during and after the Gold Rush of 1849–52. By 1860 some 10,000 Jews lived in the boom city of San Francisco; others were scattered among the mining camps in the Rockies and on the west coast.

PEDDLING

The Jews who came to the United States in early- and mid-19th century turned in large numbers to the one profession universally open to them—peddling. At a time when retail trade outlets outside large cities were few, the peddler was an important functionary of American commerce. Thousands of young men, mostly recent immigrants, trudged the countryside east of the Mississippi River with packs on their backs, successors of the "Yankee peddler." They also became purveyors of nearly all the necessities of gold prospectors in California, and peddled household and dry goods, and small luxuries among the isolated farm-

Julius Meyer, early Nebraska trader, with Indian chiefs.

Sale of *mazzot* in New York shortly after the Civil War. Engraving from *Frank Leslie's Popular Monthly*.

steads in the Middle West and South. Although many had been trained in crafts and trades in Europe, few held to them in the United States but were drawn into the grueling but lucrative business of peddling.

Isaac Mayer Wise, rabbi in Albany, New York from 1846 to 1854 described his community as composed mostly of men who departed on Sunday morning for their peddling routes through the countryside, returning only for the following Sabbath. Among the Cherokee Indians of North Carolina, these peddler-Jews were commonly referred to as "egg-eaters," probably because many of them adhered to the Jewish dietary laws and avoided eating meat of any kind until they returned to their home base on Friday evening in time to observe the Sabbath. The main source of supplies for these peddlers was the large city, but within each area they had "way stations" where they stored small stocks and which they called "home for the Sabbath." Often these way stations turned into permanent homes, as the peddler-on-foot became a peddler-in-a-wagon, then a crossroads shopkeeper and, as the village grew, a large merchant.

SOCIAL STATUS

The overwhelming majority of American Jews in mid-19th century, native and immigrant, were occupied in commerce at its various levels and in skilled crafts; many were tailors and cigar-makers. Very few tilled the soil. The numbers in the professions of the day—medicine, law, teaching, and journalism—were low.

The decades between 1820 and 1860 marked a period of broad freedom and social acceptance for American Jews. The small native bourgeois group readily entered American life and politics in such centers as Charleston, Philadelphia, and New York City. There was very little actual anti-Semitism. Anti-Semitic feelings might be expressed in an attack on Jewish businessmen in the California legislature during a debate on a Sabbath closing law; unpleasantly phrased insistence that the United States was "a Christian country"; or a biased courtroom address by a lawyer against a Jewish adversary. The antagonisms and tensions within the American society were expressed as anti-Catholicism, directed especially at Irish immigrants.

Branches of Protestant churches produced extensive missionary literature, but Jewish conversions to Christianity by such means were negligible. Linked to such proselytizing endeavors were millenarian expressions of faith that the Jews would ultimately be restored to their homeland, and words of sympathy for Jewish efforts, real or rumored, toward that end. If the biblical people of Israel still lay deep in the American mind, the contemporary Jews were, on the whole, not a preoccupation.

CULTURAL ACHIEVEMENTS

Many Jews in the post-Revolutionary period were men of education and culture, at home in the classics, in modern languages and literatures, and devotees of music and poetry. During the first decade of the 19th century, Charleston, South Carolina, with some 500 Jews, was considered the most cultured and wealthiest Jewish community in America. (It began a long decline in importance soon thereafter, and the Civil War left the city and its Jewish population decimated and impoverished.)

Both the North and the South produced a few Jewish playwrights, but aside from several plays, miscellaneous orations, addresses, and literary anthologies, Jews wrote little.

New York produced the first Jewish periodical published in the United States (1823–25), a monthly entitled *The Jew,* which sought to combat missionary influence. The first successful Jewish periodical was Robert Lyon's *The Asmonean* (1848–58). A "family journal of commerce, politics, religion, and literature," it was the prototype of the Anglo-Jewish press in succeeding decades—the privately owned weekly covering local, national, and overseas news, and carrying serialized fiction, feature articles, and editorial comments. *The Asmonean* published debates between Jewish leaders over the necessity of establishing a union of American Jews. Rabbi Samuel Isaac's *Jewish Messenger* became the voice of Orthodox Judaism (1857); its editorial policy called for a union of Jewish charities, and the establishment of a Jewish free school.

In the area of Jewish culture, the contributions of American Jewry were limited to two English translations of Hebrew prayerbooks that appeared in the 1760s, a Hebrew grammar, and post-Revolution collections of sermons and eulogies. More important was the reprinting of a number of apologetic works directed against deists and Christian missionaries.

COMMUNAL DIVERSITY

The beginning of religious diversity, and cultural and communal organization beyond the synagogue framework became apparent about the middle of the 19th century. Among the immigrants were a considerable number of persons versed in Judaism; many teachers from Europe assumed the rabbinic title and became spiritual heads of congregations. The apparatus of the synagogue was modified and enlarged. The status of the *hazzan* was raised to that of the Christian minister, and synagogue secretaries and committees became common.

The scope of Jewish philanthropic activity expanded and became structurally separate from the synagogue. Almost every local community had a Hebrew Relief or Benevolent Society, and a feminine counterpart, that enjoyed a measure of autonomy. Fraternal orders provided assistance to ill or bereaved members and their families. Jewish communal organization seldom reached above the local level, however, due to the difficulties of communications and transportation during this period, and to the apprehensiveness on the part of recently arrived German Jews over a Jewish "state within the state."

Of the many mutual-aid societies and *landsmanschaften* formed after the Revolutionary War, Hebrah Hesed Vaemet, founded in New York in 1802, is still in existence. In 1852 the Jews' Hospital in the City of New York was founded, later to be known as Mount Sinai. Poor patients were given free treatment, and both the patients and staff were Jewish and non-Jewish. Since then, virtually all communities in the United States having a Jewish population of over 30,000 have maintained hospitals under Jewish auspices.

The most important of the new fraternal orders was the Independent Order of B'nai B'rith, formed in 1843 for the purpose of combining mutual aid and fraternal features to bring harmony and peace among Jews. The rapid growth of B'nai B'rith outside the synagogue framework, and its acceptance as a representative social and benevolent organization, provided an alternate form of Jewish affiliation to the religious congregation which heretofore had been the basic institution in the Jewish communal structure.

Although Philadelphia became the first city in the nation to have two congregations (Rodeph Shalom Congregation was formed in 1802 to provide an Ashkenazi alternative to the Sephardi ritual practiced in

Mikveh Israel), and the first in the entire Western Hemisphere to break the pattern of having but one type of religious ritual in each community, it is the flourishing New York Jewish community which provides the best example of the diversification of religious and community life during this period of changing patterns in the Jewish community.

In 1825 a group of Ashkenazi Jews complained of the formality and control of Congregation Shearith Israel and broke away to form the Bnai Jeshurun Congregation. Three years later, another dissenting group of Dutch, German, and Polish Jews broke away from Bnai Jeshurun and formed Congregation Anshe Chesed. By mid-century, another six congregations were in existence in New York, at first using privately owned buildings, and then erecting their own synagogue structures. To meet the needs of the new congregations, the first ordained rabbis arrived from Europe in the 1840s.

THE PHILADELPHIA COMMUNITY

Despite New York City's numerical superiority, the Philadelphia Jewish community was in many ways the most influential Jewry in the United States during the 19th century. There, new ideas for the shaping of Jewish communal life were tested. Such creative religious and lay leaders as Isaac Leeser, Sabato Morais, Abraham Hart, Moses Aaron Dropsie, Mayer Sulzberger and Joseph Krauskopf were as concerned with the future and fate of Jewish life throughout the country as they were with developments on the local scene.

Isaac Leeser, lecturer, editor, author, and *hazzan* of the Sephardi Mikveh Israel of Philadelphia, was the first to introduce a regular English sermon into the synagogue service. In 1843 he founded the monthly *The Occident*, which was an important forum for articles on Jewish life and thought for 25 years. Leeser founded the first Jewish Publication Society of America, published the first Hebrew primer for children (1838), the first complete English translation of the Sephardi prayerbook (1848), founded the first Hebrew high school (1849), the first Jewish representative and defense organization (Board of Delegates of American Israelites, 1859), and the first, short-lived, Jewish theological seminary, Maimonides College.

Philadelphia was the site of the first Jewish teachers' seminary, Gratz College (1897), and of Dropsie College (later University), the first post-graduate institution for Jewish learning in the world (1907). The founder and first president of The Jewish Theological Seminary of America (New York) was a Philadelphia rabbi, Sabato Morais.

EDUCATION

Jewish education varied little from the 18th century, except that free public schools, Protestant in tone, were available from 1805. Jewish objections to the teaching of Christian ethics and the use of Christian textbooks in the public schools led to the expansion of Jewish day schools which taught both Hebrew and general subjects, usually under the auspices of a synagogue. By 1854 there were seven day schools operating in New York City. As in the colonial period, the education of girls was not considered too important; they were either sent to public schools, or were taught by private tutors. In 1864 the Hebrew Free School of New York was opened as a countermeasure to Christian mission schools that attracted children of poor Jewish families. The school lasted about 15 years.

In 1842 the public schools came under government control and the movement for free, universal, religiously neutral schools spread throughout the country. As they were established in city after city, the recently founded Jewish schools closed, and their children began to attend the new public institutions. By 1860 the enduring pattern was set for Jewish children: the public school combined with the Jewish afternoon or Sunday school. The first Sunday school was founded in 1838 in Philadelphia, by Rebecca Gratz; its success and the success of the schools which were modeled upon it was due both to the example of the nationwide network of Protestant Sunday schools, and to the lessened significance of Hebrew in Reform Judaism which was becoming a powerful force in American Jewish life.

REFORM JUDAISM

The most characteristic expression of the influence of German Jews upon American Jewish life was the growth of Reform Judaism. An attempt to establish a Reform synagogue had taken place in Charleston in 1824, where Isaac Harby established the Reformed Society of Israelites. Harby noted that not all who agreed with him had joined his group, but that "the Jews born in Carolina are mostly of our way of thinking," and that the only consideration that kept them in the Orthodox synagogue was "a tender regard for the opinions and feelings of their parents." This Reform group remained in existence only for a few years, but it pioneered many of the later Reform practices, and Charleston is considered the cradle of American Reform Judaism.

The growth of German Jewish communities enabled Reform Judaism to take firm root in the United States during the 1840s, beginning with the Emanu-El Reformverein in New York and the formation of Reform congregations. Few synagogues were founded outright on professed Reform principles. Usually an Orthodox congregation of German immigrants changed some relatively superficial aspects of the service, such as omitting several prayers. More far-reaching alterations would follow a few years later, with the shift to a mainly English liturgy, the elimination of the second day of festivals, and the doffing of hats.

It was less the initiative of the members of these early congregations than that of their rabbis which produced these changes. By the time of the Civil War, several dozen congregations had taken their first steps toward Reform under the movement's major leaders—Isaac Mayer Wise, David Einhorn, Bernard Felsenthal, Samuel Hirsch, and Samuel Adler. The theological thought of these rabbis satisfied the widespread desire for a Judaism which harmonized with contemporary liberalism, rationalism, and optimism. Reform sought a version of the ancestral religion that might bridge the chasm between Jews and Christians and abrogate the millennial view that the Jews were living in exile.

The main ideas of Reform were already articulated before 1860, but large-scale expansion of the movement took place in the 1860s and 1870s. Opposition came from a few Orthodox and proto-Conservative figures, most notably Isaac Leeser. Reform's opponents stressed the immutable character of Judaism as a revealed religion, and insisted that under the conditions of American freedom the Jewish religion had to be observed in full, rather than truncated. The times were not with Leeser and his companions, however.

RELATIONS WITH WORLD JEWRY

Several world events stirred the American Jewish community during the mid-19th century. The Damascus blood libel, in which accusations of ritual murder were lodged against the Jews of Damascus and atrocities were committed against them, aroused the concern of American Jewry. Several local mass meetings were held in 1840, which requested President Van Buren to protest this accusation.

In 1859 the Board of Delegates of American Israelites was formed to protect and secure civil and religious rights of Jews in the United States and abroad. It was patterned in name and structure after the Board of Deputies of British Jews. Like every central representative Jewish body created thereafter, the Board of Delegates was founded because of one or more crises. On this occasion, there was a minor problem in 1854 over the United States ratification of a treaty with Switzerland which enabled the latter country to bar foreign Jews from entry. A more serious matter was the Mortara affair of 1858, in which a six-year-old Jewish boy in Bologna, Italy was secretly converted to Christianity by a domestic servant and then abducted by papal police to Rome. The Mortara case aroused a worldwide outcry and strong Jewish protests, to no avail. The Board of Delegates of American Israelites, controlled by traditionalists and opposed by the Reformers, claimed no more than thirty congregations, perhaps one-fifth the number in existence throughout the country.

In addition, there were occasional appeals for emergency aid for overseas Jewry in distress, especially from Sir Moses Montefiore. These appeals were generally answered on the local level.

THE CIVIL WAR PERIOD

TAKING SIDES

When the Civil War broke out in 1861, the 150,000 U.S. Jews were divided in their loyalties. Each community, in general, sided with the region in which it was located.

Before the conflict, few Jews had taken part in the mounting debate over slavery. Notable exceptions were Rabbi Morris J. Raphall (New York) and Michael Heilprin, whose printed debate in 1860 over the alleged biblical legitimization of slavery attracted nationwide attention. Rabbi David Einhorn, the Baltimore Reform leader, staunchly upheld his abolitionist stance in the slaveholding state of Maryland, notwithstanding the opposition of his congregation and threats to his personal safety. On the other hand, Rabbi Isaac M. Wise probably reflected the mixed sympathies in his border city of Cincinnati by remaining silent on the issues of the war. Other rabbis were similarly silent. The Jewish community of New York was divided over the issue of slavery. Many Jews, including the members of the Manumission Society of New York City, freed their slaves; others retained them until forced to set them free.

Despite strong anti-Jewish bias in the army, some 10,000 Jews served in the war, about 7,000 in the Northern army, and 3,000 with the Confederacy forces; over 500 lost their lives. At first, Jewish chaplains were not permitted to serve, but Samuel M. Isaacs and his son Myer were among the leaders of the successful struggle to change the restrictive terms of the law, and in 1862 Jewish military chaplains were appointed to serve with the Union Army.

Jews supported the war effort by selling federal bonds, and various congregations raised money to help the sick and wounded.

As the tragedy of the war deepened, casualties mounted, and hard-

Army Jews.

The following co-religionists were either killed or wounded at the battle of Fredericksburg :

T. J. Heffernam, A, 163 N. Y., hip and arm.
Serg. F. Herrfnkneckt, 7   "   head.
M. Ellis, 23 N. J., hand.
Moses Steinburg, 142 Penn., legs bruised.
A. Newman, A, 72   "   ankle
Lt. H. T. Davis, 81   "   arm.
J. Killenback, 4 N. J., head.
S. S. Vanuess, 15 "   leg.
W. Truax, 23   "   back.
J. Hirsh, 4   "   "
Jacob Schmidt, 19 Penn., left arm.
Jos. Osback, 19   "   wounded.
W. Jabob, 19   "   left arm.
Lieut. Simpson, 19 "   left leg.
Capt. Schub, 19   "   wounded.
C. M. Phillips, 16 Maine, cheek.
Lieut. S. Simpson, 99 Penn., leg.
R. Harris, 107   "   thigh.
L. Brauer, wounded.
—— Wolf, 5 Penn., side.
R. Ellis, 2   "   leg (slight).
S. Davidson, 186 " foot.
A. Valanstein, 105 N. Y, leg.
H. Stottler, 136 Penn., leg.

Part of the list of Jewish soldiers in the Union armies, killed or wounded in the Battle of Fredericksburg, Dec. 13, 1862, published in the *Jewish Record*, *New York*.

ships intensified. The Confederacy became subject to serious anti-Semitic agitation, which focused on Judah P. Benjamin, then Confederate secretary of state, who was accused of treason and profiteering. In the North, General Grant's General Order No. 11, expelling Jewish cotton traders behind the lines, was a serious although short-lived incident. The order was promptly revoked by President Lincoln.

Military requirements provided unusual opportunities to businessmen who developed the ready-made clothing industry from large-scale orders for army uniforms. Numerous Jewish bankers of the 1870s and 1880s started with capital amassed during the Civil War years as clothing manufacturers and merchants.

United States banking was vastly stimulated by the needs of government finance, and the general prosperity was shared by Jews. Jewish financiers, mainly of German origin, acted as intermediaries between foreign finance and the United States; railway bonds, mainly distributed by Jewish bankers in Europe, served as a means of payment for munitions bought in Europe. The Seligman brothers of New York marketed a total of 200 million dollars of federal bonds on the European market and provided critically important funds to the Union Army.

POST-WAR STABILITY

Following the emancipation of the slaves and the breakup of the plantation system, Jewish peddlers and storekeepers played an important part in Southern economic growth after the Civil War. One contemporary attributed part of their success to the habit they had of addressing Negro customers as "Mister," rather than by given name.

Jewish immigration to the United States resumed after its near cessation during the Civil War period. The Jewish population rose from about 150,000 in 1860 to an estimated 280,000 in 1880, much of it due to a substantial excess of births over deaths within a young immigrant population, but even more to continued immigration. For the first time there were serious discussions in the Jewish community over the possibility of organizing Jewish immigration from Europe. In 1870 about 500 East Prussians and Lithuanians were brought over from their famine-stricken region. However, Jewish migration to the United States remained a matter of individual initiative.

GERMAN JEWRY

The years between the end of the Civil War and the onset of mass immigration from Eastern Europe during the 1880s mark the coming of age of German Jewry in the United States. They were mainly merchants, manufacturers of clothing, and other consumer goods, and bankers in large cities and the small towns of the West and South.

The large German Jewish immigration gave a pronounced German quality to United States Jewry during this period. Reform Judaism became the dominant religious form; the German language or German-accented English was generally heard; German immigrant-aid, charitable, musical, and theatrical societies developed. German Jewish periodicals appeared in many cities, from New York to San Francisco. Practically all were weeklies or monthlies—some appeared only irregularly. The most important German language publication of the time was *Deborah* (1855–1903), published as a supplement to *The Israelite,* which was edited by Rabbi Isaac Mayer Wise in Cincinnati. (*The Israelite* is the oldest Jewish journal in the United States, though by the mid-20th century it had been reduced to a local community bulletin.)

Two German language publications, *Der Freund Israels* (Baltimore) and the one-page German language supplement of *The Hebrew* (San Francisco), survived into the 20th century. For a large group of Jews in the United States, German culture was a full substitute for their ancestral Judaism, and American Jewry long spoke English with a German accent when it was not speaking its native German.

The German-Jewish merchant class climbed rapidly in the post-Civil War age of industrial and financial expansion, and the private banker gained in importance. Joseph Seligman and his brothers in New York and San Francisco were among the foremost bankers of their day. Seligman declined President Grant's offer to appoint him Secretary of the Treasury in 1869.

COMMUNITY GROWTH

The decade after 1865 marked the greatest period of synagogue construction up to that time. Reform Judaism reached the peak of its influence in the 1870s and 1880s, when it came close to being synonymous with U.S. Judaism. The Reform theological position, epitomized in the Pittsburgh Platform (see chapter 4) of 1885, remained the movement's standard statement for fifty years. The organizational strength of Reform was solidified by the founding of the Union of American Hebrew Congregations in 1873, Hebrew Union College in 1875, and the Central Conference of American Rabbis in 1889, i.e., the lay, theological, and rabbinic organizations of the movement.

While Reform attained structural maturity and theological stability, traditionalists were confined to a few synagogues and were linked by personal and family ties. Their strength was to grow later, from the East European Jewish immigration which reached the United States in unprecedented numbers.

CULTURAL CONTRIBUTIONS

Jewish participation in general cultural life remained minor, with the exception of music, which was extensively cultivated by German Jews.

Sonnet by Emma Lazarus at the foot of the Statue of Liberty.

THE NEW COLOSSUS,

NOT LIKE THE BRAZEN GIANT OF GREEK FAME,
WITH CONQUERING LIMBS ASTRIDE FROM LAND TO LAND;
HERE AT OUR SEA-WASHED, SUNSET GATES SHALL STAND
A MIGHTY WOMAN WITH A TORCH, WHOSE FLAME
IS THE IMPRISONED LIGHTNING, AND HER NAME
MOTHER OF EXILES. FROM HER BEACON-HAND
GLOWS WORLD-WIDE WELCOME; HER MILD EYES COMMAND
THE AIR-BRIDGED HARBOR THAT TWIN CITIES FRAME.
"KEEP ANCIENT LANDS, YOUR STORIED POMP!"
     CRIES SHE
WITH SILENT LIPS. "GIVE ME YOUR TIRED, YOUR
     POOR,
YOUR HUDDLED MASSES YEARNING TO BREATHE FREE,
THE WRETCHED REFUSE OF YOUR TEEMING SHORE,
SEND THESE, THE HOMELESS, TEMPEST-TOST TO ME,
I LIFT MY LAMP BESIDE THE GOLDEN DOOR!"

THIS TABLET, WITH HER SONNET TO THE BARTHOLDI STATUE
OF LIBERTY ENGRAVED UPON IT, IS PLACED UPON THESE WALLS
IN LOVING MEMORY OF
EMMA LAZARUS
BORN IN NEW YORK CITY, JULY 22º, 1849
DIED NOVEMBER 19TH, 1887.

American Jewry produced no major novelist, poet, essayist, artist, or scholar, although the poetess Emma Lazarus (1849–1887) occupies a minor niche in American literature. An essayist and poet, she is best known for the stanzas engraved at the base of the Statue of Liberty: "Give me your tired, your poor, your huddled masses yearning to breathe free..." Jewish physicians became more numerous; Abraham Jacobi (1830–1919) is known as the father of American pediatrics, and in his later years was president of the American Medical Association.

SOCIAL ANTI-SEMITISM

The phenomenon of Jewish exclusion from upper-level social circles made its first appearance during the 1870s. It erupted notoriously in 1877, with the refusal of admission to the fashionable Grand Union Hotel at Saratoga Springs to Joseph Seligman. This act aroused widespread anger and indignation, not only among Jews, but in the general press and among such liberal Protestants as Henry Ward Beecher. The social clubs for the wealthy which were being established during the 1870s and later mostly excluded Jews, and the German gymnastic and social Turnvereine, were also inhospitable.

It appears that during the early development of American cities, Jews had the broadest opportunities for social mingling and political advancement. It was quite usual for a Jew, as one of the few literate, stable settlers, to become a mayor or a leading official of a frontier town. However, once these pioneer years ended and more fixed social groupings were formed, a tendency to exclude Jews from elite social and business circles became evident.

Then, as America entered upon the last quarter of the 19th century, a phenomenon of the most profound significance for American Jewry and for the country as a whole occurred: the shift in the geographic sources of Jewish immigration to the United States from Germanic to Slavic areas of Europe.

2

COMING INTO ITS OWN

THE GREAT IMMIGRATION

The leading feature of American Jewish life during the period from 1880 to 1929 was the phenomenal growth in the number of Jews in the United States from about 280,000 in a population of 50,155,000 in 1880, to approximately 4,500,000 of 115,000,000 in 1925. Some 2,378,000 Jews arrived in the United States between 1880 and the end of free immigration in 1924. The pace of immigration increased with each decade, and peaked during the five consecutive years 1904 to 1908, when 642,000 Jews reached U.S. shores. This population movement, which formed part of the vast migration from Europe to the U.S. in general, was of tremendous sociological significance. Vast numbers of Jews who moved from Eastern Europe into the world's fastest growing economy were

Jewish population of the U.S., 1877, according to state borders of today.

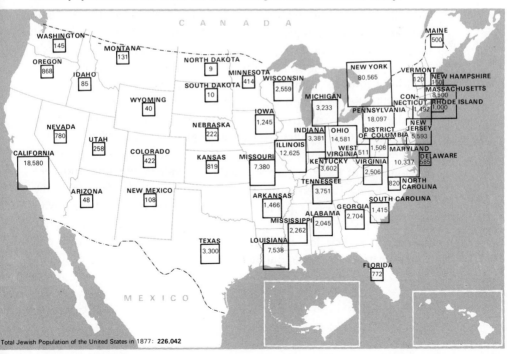

Total Jewish Population of the United States in 1877: **226,042**

33

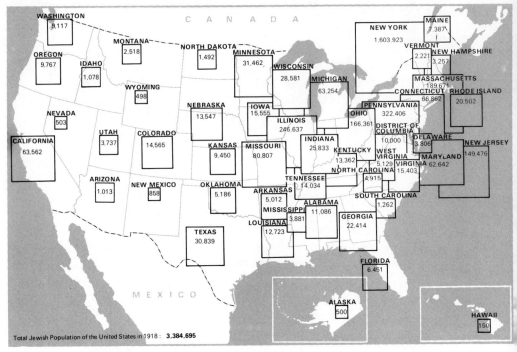

Total Jewish Population of the United States in 1918: **3,384,695**

Jewish population of the U.S., 1918, according to state borders of today.

automatically emancipated from all legal discrimination and rapidly entered Western culture.

THE "PUSH" FACTOR IN MIGRATION

Immediate events stimulating this migration included the virulent anti-Semitic Russian pogroms between 1881 and 1907, the expulsion of Jews from Moscow in 1890, and the years of war and revolution in Russia at the beginning of the 20th century. Other causes of the huge migration lay deeper, however, and were more influential.

Probably the most important cause was the growth of East European (Russian Empire, Austria-Poland, Hungary, Rumania) Jewry from perhaps 1,500,000 in 1800 to some 6,800,000 persons in 1900, generating nearly insoluble questions of sheer physical survival. The economic development of Eastern Europe failed to provide them with a sufficient livelihood, and Russian governmental policies excluded Jews from the new industrial cities, kept them off the land, and burdened them with drastically restrictive decrees. The feeling among Russian Jews grew stronger that their lot would never improve by normal political and economic processes, but required either emigration abroad or revolution at home. The Jews of Rumania, mostly 19th century immigrants from Russia who had attained a better economic position by their move, suffered greatly from arbitrary and occasionally violent treatment as aliens without rights. In Galicia, under Hapsburg rule, the Jews enjoyed emancipation from 1867, but the economic backwardness of that area fostered the highest emigration rate in Eastern Europe.

As railroad and steamship lines developed in the latter part of the 19th century, the journey from a town in Eastern Europe to the port of New York became more feasible; it might be completed in two weeks. Moreover, entry into the United States was virtually free of legal restrictions, with barely 1% of those seeking admittance being turned away, mainly because of contagious diseases. America was going through a period of rapid economic expansion as it sought to develop its large western territories, and was in need of additional manpower. It opened its gates to Europe's masses who sought a better future in the New World; Jews constituted 8% of those who came.

The proportion of Jews who returned to Europe from the immigration of the 1880s has been estimated at 25%. From that point, the rate of

Immigrants on an Atlantic liner, 1906.

return steadily declined; in 1908 it was about 8%; after 1919 it sank below 1%. Clearly, the Jewish immigrant came to stay, to a greater extent than all his immigrant contemporaries except the Irish.

Between 1890 and 1925 American Jewry had grown fifteen–fold. It had become the largest Jewish community in the world, and had established itself as a major ethnic and religious group in the United States.

DEMOGRAPHIC ANALYSIS

Almost 80% of the Eastern European newcomers were 15 to 45 years old, the age range typical of immigrants to the U.S. in general. Men outnumbered women only slightly, indicating the permanence and family character of this migration, even though families were often separated for considerable periods of time. There was a disproportionate representation of the child-bearing age, and urban districts which had a preponderance of immigrants recorded very high birthrates.

The Eastern European Jews arrived with industrial skills and the expressed willingness to be employed in any sector of the economy where opportunities were available, but they had a strong preference for settling in compact masses for reasons of economic and psychological security. Their mass influx changed the social composition of the Jewish community in the United States.

GERMAN JEWISH OCCUPATIONAL PATTERNS

The older, German Jewish stock had already acquired a basically middle-class or quasi-middle-class status, and their pattern of employment reflected a high percentage of self employment and concentration in the area of services. Joined by immigrants from England and France, this group had shifted from predominantly mercantile occupations to law and politics, banking and finance, publishing, medicine, and literary and academic pursuits. A group of them were prominent as collectors and patrons of the arts, and as philanthropists. A conspicuous activity of German Jews in the United States was the establishment of department stores, among them some of the world's largest. Of particular importance to the occupational patterns of American Jewry was the establishment of Sears, Roebuck, under the ownership of Julius Rosenwald. A retail enterprise which published huge catalogues for mail-order

service, Sears, Roebuck cornered the market that had been serviced by
the itinerant country peddler. The latter was dealt another blow by the
invention of the automobile which enabled his rural customers to go to
the store and eliminated their dependence on door-to-door salesman.

A noticeable migration took place among the Jews from small towns
to metropolitan centers. During the 1870s Jewish settlement had been
widespread. In hundreds of small towns in California, along the Mississippi River, and throughout the South and Middle West there were
small Jewish communities. It appears that during the 1880s most
Jews quit these towns. The great expansion of industrial cities, and
the depression of the agricultural economy upon which the small
towns were founded, as well as the anti-Semitic undertones in such small-
town political and social movements as religious fundamentalism and
populism, helped to make Jews of the 20th century a metropolitan group.

EAST EUROPEAN JEWISH OCCUPATIONAL PATTERNS

The new Jewish immigrants clustered in distinct urban neighborhoods
in major cities, and the Jewish population of the United States now
became a predominantly industrial and labor-oriented community. The

The Lower East Side, c. 1912.

streets where the immigrants lived were generally older slum districts close to the downtown area. They became all but exclusively Jewish in population, and the merchandise in the stores, the Yiddish heard on the streets, and the festive atmosphere on the Jewish Sabbath and holidays reflected the character of the inhabitants. Every large city had such an area between the 1890s and 1920. The largest of them, the Lower East Side of New York City, sheltered an estimated 350,000 Jews in 1915 in less than two square miles. These neighborhoods were very seriously congested and had dangerous problems of health and sanitation. Yet, their prevailing atmosphere was one of hope and confidence, and they supported a rich and varied cultural life.

The immigrants' prime motive in coming to the U.S. was to better their material conditions. European fables about "the golden land" notwithstanding, their lot was a hard one. Although they made their living from a wide variety of trades, they generally tended to cluster in certain occupations.

The East European Jewish immigrant generally joined the working class. He worked mainly in the ready-made clothing industry, which was growing with remarkable rapidity as the use of the mechanical cutting knife made possible more rapid and economic production of the basic parts of garments, and as the demand for ready-made clothing grew among the booming urban population. The number of Jews employed in the needle trades as workers, entrepreneurs, and salesmen may have reached 300,000 around 1915. The ready-made garment industry was composed mainly of shops where workers labored on one or two parts of the total product. In such important centers as Rochester, Cleveland, and Chicago, clothing was produced in substantial factories, owned mostly by Jews. On the other hand, in 1910, in the Borough of Manhattan within New York City, there were 11,172 clothing firms employing 214,428 persons; 78% of them in 1913 averaged five employees each. These were the notorious sweatshops—tiny, dirty, unventilated, frequently located in the employer's dwelling, where the employee often worked for 16 hours a day during the busy period of this highly seasonal industry. With all their evils, the workshops did enable thousands of immigrant wage workers to enter the garment business on their own. Failure only meant that the unsuccessful entrepreneur returned to wage work, while success in the ferociously competitive industry might lead to independence and wealth.

New York City was the great center of the clothing industry; Chicago was a second major center, especially for men's clothing; and Philadelphia, Baltimore, Rochester, Boston, and Cleveland were also important centers. After 1900 successful Eastern European immigrant entrepreneurs moved into the leadership of the industry, as the earlier German Jewish capitalists tended to leave it for other fields.

THE JEWISH LABOR MOVEMENT

Highly decentralized low-cost, ready-made clothing production was as nearly Jewish an industry as ever seen in the United States, although large numbers of Italian, German, and Irish workers, especially women, also held jobs in it. It inspired the Jewish trade union movement which began in the 1880s, developed slowly, and made greatest headway in New York City. Unlike most American labor organizations, the Jewish unions were socialist in ideology, deriving their leadership from the numerous Jewish socialists (of varying shades of political radicalism) who arrived in the United States among the waves of Eastern European immigrants. They were staunch opponents of the nonpolitical unionism embodied in the American Federation of Labor, led by Samuel Gompers, himself a Jewish immigrant from England.

In 1888 several small Jewish labor organizations formed the United Hebrew Trades as their central body. This group later comprised a majority of the Jewish workers in the United States. Louis Miller of the United Hebrew Trades and two other representatives from Jewish labor organizations were present at the first congress of the Second International (1889). Miller submitted a report on the activities of Jewish trade unions, the first time that an international socialist conference received information about the existence of an independent Jewish labor movement. The "Jewish issue" was raised at the following congress of the International (Brussels, 1891) by Abraham Cahan who represented 30,000 "Yiddish-speaking workers" from the United States. After debate, the congress adopted a resolution affirming that the only struggle that socialist and workers' parties recognized was that of the proletariat against capitalists, and that the Jewish proletariat could achieve emancipation only through the workers' organizations in their countries.

The success of the International Ladies' Garment Workers Union in the great cloakmakers' strike (see chapter 3) turned the Jewish labor

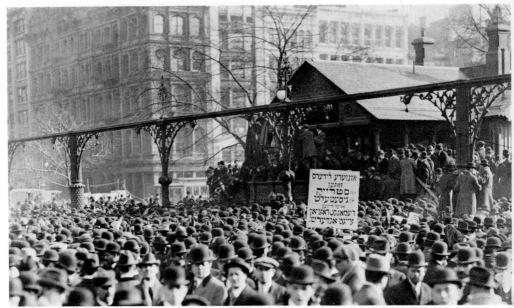

N.Y. garment workers demonstrate against a proposed strike settlement, 1913.

movement into a powerful force. (The scene of workers pouring into the streets from their shops at the appointed hour reminded the chairman of the cloakmakers' strike of the Jews leaving Egypt!) This strike was followed by others, the most important being a series of Chicago men's clothing strikes between 1910 and 1920. Here, leaders of the United Garment Workers, whose preponderant ethnic elements were not Jewish and did not work on ready-made clothing, made an unauthorized deal with the employers. This brought about the secession of the Jewish ready-made tailors (and others), and the founding of the Amalgamated Clothing Workers of America, led by Sidney Hillman. The strikes were the proving ground for Hillman, an immigrant labor leader from Lithuania, who was instrumental in getting the principle of the union shop accepted. This experience was fundamental in shaping his concept of "industrial constitutionalism," that is, the idea of a structured harmony between labor and management, that was to be Hillman's main contribution to the American labor movement during his years of leadership in the Amalgamated Clothing Workers of America and in the Congress of Industrial Organizations (CIO).

IMMIGRANT CULTURAL LIFE

JEWISH SOCIALISM

The philosophy of Jewish socialism embodied the vision that the Yiddish-speaking masses needed special organizations in order to better their economic and cultural conditions, and that the task of the Jewish intelligentsia was to devote itself to these masses. The Jewish socialist tradition eventually lost its impetus in America because of the unparalleled opportunities offered by American society. But during its relatively brief years of activity, the movement was of enormous significance to countless numbers of Jews to whom it offered new vistas of education, the ideals of democratic socialism, and the chance to achieve a decent standard of living.

Very few Jewish immigrants, especially before 1900, had come from educated stock: they were mainly from the poorer working classes. Yet, virtually all knew the rudiments of Jewish law and ritual, Bible and frequently some Talmud and rabbinic literature. (Few women, however, had any education.) Only a minority maintained their East European Orthodox religious practices in the face of the overpowering force of the urban, industrial, secular life into which they were cast. The younger intelligentsia embraced socialism in one of its numerous contemporary forms, and, in smaller numbers, advocated Zionism or Hebraism.

THE YIDDISH ENVIRONMENT

In the United States, the Jewish socialist labor movement helped foster a secularist Yiddish environment which offered an alternative to Jewish religious tradition, but preserved strong folk loyalties. At the beginning of the 20th century, Yiddish was the spoken language of the vast majority of world Jewry. The Yiddishist movement aimed to preserve a secular national culture in that language. There was a Yiddish press and a rich diet of Yiddish literature, scholarly Yiddish lectures, and numerous Yiddish theatrical troupes. Somewhat later, there were Yiddish films and radio programs, and in 1931 New York City could boast of the world's only full-time Yiddish radio station in WEVD, established by the Yiddish newspaper, the *Forward*. (By the 1970s, much of its programming was in English, and to an increasing extent in Spanish.)

By the mid-1920s, about 80,000 families, mainly members of Jewish unions and small businessmen, belonged to the Arbeiter Ring (Workmen's Circle), a Yiddish-language fraternal organization that provided families with financial aid in time of sickness or death, and supported a diversified Yiddish cultural program. The Workmen's Circle, as well as other Yiddish groups such as the Sholem Aleichem Folk Institute and the "Central Farband" of the General Jewish Workers' Union (Bund), sponsored Yiddish afternoon schools which provided an education for thousands of poor Jewish children.

THE YIDDISH PRESS

The Jewish immigrants found themselves in an alien society in which they had to struggle to keep afloat economically. The Yiddish press provided a rudder to guide them through the rocky shoals of the unfamiliar American milieu. New York City, whose preeminence as the center of Jewish immigration and Yiddish culture in the United States was unchallenged, was the home of the American Yiddish press. The rise, golden age, and decline of that press parallels the arrival and acculturation of the great East European Jewish immigration.

The first attempt to publish a Yiddish newspaper was made in 1870 when J.K. Buchner, an immigrant from Prussia, published his *Juedische Zeitung* which aspired to keep the reader abreast of all aspects of "politics, religion, history, science, and art"—a foreshadowing of the broad scope and sense of mission that was to characterize the U.S. Yiddish press in years to come. With the help of a political subsidy from Tammany Hall, the paper appeared irregularly until at least 1876.

The title "father of the American Yiddish press" belongs to Kasriel Sarasohn, a Russian immigrant who, in 1872, began publishing the short-lived *New Yorker Juedische Zeitung.* He also founded the weekly *Juedische-Gazetten* (1874), and the first Yiddish daily in America, the *Tageblat* (1885–1928). The latter, a politically and religiously conservative newspaper, exerted great influence upon the immigrant generation. (Sarasohn also published a Hebrew weekly, *Ha-Ivri,* 1891–98.)

The rise of political activism among Jewish immigrants in the late 1880s and 1890s was reflected in the development of the Yiddish press. Thus, in 1894, on the heels of a garment-workers' strike, the first socialist daily, the militantly left-wing *Abendblatt,* made its appearance; and in 1897 an ideological quarrel that split the American Socialist Labor Party into left-wing and right-wing factions was reflected in the appearance of the *Jewish Daily Forward,* a politically more moderate newspaper. The *Forward* was edited for nearly half a century by Abraham Cahan, a man intellectually and emotionally situated at the confluence of three worlds —the Jewish, the American, and the Russian–Socialist. At its zenith in the 1920s, it was the wealthiest and most widely read Yiddish newspaper in the United States, with eleven local and regional editions reaching as far west as Chicago. It combined conscientious journalism with a partisan commitment to democratic socialism and the Jewish labor movement. (The paper reached a peak circulation of nearly 200,000 during World War I.)

The Orthodox *Jewish Morning Journal* (1901–72) was for years the only morning Yiddish paper. It was also unique in its support of the Republican Party. In 1916 it reached its peak circulation of 111,000.

Topical Yiddish periodicals also proliferated in New York: humor magazines, literary publications, journals of opinion, theatrical reviews, trade journals, and papers catering to specific groups and neighborhoods.

The *Jewish Day (Der Yidishe Tog)* was founded in 1914 by a group of New York City intellectuals and businessmen under the slogan "the newspaper of the Yiddish intelligentsia." Like the other Yiddish press, it reached its peak circulation during World War I and then began a sharp decline. (In 1953 it merged with the *Jewish Morning Journal,* and managed to hang on in an era of dwindling Yiddish readers and spiraling economic costs, until 1972, when the *Day–Morning Journal* finally closed its doors.)

The first decade of the 20th century witnessed several attempts to establish Yiddish dailies in other American cities where immigrants had settled in large numbers, and where Yiddish weeklies had been in existence since the early 1890s. The most notable were the *Chicago Daily Courier* (1887–1944; daily after 1892) and the *Cleveland Jewish World* (1908–43). The other papers were unable to compete for long with the Yiddish papers that were trucked in from New York every day.

THE ANGLO-JEWISH AND HEBREW PRESS

The period of mass immigration also saw the appearance of several English-language weeklies covering local and world news of Jewish

First issue of the N.Y. Hebrew daily, *Hadoar*, Nov. 1, 1921.

interest. Many of them had as their primary object the projection of their editors' opinions, a characteristic they shared with much of the general press of the time. As the daily American press, especially in the New York area, began to give more space to Jewish news, the Anglo-Jewish press tended toward increasing parochialism, and many papers became organs of the local Jewish community or Jewish institutions. The Anglo-Jewish press obtains the bulk of its news of Jewish interest from the Jewish Telegraphic Agency, which is supported by the Council of Jewish Federations and Welfare Funds.

The last decades of the 19th century also saw the appearance of a Hebrew periodical press. Unlike the Anglo-Jewish and Yiddish publications which served large bodies of readers, the Hebrew press was restricted to a relatively small group of subscribers. The first Hebrew periodical, a newsletter, *Ha-Zofeh ba-Arez ha-Hadashah (The Observer in a New Land),* appeared irregularly from 1871 to 1876. Other Hebrew periodicals, most of them one-man operations, made brief appearances in the following decades.

The longest-lived of all Hebrew periodicals in the United States has been the weekly *Hadoar* (founded 1921; originally a daily). Its circulation in 1970 was about 5,000.

THE LANDSMANSCHAFTEN

The most widespread immigrant organization was the *hevrah* (society), usually founded on a hometown (*landsmanschaft*) basis; in New York City alone at least 1,200 existed about 1915. In addition to providing a fraternal social atmosphere for their members who knew each other from Europe, the *landsmanschaften* invariably provided funeral arrangements and burial rights. Sick benefits and occasionally unemployment payments were also granted. The societies probably reached their peak during the World War I years, when these organizations dispatched millions of dollars in relief supplies and cash to cities and towns in Eastern Europe. After the war, the *landsmanschaften* financed relief work carried on by the Joint Distribution Committee, Hadassah, and other organizations, and also used their membership and money to oppose anti-Semitism and discrimination in the United States. A large proportion of such *landsmanschaften* was affiliated with central organizations, such as the Arbeiter Ring, the Farband, the Federation of Galician Jews, etc.

Although the membership and activities of the *landsmanschaften* declined after 1930, due in part to the dying off of the immigrant generation, hundreds of thousands of European-born Jews still belonged to them in the period immediately prior to World War II. They attempted to assist Jews in Europe and to bring groups of immigrants into the United States and Palestine.

The *landsmanschaften* experienced a minor revival after World War II, brought about by the need to aid, with food, medical supplies, and clothing, the survivors of the Holocaust and the new immigrants to Israel. However, this revival was short-lived. In Chicago, for example, the 600 *landsmanschaft* societies which had 40,000 members in 1948 had dwindled to 60 societies in 1961.

Many of the *landsmanschaften* maintained synagogues that were Orthodox and Yiddish-speaking, and preserved East European habits of worship. These *shuls*—New York City alone had over 500 in 1916—were unesthetic and tiny, and few of them survived their immigrant founders and the movement of Jews from their original neighborhoods of settlement.

A TRANSITORY GENERATION

The entire immigrant milieu thus described was transitory. Children of the Jewish garment workers did not, as a rule, follow their fathers' occupations but entered other areas of economic endeavor. The striking feature of the Jewish proletariat in the United States was that it was a one-generation phenomenon. Aided by the availability of educational opportunities and the rapidly changing structure of the American economy, the almost exclusively urban Jewish population found outlets for its livelihood in self-employment and in the service sector. The percentage of those employed as unskilled laborers, in domestic service, and as low-paid industrial workers declined swiftly.

As a result, the proportion of Jews in the trade unions was more than halved by the 1920s. By the 1930s, Jews constituted only two-fifths of the membership of the International Ladies' Garment Workers Union: the number of Jews in the Amalgamated Clothing Workers dropped, although the leadership continued to be Jewish. (While certain white-collar unions, such as the Teachers Union in New York, were still predominantly Jewish in membership in 1971, they were neither socialist in content nor Jewish in any meaningful way.)

The use of Yiddish also declined, for the native-born generation's language was English. This dealt a blow to the Yiddish press and the cultural activities of the Jewish labor organizations. The ideology of Abraham Cahan, editor of the *Forward* and perhaps the dominant figure in American Jewish Socialism, who believed that the goal of the Jewish labor movement was to make good Americans of its members, was achieved; but, ironically, the movement itself declined once "Americanization" was completed.

Indeed, the entire immigrant environment—problem-ridden, colorful, and dynamic—existed only as long as the stream of newcomers continued to arrive; that is, until the restrictive immigration law of 1924. Then, lacking replenishment from overseas, the immigrant Jewish life of *landsmanschaften,* Yiddish theater, tiny *shul* and *ḥeder,* burial- and loan-societies, eventually died out. By the 1940s, it was a relic of the past.

IMMIGRANTS AND NATIVES

The immigrants from Eastern Europe were a breed apart from their more established co-religionists of German origin. The latter had become acculturated to a great degree. Upon their arrival, many had found amenable surroundings in the larger colony of gentile German immigrants. Their American-born children strongly identified with and looked to their economic peers in the American business world for their social environment. Some of the rabbis among the Central European Jews had participated in the early stirrings of Reform Judaism in Europe and believed in the desirability of acculturation, even in religious practices. Large numbers were following the pattern of the colonial Jews, in that by the third generation the rate of intermarriage was large enough to bring into question the continued Jewish existence of many of these families. Moreover, by the end of the 19th century, one could adopt secularism as a way of life, and vanish as a Jew without accepting any other religious identity.

The East European immigrants, however, brought with them the identity of a deprived national minority, sustained by great forces of religious, cultural, and communal cohesion. Political action in the name of Jewish interests, Jewish efforts toward social reform, pressure on society at large to regard the Jewish community as equal to other communities by right—in short, the total stance of a group fighting to express itself in all its peculiarities and to be accepted by society—all this became the new mode of American Jewish life among the immigrants and most of their children in the 20th century.

The symbiosis of the two elements, the German and the East European, was ridden by conflicts and prejudices, and by distinctions in wealth and status, the latter a function of the degree of "Americanization" or the duration of residence in the United States.

WARDS OF CHARITY AND PATRONS

Unlike the many other immigrant groups which reached the United States at the same time as the East European Jews, the latter enjoyed important patronage and the protection of their established co-religionists. Notwithstanding irritation over the "clannish," "backward" character of the immigrants, their alleged ingratitude for the philanthropy they received, and their political radicalism, the native Jews, guided by the ideals of middle-class liberalism, regarded the new arrivals as their wards, to be helped, chided, and guided.

The German Jewish elite provided most of the social services for the American Jewish community during the period between 1881 and World War I. The Hebrew Relief Society which existed in dozens of cities became a social agency for the relief of distress and for family aid, usually changing its name between 1910 and 1925 to Jewish Social Service Association. Such institutions as the Educational Alliance in New York, the Council Educational Alliance in Cleveland, the Jewish People's Institute in Chicago, and the Abraham Lincoln House in Milwaukee all demonstrated the interest of native Jews in bringing social and cultural amenities—art, music, sports, health education, and lectures—to immigrant Jews, particularly the youth, thus hastening their "Americanization."

There were occasional criticisms of the Americanization program. Perhaps it was not in the best interests of the immigrant to Americanize him and thus sever his ethnic, cultural, and religious roots.

This viewpoint was stated by Solomon Schechter, who headed the Jewish Theological Seminary of America. In a letter of resignation from the board of the Educational Alliance in New York City, he expressed opposition to its goals:

> The great question before the Jewish community is not so much the Americanising of the Russian Jew as his Judaising. We have now quite sufficient agencies for his Americanisation. But the problem is whether we are able to keep the immigrant within Judaism after he has become Americanised. . . .

Feelings between the native Jews and the immigrants were, however, none too cordial, and strong anti-immigrant sentiment was to be found among working-class native Jews, such as cigar makers and skilled tailors. Moreover, the indifference or antagonism of the "uptown" Jews to the cultural heritage and aspirations of the "downtown" newcomers generated an undertone of tension which occasionally erupted into conflict.

For their part the immigrants had unflattering perceptions of the "uptown" Jews, whom they regarded as snobbish and patronizing, excessively assimilated, and lacking Jewish kindness. Yet the natives did provide the immigrants with a model for being American and Jewish.

Immigrants and their problems were the main content of Jewish communal life and concerns from the 1880s until the 1930s. The intellectualism and Jewish fervor common among the newcomers, and such achievements as their labor movement and the New York City Kehillah, showed some natives—of whom Louis D. Brandeis might be cited as the outstanding example—a more authentic, passionate way to be a Jew. Quite a few native Jews were thus drawn into the cultural life and social movements of the immigrant milieu, including Zionism.

By the 1920s the German group began to lose its hold over Jewish communal life. As the new immigrants and their children shed their sense of being alien, and achieved some power in their own right, they were ever less willing to accept the tutelage of the "uptown" group.

ORTHODOX AND REFORM JUDAISM

A subtler issue between natives and immigrants involved religious life. The Reform temples of native American Jewry were cold and uninviting to the newcomers; the unesthetic *landsmanschaften* synagogues attracted only their own small group of members.

East European Jewish immigrants brought about the firm establishment of Orthodoxy in the United States, although only a minority of the immigrants and few of their children actually remained Orthodox Jews. Several hundred East European rabbis settled throughout the country, but their influence was far more limited than it had been in their native lands.

At the other extreme, Reform Judaism was reaching its greatest distance from Jewish tradition at the turn of the 20th century. Proposals were considered at length for a Reform synod to settle matters of belief and practice, but they were not accepted. Extensive discussion took place over shifting observance of the Sabbath from Saturday to Sunday, and several large congregations did so. The Reform rabbinate began to take an active interest in contemporary social problems, and there was considerable preoccupation with the inroads made by Christian Science and Ethical Culture.

After the 1890s Reform Judaism tended to lose contact with the mainstream of American Jewish life and affairs. Its leading laymen, who included almost all the leaders of U.S. Jewry, participated in Jewish life mostly outside the framework of religious organizations. It was only during the 1920s that Reform interest in tradition and Jewish peoplehood revived, largely as a result of the developments in Palestine, and the increasing influence of East European Judaism.

THE EMERGENCE OF CONSERVATIVE JUDAISM

As prominent figures in both the older and immigrant Jewish communities worried over the young people in both groups who were rejecting the religious practices of their fathers in favor of secularism ("uptown") and radical social doctrines ("downtown"), or turning toward hedonism ("uptown") and criminality ("downtown"), it became apparent that a modernized form of traditional Judaism was required for the rising generation in the American society. Against this background of concern, the moribund Jewish Theological Seminary was reorganized in 1902. Originally opened in New York in 1887 with the avowed purpose of "the preservation in America of the knowledge and practice of historical Judaism," it sought to establish a school to train rabbis and teachers who would preserve traditional Jewish values and practice against the onslaught of "radical" reformers.

The Seminary was substantially endowed, mainly by wealthy native-born Jews, and under the leadership of Solomon Schechter an outstanding faculty and library were assembled. The growth of the seminary was slow but its faculty deeply influenced many of the younger intelligentsia, and the institution provided an alternative to the growing assimilationist tendencies of Reform, and the over-identification of Orthodoxy with East European immigrant life and customs. Conservative Judaism was hampered, however, by its lack of a strong congregational constituency and its dependency for recruits on acculturated immigrants.

ḤEDER AND SUNDAY SCHOOL

Well before massive East European immigration began, U.S. Jews were committed to the public school for the education of their children. Catholics rejected the religiously neutral public schools and erected a parochial school system, but Jews gladly saw their children educated in the public schools. Specifically Jewish education became the responsibility of congregations, most of which maintained Sunday schools in which the course of study lasted three years, and the teaching usually involved a

Drawing by Jacob Epstein of immigrants' Hebrew school, 1902.

moralistic interpretation of Bible stories and an inculcation by catechism of the principles of Judaism.

The East European immigrants transplanted to the United States the traditional Jewish educational institutions of their native lands. Their willingness to adjust to American life was manifest in their acceptance of the public school for their children, but they also wanted their children to remain Jews. For this purpose they recreated the European education they knew—the *ḥeder,* a private, one-room school, open every weekday of the year. The teachers in the *ḥeder* were, in most cases, untrained in pedagogy, and the parents were too overwhelmed with their struggle to make economic headway in their new surroundings to take the time to consider the quality of their children's education, as they had done in their country of origin. The curriculum in the *ḥeder* consisted of mechanical reading of prayers, study of the Pentateuch portion of the week, recitation of portions of the liturgy, and *bar mitzvah* preparations for the boys. Virtually nothing was done about educating the girls.

THE TALMUD TORAH

A new direction became prominent in Jewish education in the form of a curriculum which combined religion, modern Hebrew, and Zionism, and which was adopted by the communal afternoon Hebrew schools known as the *talmud torahs*. These schools were generally founded by residents of a given neighborhood, financed by a paid membership, and staffed by more competent teachers than the *ḥeder* enjoyed. Their more ambitious curriculum included Hebrew language and literature, history, Bible, customs and ceremonies, prayers, music, and arts and crafts. These schools, the first of which was founded in Brooklyn, New York, in 1893, exercised great influence on Jewish education in the early 20th century. (They began to decline in number and function in the 1940s, due mainly to the increasing number of new suburban synagogues which maintained their own afternoon Hebrew schools.)

Despite the modern curriculum and the improved methods of pedagogy, the *talmud torahs* had to struggle against widespread parental indifference to any Jewish education beyond lessons to prepare sons for *bar mitzvah* which symbolized identity and continuity.

In 1910, the Bureau of Jewish Education of the Jewish Community of New York was founded, after a community survey of Jewish education in the city ascertained that fewer than one-quarter of the Jewish children of school age received a Jewish education in some form during a given year. The Bureau sought to standardize education, initiated educational experimentation, and inspired a group of young American Jews to prepare for professional careers in Jewish education. By 1930 similar bureaus for Jewish education existed in all large Jewish communities.

COMMUNAL STRUCTURE

Before 1890 U.S. Jewry consisted essentially of dozens of local communities. The *de facto* leaders were lawyers, substantial merchants, and bankers in the largest cities. These local elites were the pillars of the Reform temples, the B'nai B'rith lodges, the Hebrew Relief Societies, and the Jewish social clubs. The sole nationwide organizations were B'nai B'rith (and several other internally oriented fraternal bodies) and the Reform movement's Union of American Hebrew Congregations.

Mass immigration and increasing manifestations of anti-Semitism, however, brought charity and the defense of Jewish rights to the foreground of American Jewish concerns, while the development of nationwide transportation and communications provided the means of making American Jewry an organic, nationwide body.

ANTI-SEMITISM

Official or governmental discrimination against Jews, on the European model, did not exist in the United States. However, beginning in the 1870s, anti-Semitism in the form of social discrimination became increasingly evident, and was accompanied by the development of ideological anti-Semitism.

The rapid economic rise to affluence of the first generation of German immigrant Jews impinged upon the prestige enjoyed by wealthy non-Jews, who reacted by seeking to assert their social positions by manufacturing exclusiveness. In 1876 an advertisement printed in the *New York Tribune* advised that a certain resort hotel was barring Jews. This was the beginning of a growing tendency toward the exclusion of Jews from areas involving leisure-time facilities. Summer resort advertisements noting "we prefer not to entertain Hebrews" were common after the 1880s. From the resorts, social discrimination worked back into the cities. Important social clubs barred Jewish members; private schools were closed to Jewish children; in general, Jews were not welcome at any institution or association where membership conferred prestige and status.

Behind the groundswell of social discrimination lay the profound social changes of the "Gilded Age" of the late 19th century. The older, socially elite groups were faced with a growing struggle for place and power as their security was threatened by rapid industrialization, and the new elements which rose into middle- and upper-class status appeared as crass *nouveaux riches*. Social discrimination thus served the dual purpose of keeping Jews "in their place" while enhancing and defining the social status of the older elite and the newer non-Jewish wealthy class.

Other tensions arose as over 1,500,00 East European Jews arrived in the United States in the three decades from 1881 to 1910. Non-Jews fled from, or battled to retain, neighborhoods becoming crowded with masses of foreigners. The presence of these large numbers of new arrivals, the competition engendered by their rapid rise in economic status, and their pressure to achieve social integration led to the development of anti-Jewish stereotypes.

An ideological anti-Semitism first appeared in the 1890s as a by-product of American nativism and in response to the perceptible cultural gap between the older population and the massive numbers of Jewish immigrants from Eastern Europe. Men like Henry Adams, representing Eastern patrician intellectuals, and Ignatius Donnelly, representing Western agrarian radicals, while far apart in basic orientation, both viewed the Jew as conniving and grasping, and as the cause and symbol of their discontent. The anti-Jewish stereotype which emerged clearly during this period contained elements of earlier Christian anti-Semitism, the Shylock image, the wielding of undue power through manipulation of gold, and an identification of Jews with the hated, feared city.

Substantial discrimination began to appear in housing and educational opportunities at colleges and universities, and especially in jobs in the highly structured bureaucracies of heavy industry, insurance, and banking.

BEGINNINGS OF NATIONAL ORGANIZATIONS

Leaders of the Jewish community reacted to these anti-Semitic manifestations on two levels. They created a network of social and philanthropic institutions within which they could live a life that largely paralleled that of their non-Jewish peers, and accepted a social isolation that was partly self-willed and partly enforced by the outside society.

Beginning in 1895 in Boston, local Jewish charities set up federations for unified fundraising and allocation. This federation method was soon taken up by every larger community, and essentially covered the United States with the founding, in 1917, of the Federation for the Support of Jewish Philanthropic Societies in New York City. These bodies tended to assume local Jewish leadership, developing a quasi-ideology that philanthropy was the one tie uniting Jews of all kinds.

On another level, the Jewish community sought to fight anti-Semitism, especially when it appeared to involve public matters. Led by the more established German Jewish group, American Jewry formed defense organizations on a national level: the American Jewish Committee in 1906, the Anti-Defamation League of B'nai B'rith in 1913, and the American Jewish Congress in the 1920s.

The American Jewish Committee was the most influential national Jewish spokesman. Centered in New York City, it drew its membership, by invitation, from the leading Jewish bankers, merchants, lawyers, and politicians of every city, and enjoyed the able leadership of such wealthy and well-connected men as Jacob H. Schiff, Mayer Sulzberger, and Louis Marshall. The elitist viewpoint of the Committee frequently was in conflict with such movements as Zionism and Jewish trade unionism which drew their strength from the immigrant masses.

WORLD WAR I

World War I proved decisive in welding together the various segments of U.S. Jewry and affirming their place in U.S. society. When the war started, there was considerable Jewish sympathy with Germany as the enemy of Russian czarism, a bastion of socialist strength, and the ancestral land of a large proportion of U.S. Jewry. Reflecting the anti-Russian sentiments that were widely prevalent in the Jewish community, most Yiddish papers, whose readership then reached 600,000 throughout the country, took a pro-German position. Only the newly founded *Jewish Day* supported the Allies from the outset.

CHANGING SYMPATHIES

As the war raged, however, Jewish opinion moved with U.S. opinion in general toward a pro-Allied policy. The decisive year was 1917. The overthrow of Russian czarism, the idealistic motivation of America's entry into the war, and the British conquest of Palestine, followed by the Balfour Declaration giving the land of their forefathers back to the Jewish people, stirred a fever of enthusiasm. The Yiddish Socialist daily, *Forward,* remained editorially alone in refusing to condemn the Bolshevik Revolution in 1917, and was almost closed by the U.S. government. Before long, however, it took a hostile stand against Russian communism.

Approximately 250,000 Jews served in the U.S. Armed Forces in 1917 and 1918, a majority of them young immigrants. Military experience provided an intensive education in acculturation to the broader American milieu for Jews who came from urban immigrant neighborhoods. Congress authorized the commissioning of Jewish chaplains to serve the large number of Jewish servicemen, and the National Jewish Welfare Board (JWB) was founded in 1917 to enlist such chaplains and to provide religious materials for their use.

POPULARIZATION OF ZIONISM

During the World War I period, Zionism acquired an influence in U.S. Jewish life which it had not previously enjoyed. (The organized movement dated from 1897, but there had been Zionist groups as early as 1882.) The leadership was composed of several acculturated businessmen and Jewishly-conscious academicians, including figures as diverse as Richard J. H. Gottheil, who taught Semitic languages at Columbia University and was director of the Oriental Department of the New York Public Library; Harry Friedenwald, who taught ophthalmology at the Baltimore College of Physicians and Surgeons and wrote on medical history; Israel Friedlaender, professor of Bible at the Jewish Theological Seminary of America; Judah L. Magnes, president of the New York City Kehillah; Stephen S. Wise, rabbi of New York City's Free Synagogue; and Henrietta Szold, founder of the women's Zionist organization, Hadassah. Funds and outlets for activity were extremely limited, however, and membership was comprised mostly of young people of immigrant parentage.

The anticipation of the dissolution of the Ottoman Empire as a result of the war aroused new interest in the Zionist idea. The entry of Louis D. Brandeis into the Zionist ranks and his assumption of active leadership in 1914 also attracted new blood to the movement.

The Zionist idea began to stir U.S. Jewry, for it appeared to be a Jewish counterpart of the "self-determination of nations" propounded by President Woodrow Wilson. Zionist ideology was adapted to the American Jewish outlook by stressing Palestine as a refuge for oppressed Jews, and a place where an ideal society would be built.

American Zionism entered into a prolonged decline after Brandeis was named to a seat on the Supreme Court, and after he and his group withdrew from Zionist activities following an unsuccessful battle with other elements in the World Zionist Organization over the issue of whether Palestine was to be developed by large-scale public corporate enterprise or mass contributions to a general development fund (see ch. 4).

The American Jewish Committee's leadership of the Jewish community was challenged for the first time by the movement for an American Jewish Congress which sought to include the realization of the Zionist goal among post-war Jewish demands. A nation-wide election was held by U.S. Jews, to choose delegates to represent them at the post-war peace conferences. The majority of delegates chosen were pro-Zionist. Bowing to public sentiment, the American Jewish Committee joined the Congress delegation.

POST-WAR XENOPHOBIA

Although incidents of anti-Semitism were only sporadic during the period of America's participation in World War I, a new wave of nativist nationalism gripped the land with the coming of peace, as the artificially stimulated unity of the war cracked under the impact of post-war disillusionment, and a sense of imminent danger from internal and external subversive forces seized the nation. The old way of life appeared to be disappearing under the onslaught of the foreign-born, the city, the new moral relativism, and liberal religion. Many Americans adopted ideologies stressing coercive political and religious fundamentalism and sought scapegoats for the ills, real and imaginary, that beset them.

The United States' turn toward isolationism, the "Red Scare" of 1919–21, and the surge of nativism and anti-urbanism during the 1920s bore serious consequences for U.S. Jewry as a great wave of anti-foreignism and fervor for "Americanization," propagated in the press, books, and public schools, bore down hard on Jewish cultural distinctiveness. The noted American historian, Oscar Handlin, has described "the portentous period between 1913 and 1920" during which "great numbers of Americans became obsessed with fear of the Jew."

Anti-Jewish attitudes were rooted in older stereotypes and in renewed economic anti-Semitism which was an element in Populism, the movement of protest against capitalism and monopoly, which was powerful in the southern and western states at the turn of the century. Jewish capital was identified with "Wall Street" and with the oppression of farmers and small businessmen by the financial system. Some of the populists, such as Burton K. Wheeler (later Senator from Montana), were to remain anti-Jewish on such economic grounds into the 1930s.

Lynching of Leo M. Frank, 1915, Atlanta, Georgia.

In 1913 American Jews had been shocked when Leo Frank, a factory manager in Atlanta, Georgia, was convicted of the slaying of one of his female employees. The evidence against Frank was flimsy and the circumstances surrounding his trial and conviction indicated that mob anti-Semitism was involved. In 1915, a lynching party abducted Frank from jail and hanged him.

The emergence of overt anti-Semitism in the Frank case was a harbinger of an upsurge of anti-Jewish feeling, expression, and actions during the 1920s.

THE "RED SCARE"

Foreign radicalism became the chief target in the post-war "Red Scare." Because a certain number of Jews were members of politically radical groups, the canard of an international Jewish plot to overthrow Western civilization spread. The Jews as a body were generally labeled as Bolsheviks in a process of damnation-by-association which was to remain a permanent part of anti-Semitic propaganda.

Actually, the October (1917) Bolshevik Revolution and the establishment of the Communist International inaugurated a period of schisms within the Jewish socialist movement, as within virtually all socialist parties. It became necessary to choose between affiliation to the victorious communist movement, and continued adherence to democratic socialism. For Jews, this choice was particularly difficult, for the Russian Communist Party, while opposed to anti-Semitism, took an assimilationist attitude towards the Jewish question and was hostile both to Zionism and Jewish nationalism. The Comintern did not recognize the existence of a Jewish problem, and it denounced Zionism as an idea leading directly to counter-revolutionary results, aiming as it did at settlement in Palestine, which eventually would only serve to "strengthen British imperialism there."

The Bolshevik Revolution led to factional disputes within the two main American socialist parties in existence in 1917—the Socialist Party, and the Socialist Labor Party, both of which had significant Jewish memberships. Some of the more moderate Jewish socialist and labor leaders temporarily sided with the Bolsheviks after the October Revolution, in part because the alternative to Bolshevism was the violently anti-Semitic "white" counter-revolution. But they soon adopted a firm anti-communist stand. Other Jewish socialists threw their lot in permanently with the communists.

A Jewish Federation of the Communist Party was founded in 1919, and three years later a communist-sponsored Workers' Party came into being. In 1922, too, the *Freiheit,* a Yiddish newspaper of communist ideology, made its appearance. Some socialist leaders who were steeped in Jewish culture lent their support to communism largely because of their belief in the prospects of a national Yiddish culture developing in the Soviet Union. The Arbeiter Ring, one of the most important repositories of socialist sentiment in the United States, was a decisive factor in defeating Communist Party ambitions in the Jewish community.

The concern of the Jewish community over charges that it was part of an international Bolshevik conspiracy to destroy Christendom and dominate the world was heightened considerably by the appearance of an American edition of the spurious *Protocols of the Elders of Zion* in 1920, followed by a work based on it, *The Cause of World Unrest.* These libels, concocted in Paris in the last decade of the 19th century by an unknown author working for the Russian secret police, and then distributed throughout the world, were discredited by serious investigators, but they nevertheless remained alive, and continued to stir up anti-Semitic sentiments.

HENRY FORD'S DEARBORN INDEPENDENT

Simultaneous with the spread of social anti-Semitism and political and economic stereotypes of the Jew, doctrines of the inferiority of specific racial types became widely accepted in academic as well as popular thinking. This philosophy had a vigorous proponent of unlimited financial means in the automobile magnate Henry Ford. Ford published a magazine, *The Dearborn Independent,* which launched an anti-Semitic propaganda campaign without precedent in the United States. It lasted, with varying intensity, for almost seven years.

Charging American Jews with a plot to subvert traditional American ways, Ford's propaganda found acceptance in rural areas and small towns, but met a negative reaction in the large urban areas and among leading American policy and opinion makers. Notwithstanding such condemnations as a declaration, signed by 119 leading Americans, headed by President Wilson and former president Taft, denouncing the anti-Jewish calumnies, Ford's campaign continued unchecked. At last, in 1927, under pressure of an unofficial consumer boycott and several lawsuits, Ford issued a public apology through Louis Marshall, head of the American Jewish Committee.

Ford also published millions of copies of *The International Jew,* based on the calumnies of the Elders of Zion, until forced to desist in

Headline of one of the anti-Semitic articles in Henry Ford's weekly, May 22, 1920. All Ford dealers were required to sell the paper.

1927. But its ideas persisted as staple items in the arsenal of American anti-Semitism in succeeding decades.

THE KU KLUX KLAN

The most significant expression of American nativism during the 1920s was the spectacular revival of the Ku Klux Klan, the hooded Southern society. Refounded about 1915, it spread far beyond its original locale to the Middle West and even to the East.

Although its primary targets in the defense of "one hundred percent Americanism" were Catholics and Negroes, Klan propaganda also included Jews as one of the chief obstacles to preservation of the "real America." Thus, the Klan of the 1920s was the first substantial, organized mass movement in which anti-Semitism was utilized. Politically ineffective except as an adjunct to the immigration restriction movement, the Klan never proposed a specific anti-Jewish program, but encouraged sporadic boycotts of Jewish merchants and similar harassments.

At the height of its popularity in 1924, the Klan numbered over four million members throughout the country. However, public revulsion led to the organization's loss of power and virtual disappearance in the late 1920s.

THE JOHNSON ACT

One of the most serious issues faced by the Jewish community during the first quarter of the 20th century was the movement for restriction of immigration to the United States. Although there was no direct anti-Semitism reflected in the legislation resulting from restrictionism, it was clear that the intellectual fathers of the movement, who included Henry Cabot Lodge, Senator from Massachusetts, considered Jewish immigration deleterious to the welfare of the nation. Edward A. Ross, for example, predicted "riots and anti-Jewish legislation" if unrestricted immigration continued. Madison Grant, a thoroughgoing racist, condemned the Jews in his book, *The Passing of the Great Race* (1916), for mongrelizing the nation. The campaign for immigration restriction reached its height after World War I, when various writers, including Kenneth Roberts, a popular novelist, urged limitation of Jewish immigration.

By far the most important result of the restrictionist movement was the Johnson Act of 1924. An earlier immigration act of 1921 had established the principle of the "national origins quota," by providing that the number of immigrants to be admitted in any year was not to exceed 3% of their respective native lands' stock (i.e., immigrants and their children) residing in the United States in 1910.

The provisions of the Johnson Act were based on a belief in "Nordic" (Northern and Western European: English, Irish, German Scandinavian) superiority over Mediterraneans, Slavs, Orientals, and Jews. It not only limited yearly immigration to 154,000, but gave overwhelming preference to immigrants from Northern and Western Europe. This was accomplished by setting the quota at 2% of the foreign stock living in the United States in 1890, a census year before "undesirable" Slavic and Mediterranean elements were heavily represented in the population. Thus, only 5,982 immigrants could be admitted yearly from Poland, 2,148 from Russia, and 749 from Rumania. A prospective immigrant was categorized for quota purposes by his land of birth so that, for example, a Jew born in Poland who spent his life in England was a Pole under the Johnson Act. The only means of reaching the United States outside the quota was by affidavits guaranteeing support, submitted by relatives in the U.S.

The quota system, worked out in detail during the late 1920s, closed off the great stream of Jewish immigration to the United States. The effect of the Johnson Act was to hasten the day when the majority of U.S. Jews would be native-born, which was reached around 1940.

SOCIAL AND OCCUPATIONAL DISCRIMINATION

The immediate post-war years were a period of massive movement of Jews out of the immigrant neighborhoods into newer, more attractive urban districts, and out of immigrant trades into independent business, and commercial, clerical, and professional occupations. During the prosperity of the 1920s, large numbers of young Jews, children of immigrant parents, also sought to enter the professions of law, medicine, dentistry, teaching, and to some extent, social work.

As Jews continued to be the most rapidly rising ethnic group in American society, they were faced with increasing social discrimination in many areas of life. Jews with high incomes found themselves unwelcome in the fashionable sections of the cities and in many suburban developments. Discrimination hit hardest in the area of higher education, which Jews sought in larger numbers and earlier than any other immigrant group, for they viewed education as the key to economic and cultural advancement. Eastern colleges, in particular, were faced with increasing waves of Jewish students, and reacted by establishing quota systems—usually between 5 and 10%—under a variety of guises.

In 1922 President A. Lawrence Lowell of Harvard College publicly announced that Harvard was considering a quota system for Jewish students in order to preserve the representative character of the leading academic institution of the United States. The quota system thereupon became an open issue. The student body at Harvard supported Lowell, but the faculty committee that was appointed to set up the quota system was unanimous in opposing it and in insisting that applicants to the college be considered solely on the basis of merit. Defeated in its most blatant form, the quota system survived indirectly through various unofficial admissions techniques, at Harvard and at most other leading colleges, until after World War II. As late as 1945, Dartmouth president E. M. Hopkins justified a quota for Jewish students by emphasizing that "Dartmouth is a Christian college founded for the Christianization of its students." (A 1946 B'nai B'rith survey indicated that while Jews formed about 9% of the American college population, 77% of them were concentrated in fifty of the largest schools.)

The most rigorous anti-Semitic restrictions were enforced in the medical schools (in 1920 there were 214 Jewish students in the medical schools of New York State; by 1940 there were only 108 in the same schools), and many capable Jewish students were forced to study abroad. Anti-Semitism in the medical profession also applied to opportunities for specialty training and appointment to hospital staffs, even in public institutions. The Jewish hospitals founded late in the 19th century for the needs of Jewish patients devoted themselves in the 1920s to alleviating the plight of the Jewish physicians. College and university faculties were, with few exceptions, closed to Jews, and Jewish teachers could usually secure employment in public schools only in the largest cities where positions were filled through open, competitive examinations.

Jews encountered considerable resistance as they attempted to move into white-collar positions. Employers increasingly specified that Christians were preferred for office, sales, and executive positions.

Banking, insurance, and public utilities firms were in the forefront of anti-Jewish prejudice.

CULTURAL BLOSSOMING

In contrast to these restrictions, the 1920s were the ripest years of internal Jewish culture. There were 11 Yiddish theaters in New York City and 17 elsewhere in the United States. During a one-month period in the fall of 1927, 645 performances of 85 plays, many of high artistic quality, were presented. The Yiddish school system also reached its peak during these years, enrolling approximately 12,000 children. The first Jewish literary magazine, the *Menorah Journal*, began publication in 1915, with the goal of "fostering the Jewish 'humanities'."

American literature began to take note of the Jewish community, and novels about Jewish immigrant life appeared. Individual Jews became nationally known figures in the world of publishing and literary criticism. And the new entertainment industry of motion pictures was being developed, in large measure, by immigrant Jews.

THE DEPRESSION ERA

The economic depression, which began in 1929 and did not fully end until World War II, struck hard at all Americans. Mass unemployment severely affected thousands of small Jewish businesses, many of which were established by immigrants only a few years earlier, and which now went into bankruptcy. Established businessmen and Jewish communal leaders often fared no better.

COMMUNITY LIFE EBBS

One result of these economic disasters was the abandonment by Jewish philanthropies of the claim that "Jews take care of their own," for the numbers requiring relief were far too great for any but governmental support. Against the background of unemployment and business crisis, the income of Jewish community institutions drastically declined. The income of charitable institutions dropped by more than half; campaigns for overseas aid were virtually given up from 1930 to 1935; and synagogues and schools could not pay their employees.

Few of the 3,728 Jewish congregations in the United States flourished financially or spiritually. Synagogue membership and contributions sharply declined, and many congregations were burdened by mortgages on buildings erected during the 1920s. Reform Judaism became quite vigorous in its espousal of a liberal political program emphasizing trade unionism and international peace, and the Conservative movement spoke similarly. The Orthodox were disorganized and inarticulate, losing strength as their immigrant constituents died without leaving replacements.

Despite the rise in the Jewish school population (a 100% increase between 1908 and 1935, reflecting both the growing Jewish population and the parents' greater desire for their children's Jewish education), Jewish schools were hit hard. Enrolled students failed to pay tuition, and communal sources of funds dwindled and disappeared. This economic blow came at a period of great efforts in Jewish education, which witnessed the early development of the Jewish day school movement, the improvement of the Sunday school curriculum, the establishment of Jewish educational programs on the secondary school level, and the rise of the Conservative movement's congregational schools.

ECONOMIC DISCRIMINATION

Discrimination against Jews in employment became much sharper as jobs became fewer. Many Jews entered the expanding civil service rolls which offered employment to professionals and to technically trained individuals on terms of equal opportunity. The large number of Jews in the teaching and municipal social work fields, which was to be a factor in Negro-Jewish relations in the 1960s, stemmed from this period.

Widespread Jewish communal concern that under conditions of depression and anti-Semitism U.S. Jewry would soon consist of a few large businessmen, many independent salesmen, a large proletariat drifting unwillingly into factory labor, and an element of restless, bitter intellectuals, prompted much talk and a few efforts to "balance" Jewish occupational distribution, none of which came to anything.

Jewish youth, aided by their often impoverished families, continued to go to free colleges, especially in New York City, and to somewhat more costly state universities, while the prosperous went to private institutions. The percentage of college students in the Jewish community continued to be far higher than in the general population. In New York City 49% of all college students were Jewish, while the 105,000 Jewish college students in the entire country were just over 9% of total college enrollment. Student ambitions turned toward business and the professions. This foretold the Jewish economic future of the 1950s more accurately than did the predictions of the sociologists and economists.

THE GERMAN-AMERICAN BUND, AND FATHER COUGHLIN

The combined impact of the depression and the triumph of Nazism in Germany produced an outpouring of anti-Semitic propaganda and the birth of anti-Semitic organizations in the United States. The major themes of this agitation repeated the old charges of a Jewish international conspiracy, to which was added alleged Jewish responsibility for the depression.

Nazi-inspired anti-Semitism was diffused by such groups as the Friends of New Germany and the German-American Bund. The latter never achieved wide membership and was discredited when its leader, Fritz Kuhn, was convicted of embezzlement. More serious was the revival of native American anti-Semitism of the fundamentalist, pseudo-agrarian type.

The most potentially dangerous anti-Semitic leader of the 1930s was Charles E. Coughlin, a Roman Catholic priest. Coughlin, whose weekly radio broadcasts reached millions of listeners, launched an open anti-Semitic attack in 1938. His magazine, *Social Justice,* reprinted *The Protocols of the Elders of Zion,* with Coughlin's commentary placing responsibility for the world's plight on the Jews. Street riots and disturbances occurred when vendors sold his publication in the large cities. Coughlin was supported in his campaign by some official Catholic publications, including the *Boston Pilot* and the *Brooklyn Tablet.* The organizational expression of this predominantly Irish Catholic version of anti-Semitism was the Christian Front which held street-corner meetings and sponsored boycotts of Jewish merchants.

The impetus of Nazism added to the native American populist tradition with its suspicions of the big cities and intellectuals, and made it seem, for a moment in the 1930s, as if anti-Semitism might become a substantial force in the United States. But all these groups collapsed during World War II.

COMMUNAL RESTRUCTURING

The depression changed the mood of Jewish life and profoundly shook the communal structure of American Jews. The old leaders, many of them of German Jewish origin, were dying out and their children were for the most part uninterested in the Jewish community. Many leaders' personal wealth and status declined sharply. The depression and the Jewish crisis in Germany and Europe shook established Jewish values and practices and opened the way for communal restructuring and a newer leadership, drawn from Eastern European immigrant origins.

Jewish labor and socialist groups decisively joined the community after decades of abstention on account of class differences. The Jewish Labor Committee, established in 1934 to combat totalitarianism and aid refugees, collaborated with other Jewish bodies. Many labor groups gave up their anti-Zionist stance because of the socialist character of Jewish Palestine and their disillusionment with the international socialist brotherhood.

The Zionist movement was weak during the 1930s, and the income of its two fundraising arms, the Palestine Foundation Fund (Keren Hayesod) and the Jewish National Fund (Keren Kayemeth), dropped. The raising and allocation of philanthropic funds was, in fact, the key issue in U.S. Jewish communal life. Zionists waged a prolonged campaign to increase the proportion given to Palestine from the welfare fund drives conducted in most cities. In their attempt to increase the allocations to Palestine, Zionists encountered consistent opposition from the controlling oligarchy of large givers who generally favored European relief and distrusted Zionist projects.

These developments at the national level were made possible in many cities by the newly founded Jewish community councils. (There was a General Jewish Council of Jewish defense organizations from 1938 to 1941 which subsequently became the National Community Relations Advisory Council.) Synagogues, B'nai B'rith lodges, and Zionist societies were heavily represented and the tone was pro-Zionist. The Jewish community councils were deeply involved in the overseas philanthropic campaigns, or in Jewish welfare funds as they were known locally, in addition to their functions of promoting Jewish education, settling internal disputes, and watching over Jewish rights in their cities. They became the representative local Jewish organizations during the 1940s and strongly influenced American Jewish philanthropic allocations toward Palestine.

POLITICAL ACTIVITIES IN THE 1930s

The 1930s were marked by economic reform in American domestic life, and by a small qualitative upsurge in Jewish migration to the United States. Both of these factors had great influence on the Jewish community, and marked the beginning of a new era of maturation.

INTELLECTUAL MIGRATION

The increasing persecutions of the Nazi regime drove ever greater numbers of its Jewish victims to the United States. This immigration was limited, however, by economic conditions and by the difficulties in

Mr. Ussishkin, Dr. and Mrs. Weizmann, Prof. and Mrs. Einstein, and Dr. Mossinsohn, arriving in N.Y., 1921.

obtaining visas. Thus, total Jewish immigration to the United States from 1933 to 1937, which derived mostly from Germany, did not exceed 33,000. The National Coordinating Committee for Aid to Refugees and Emigrants Coming from Germany was established in 1934, and became the National Refugee Service in 1939. As the situation in Europe worsened, the number of immigrants from Germany and the lands it had occupied increased, totaling 124,000 between 1938 and 1941.

Several thousand of these refugees were scientists and academic intellectuals, whose symbolic leader was Albert Einstein. A few hundred of them wielded tremendous intellectual influence on research and teaching in the U.S. in such fields as music, art history, psychiatry and psychoanalysis, history, sociology, and incomparably in nuclear physics. This intellectual migration, nearly all Jewish, marked the transfer of the world's intellectual leadership from Europe to the United States.

Refugee immigrants generally encountered great difficulty in adjustment, owing mainly to depression conditions, and most of them had to start and long remain at an economic level beneath that which they enjoyed in Europe. They concentrated in New York City, focusing on particular neighborhoods, and tended to establish their own congregations, welfare organizations, and social clubs.

The German Jewish Club published a weekly newsletter, *Aufbau* (Reconstruction), which developed into a newpaper of high journalistic standards, emphasizing analysis of political and cultural events in the United States and abroad from a Jewish point of view. (Its circulation in 1970 stood at 25,000.)

THE NEW DEAL

As the Democrats became the party of urban-oriented reform, exemplified in 1928 by the candidacy of Alfred E. Smith, Jews, like other ethnic groups, moved into its ranks en masse. The New Deal and its leader, President Franklin D. Roosevelt, attracted enthusiastic Jewish loyalty. Roosevelt, who had strong ties with New York City reformers, many of them Jews, was greatly admired; throughout his presidency (1933–45) 85% to 90% of Jewish votes were cast for him and candidates who supported him. Jews appeared in politics with unprecedented prominence: one cabinet member (Henry Morgenthau, Jr., Secretary of the Treasury), three Supreme Court justices (Brandeis, Cardozo, and Frankfurter as

Brandeis' successor), four governors, and several hundred mayors, judges of lower courts, and high appointive officials.

Such New Deal legislation as bank deposit insurance, the protection of trade unionism, relief (welfare payments for low income families), government-sponsored public work projects, establishment of wage and hour standards, and social security, directly benefited the mass of working-class and lower-middle-class Jews.

"POPULAR-FRONT" COMMUNISM

Besides overwhelming Jewish support for the New Deal, the vogue of "popular front" Communism attracted many Jews during this period. Troubled by the seemingly insoluble economic crisis and menaced by nativist manifestations of anti-Semitism, the security of employment in Soviet Russia and its "prohibition" of anti-Semitism made that country appear a utopia to thousands. Communism appealed to some segments among garment workers and to professionals, like teachers and social workers, who were sensitive to social ills and encountered great difficulty in establishing themselves economically. Many American Jewish intellectuals, some of whom publicly recanted later, were active Communist Party propagandists.

However, Jewish membership in the Communist Party, which had been as high as 15% during the 1920s (the percentage of Jews among the Party leadership was undoubtedly higher) began to drop as a result of the Party's support of the Arab cause in Palestine, and fell sharply when the American Communist Party supported the Hitler-Stalin friendship pact of 1939. Finally, post-World War II revelations of Stalinist atrocities and of systematic Soviet anti-Semitism put a permanent end to Communism as a serious force in American Jewish life.

WORLD WAR II

During the public debates between 1939 and December 7, 1941, concerning American foreign policy during World War II, U.S. Jews were generally found on the side favoring maximum aid to England and France, and later Russia. Although Jewish sympathies were not with Great Britain, whose imperialism and White Paper of 1939 on Palestine were deeply resented, their fear and loathing of Nazi Germany far out-weighed any anti-British feelings they may have had.

THE AMERICA FIRST COMMITTEE

These years also witnessed the formation of a powerful isolationist movement in the United States. One of its most vocal organizations was The America First Committee, organized in 1940. The Committee attracted anti-Semites to its banner, and at an America First rally in September 1941, Charles A. Lindbergh, hero of American aviation, gave a speech in which he called the Jews the most dangerous force pushing the United States into war. Although his speech was followed by the protest resignation of the more liberal members of the Commit-tee, Lindbergh and the conservative faction persisted in their propa-ganda. Similar remarks were heard on the floor of Congress from such isolationist Senators as Burton K. Wheeler and Gerald Nye.

FIGHTING NAZISM

The attack on Pearl Harbor and the entrance of the United States into the war proved a blow against anti-Semitism, which was identified with the Nazi enemy.

Approximately 550,000 Jews, including many recent immigrants who were refugees from Nazi Germany, eventually served in all branches of the U.S. armed forces. And refugee scientists played an indispensable role in the development of atomic and other advanced weapons.

Some 311 rabbis were commissioned as chaplains and served in the armed forces; seven died in service. The National Jewish Welfare Board's Committee on Army and Navy Religious Activities provided the chaplains with religious literature, equipment, and kosher food in a supply line that reached around the world. Two tasks of special impor-tance performed by Jewish chaplains were their work with Jewish civilians in the first penetration of areas cut off from Jewish contacts during the Nazi occupation of Europe, and their aid to concentration camp survivors.

(Since World War II, the JWB has provided chaplains to serve in Korea and Vietnam, at military bases, service academies, federal hos-pitals, and other non-military installations. In 1970 Jewish chaplains

"The Four Chaplains on the S.S. Dorchester" by Dudley, depicting a classic incident of wartime heroism, a Jewish chaplain and three Christian chaplains praying together as the torpedoed ship goes down.

were serving in 611 domestic installations and hospitals, and in more than 40 foreign countries.)

AID FOR EUROPEAN JEWS

While battles raged throughout the world, European Jewry was being systematically murdered by Nazi Germany. Information became public during the fall of 1942, and subsequent stages in the Nazi "final solution" were widely known. U.S. Jewry, fearful of appearing to ask for "special treatment" or of encouraging propaganda that World War II was a "Jewish war," shied away from demanding direct U.S. intervention to save Jews under Nazi rule. The view was taken that an early Allied victory was the sole means to rescue European Jewry.

High Holidays service at a military base in Texas, 1956.

Early in 1944, following a direct approach by Secretary of the Treasury Henry Morgenthau, Jr., who was profoundly disturbed by State Department indifference and hostility to all proposals for the rescue of European Jews, President Roosevelt established the War Refugee Board. The board energetically attempted, with some success, to work through neutral countries and third parties to prevent further Nazi murder of Jews and others. Within the U.S. Jewish community, a Va'ad Ḥaẓẓalah (Rescue Council) under Orthodox leadership worked to rescue Jews, mainly by ransom.

As the war drew to a close, and the full dimensions of the European Holocaust were revealed, the American Jewish community faced its greatest challenge—to provide the vast sums required to rescue the surviving remnant of European Jewry, and to build up the Jewish state in Israel. They launched the greatest fundraising campaign in history and mobilized themselves to a heroic financial effort. Fundraising goals were raised by the continuous education of the Jewish community to the dimensions of the needs and its responsibility to meet them. Success in fundraising campaigns was to a great extent due to the willingness of the volunteer leaders to elevate the levels of giving by setting an example with their own contributions. The Jewish community responded to the challenge by raising funds unequalled in the annals of philanthropy.

Recognition of the need to provide a refuge for European Jews won the American Jewish community to a general acceptance of Zionism (see chapter 6). Anti-Zionist views became more isolated—and more aggressive. The American Council for Judaism was founded late in 1942 upon an ideology of opposition to Jewish nationalism. It conducted an assiduous anti-Zionist propaganda campaign which was vigorously countered by Zionists. The American Jewish Committee was non-Zionist in the political sense, and advocated free Jewish immigration to Palestine under a rather vague international trusteeship. It lost much of its once great influence in the American Jewish community over that issue.

A COMMUNITY IN HIBERNATION

The domestic activities of the American Jewish community remained in relative suspense during the war. Jews shared in U.S. prosperity as unemployment almost vanished. Charitable aid became superfluous, and business flourished.

However, anti-Semitism continued in sectors of public opinion, and manifested itself in petty street molestations of Jews, especially in Boston and somewhat in New York. In 1944 a public opinion poll showed that 24% of the respondents still regarded Jews as a "menace" to America, and one-third to one-half would have supported a hypothetical anti-Semitic campaign. President Roosevelt's alleged remark to "clear it with Sidney" (Sidney Hillman, Roosevelt's chief labor advisor during the war years) was used with special malice by anti-Semites during the 1944 election campaign.

A wave of post-war anti-Semitism was expected, especially if there were to be a depression during the difficult transition period from a wartime to a peace economy. The post-war years, however, proved to be a period of general economic expansion, and the American Jewish community struck deeper roots into the cultural, political, and economic life of the United States.

3

THE LARGEST JEWISH COMMUNITY
IN HISTORY

No history of the Jewish community in the United States would be complete without special attention being focused on the unique relationship that has existed between that community and the city of New York. It was at Manhattan Island that the first Jews to settle on the North American continent landed, and after an initial period of difficulties, the city proved hospitable to its Jewish residents. As New York prospered, so did its Jewish community; as the city grew to become the leading metropolis of the country, its Jewish citizens came to occupy positions of influence and power in its economic, civic, and cultural life.

As the Jewish community sank roots into New York, its identification with the city became so complete that it would be difficult to imagine any aspect of New York City life without its Jewish component. Jewish involvement made itself felt not only in commerce, politics, education, and the arts, but in numerous areas of everyday life, in its impact on local speech, gestures, food, humor, and attitudes. On the other hand, it is doubtful if anywhere else in the history of the Diaspora a large Jewish community has existed in so harmonious a symbiosis with a great metropolis, without either ghettoizing itself from its surroundings or losing its own distinct sense of character and identity.

From the first 23 refugees from the Brazilian Inquisition who reached the town of New Amsterdam, the Jewish population of New York City expanded to become the single largest Jewish community in history. In the 1960s the Jewish population in the metropolitan area was estimated at 2,400,000, about a sixth of world Jewry. It surpassed the number of Jews within the boundaries of the U.S.S.R.; and was approximately equal to the Jewish population of the State of Israel.

During the first two centuries of Jewish settlement in New York City, the Jewish community remained small, fluctuating between 1 and 2% of the population. In the decades preceding the Civil War, the arrival of large numbers of German and Polish immigrants increased the number of Jews to 40,000, or approximately 4% of the population. It was the great migration of Eastern European Jews to the United States beginning in the last decades of the 19th century that sparked the tremendous growth in New York Jewry.

POPULATION EXPLOSION

Beginning in the 1870s and continuing for half a century, the great population shift from Eastern Europe to the United States radically altered the demography, social structure, cultural life, and communal order of New York Jewry. During this period, more than a million Jews settled in the city. They were overwhelmingly Yiddish-speaking and impoverished, the products of intensive Jewish group life and wretched economic conditions. Meeting the harsh problems of economic survival and social integration and maintaining their ethnic heritage exacted vast physical, emotional, and intellectual efforts.

Immigrants at the Ellis Island depot, N.Y., c. 1907.

ETHNIC INTERACTION

On their arrival in the city the East European Jews (Russian Jews, as they were commonly called) found a Jewish settlement dominated by a group strikingly different from theirs in its cultural background, social standing, and communal outlook. By the 1870s this older settlement of German Jews had become, with some important exceptions, middle-class in outlook, mercantile in its economic base, and Reform Jewish in its group identity. Successfully integrated in the economic life of the city and well advanced in its acculturation to the larger society, the established Jewish community drew its leadership from a socially homogeneous elite of bankers, merchant princes, brokers, and manufacturers.

The two groups—the prosperous and Americanized "uptown Jews" and the alien and plebeian "downtown Jews"—confronted and interacted with one another, a process which significantly shaped the course of Jewish community development during the decades preceding and following the turn of the century.

Two-thirds of the city's Jews in 1870 were German-born or children of German-born parents. Together with the smaller subgroups—descendants of the 18th century community, clusters of English, Dutch, and Bohemian Jews, and a growing contingent of Polish Jews (who formed a distinctive subcommunity)—the Jewish population numbered 60,000, or 4% of the inhabitants of the larger city (Manhattan and Brooklyn). Only fifty years later, New York (all five boroughs) contained approximately 1,640,000 Jews (29% of the total population), and they comprised the most numerous ethnic group in the city. (The Italians, the second most numerous, formed 14% of the population. Their arrival in the city paralleled the Russian Jewish migration, and their initial areas of settlement adjoined the Jewish immigrant neighborhoods.) By 1920, 45% of the Jewish population of the United States were living in New York.

As the main port of entry for immigrants, New York served as a transit point and temporary domicile for an undetermined number of new arrivals. The city also attracted a portion of those who entered the country through other ports, particularly Philadelphia and Baltimore, or who came to the city after having lived inland for a time. Of all immigrant groups, Jews ranked first in their preference for New York. Of the 1,372,189 Jews who passed through the port of New York between 1881 and 1911, 73% settled in the city. The table below indicates the population growth of New York and of its Jewish community.

NEW YORK CITY POPULATION GROWTH AND JEWISH POPULATION GROWTH: 1870–1920

Year	Total Population of Greater New York	Estimated Jewish Population	Percentage of Jews in Total Population
1870	1,362,213	60,000	4%
1880	1,912,698	80,000	4%
1890	2,507,414	225,000	9%
1900	3,437,202	580,000	11%
1910	4,766,883	1,100,000	23%
1920	5,620,048	1,643,000	29%

RESIDENTIAL PATTERNS

This growth was accompanied by population dispersion within the city. In 1870 nearly two-thirds of the inhabitants of Greater New York resided in Manhattan. Fifty years later Manhattan's population had grown two and a half times, but it contained only two-fifths of the city's inhabitants. During this period Brooklyn's population multiplied fourfold, the Bronx's fifteenfold, Queens' ninefold, and Richmond's threefold.

THE LOWER EAST SIDE

On Manhattan's Lower East Side—bounded by Catherine Street, the Bowery, Third Avenue, 14th Street, and the East River—the population reached a peak of 540,000 in 1910. At the height of its congestion one-fourth of Manhattan's residents occupied one-twentieth of the island's space, an area of 1.5 sq. mi. For most of 50 years these East Side blocks, already overcrowded in 1870, were the reception center for the flood of Russian Jewish immigration. Only after 1900, when the immigrants themselves established new neighborhoods in areas like Harlem and Brownsville, did some newcomers go directly there, bypassing the Lower East Side.

The Jews constituted the most conspicuous element in this dual phenom-

THE MOST CROWDED SPOT IN AMERICA, NEW YORK'S GHETTO.

Cover of *Leslie's Weekly,* New York, April 23, 1903, showing the corner of Orchard Street and Ludlow Street.

enon of rising congestion and rapid dispersion. In 1870 the less affluent, and those whose occupations required it, lived in the southern wards of the Lower East Side along the axis of East Broadway. Germans, Irish, and native Americans constituted a majority of the district's population. The northern tier of wards, stretching from Rivington to 14th Streets, was heavily populated by Germans. Two-story frame houses were the prevailing type of residence, though many of these had already been converted to multiple-family use. By 1890, with Russian Jews pouring in, the great majority of the earlier inhabitants, including the German Jews, left the 80 square blocks of the southern wards. Ten years later they were in the process of abandoning the entire region below 14th Street to the rising tide of Jewish immigrants.

The characteristic type of residency in the enlarged Jewish neighborhood was now the "dumbbell" tenement. (The dumbbell shape met an 1879 municipal regulation requiring an airshaft between contiguously built tenements.) These tenements were five to eight stories in height, and occupied from 75 to 90% of a plot 25 feet wide and 100 feet deep. Each floor contained four apartments, a total of 14 rooms—of which only one in each apartment received air and light from the street or from a cramped backyard. The most congested area of all was the tenth ward, the heart of the Jewish East Side. In the 46 blocks between Division, Clinton, Rivington, and Chrystie Streets which made up the ward—an area of 106 acres—there were 1,196 tenements in 1893. The population was 74,401, a density of 701.9 persons per acre.

MOVING "UPTOWN"

The German Jews who left the Lower East Side joined their more prosperous brethren who had moved halfway up the east side of Manhattan in the years following the Civil War. They settled in the region between 50th and 90th Streets, which included the beginnings of Yorkville with its heavy concentration of Germans. Smaller contingents settled in the upper-class neighborhood of Harlem, north of Central Park, and scattered numbers reached the zone of well-situated brownstone homes west of Central Park.

The relocation of synagogues and the establishment of other Jewish institutions underscored this process of removal and social differentiation: the geographical division of the Jewish populace into "uptown"

The present synagogue of Congregation Shearith Israel, designed by Arnold Brunner and built in 1897 (left). The Central Synagogue, erected in 1872, the oldest building in continuous use as a synagogue in N.Y. (right).

and "downtown." As early as 1860 the venerable Shearith Israel had moved from a rapidly declining downtown area to 19th Street near Fifth Avenue, and in 1897 it moved once more to Central Park West and 70th Street, its present site. Temple Emanu-El, the leading Reform congregation in the city, moved from East 12th Street to Fifth Avenue and 43rd Street in 1868. Ahavath Chesed occupied its fourth site in its 26-year existence when it moved to Lexington Avenue and 55th Street in 1872. (Known as the Central Synagogue, this is the oldest building in continuous use as a synagogue in New York.)

In 1872 uptown Jews transferred one of their most esteemed philanthropic institutions, Mount Sinai Hospital, to 67th Street and Lexington Avenue, and by the turn of the century additional institutions supported by the older community were operating in the area. The Baron de Hirsch Trade School, the Clara de Hirsch Home for Working Girls, and the Young Men's Hebrew Association (YMHA) at Lexington and 92nd Street were the most prominent. Also located in the mid-East Side area were a number of private clubs which catered to the social needs of the wealthier Jewish businessmen.

Fourteen synagogues served the growing Yorkville settlement, half of them Reform or Conservative. The Orthodox congregations mainly served a Central European element, though affluent East European Jews were moving into the area and joining them.

JEWISH HARLEM

The Jewish settlement in Harlem developed along broadly parallel lines, though with some differences. Less accessible to the center of the city, and hence beyond the reach of most middle-class families, Harlem became a residential suburb for the wealthy and grew more slowly at the start. In 1874, when Temple Israel was established, it was the sole congregation in Harlem. Fourteen years later, when it dedicated its new synagogue on Fifth Avenue and 125th Street, three other small congregations were serving the community as well. By 1900 the number of permanent synagogues had grown to 13. Significantly, four of these had been founded by East European Jews—a sign that the movement of Russian Jews from the Lower East Side to Harlem was already well under way.

URBAN SPREAD

The completion of the first elevated railway in the late 1870s inaugurated a new age of transit which opened cheap, semi-rural land to intensive urban development. Along a network of expanding elevated and subway routes Russian Jewish immigrants moved out of downtown New York City in two great streams—north to Harlem and thence to the Bronx, and southeast across the East River to Williamsburg and Brownsville. By the 1880s three elevated lines were running the length of Manhattan. In 1904 the first subway was completed, and put the West Side, Washington Heights, and sections of the Bronx within the reach of families of modest means. In like manner the transit net spread to Brooklyn, with the construction of the Brooklyn, Williamsburg, and Manhattan Bridges, and subway tunnels under the East River.

A significant factor in the Jewish immigrant's geographic mobility was his rising expectations for economic progress. The physical conditions the new immigrant encountered on the Lower East Side were tolerable while he made his initial adjustment and saved to bring to the United States the family he left behind in Europe. With this achieved, the Jewish immigrant family looked for improved housing and environmental conditions, particularly as they might affect the young.

For the working class, moreover, the Lower East Side was losing its "walk to work" advantage. By 1910 the clothing industry, the main employer of the Jewish immigrants, was moving to the West Side above 14th Street. This development reflected the decreasing role of the sweatshop. Once the tenement-flat sweatshop (see below) based on cheap labor drawn from the neighborhood was restricted or eliminated, a major feature which had attracted newly arrived Jewish immigrants to the Lower East Side disappeared. The gradual elimination of the sweatshop belonged to a general improvement in labor conditions which was noticeable after 1900, when municipal housing regulations did away with some of the worst abuses in the tenement sweatshops, and was especially marked in the 1910s due to the new militancy and effectiveness of the labor unions (see below). A shorter work week and higher wages created the margin in time and money needed to leave downtown for more congenial surroundings. In many cases the move became possible, or was hastened, when children became old enough to add to family earnings.

A study of pensioned clothing workers shows that 88% of the Russian Jews left the Lower East Side after residing in the area, on the average, for 15 years. In all likelihood those who became entrepreneurs lived on the Lower East Side for a briefer time. Indeed, between 1910 and 1915

Shop for religious articles on the Lower East Side.

the population of the Lower East Side declined by 14%, and between 1915 and 1920 by a further 11%.

The most graphic instance of the growth of a new area of settlement is the case of the Brownsville-New Lots district of Brooklyn, where a small group of Jews of German origin had settled. In 1886 real-estate promoters began dividing the farmland into lots for sale and between 1890 and 1900 the Jewish population increased from less than 3,000 to more than 15,000. Five years later it had passed 49,000, and by 1916 the Brownsville-New Lots Jewish population had reached 225,490 and was served by 72 synagogues, all of which were Orthodox.

JEWISH NEIGHBORHOODS

By 1920 a socioeconomic hierarchy of Jewish neighborhoods had come into being. The Lower East Side and Harlem were losing their Jewish population at a rapid pace to the East Bronx and Washington Heights. More affluent Jews were moving from the East Bronx to the northern sections of the borough, and from Brownsville and New Lots in Brooklyn to the more rural areas of Eastern Parkway, Boro Park, Coney Island, and Flatbush. The move to more desirable sections of the city also meant severing ties with the *landsmanschaften* and local synagogues, and escaping some of the traditional group pressures that existed in the older immigrant neighborhoods. In their new neighborhoods, Jews lived alongside non-Jews.

ECONOMIC PATTERNS

In a number of fields the Jews of New York loomed large in the economy of the city. One group of German-Jewish families played an outstanding role in revolutionizing the retail trade of the city. In the decade after the Civil War, fathers and sons entered the dry goods business and transformed their establishments into great department stores, which still bear their names. Bavarian-born Benjamin Bloomingdale and two of his sons, both born in New York City, opened a dry goods store in 1872. By 1888 Bloomingdale's employed 1,000 persons in its East Side emporium. On the West Side, the department store founded by Benjamin and Morris Altman had 1,600 employees. R. H. Macy, not originally owned by

"Abraham and Straus" horse-drawn delivery wagons in the late 1890s.

Jews, was bought by Isidore and Nathan Straus in 1887. Sterns, Gimbels, and Abraham and Straus were other department stores established by Jews during this period.

A significant number of German Jews entered the field of investment banking. Closely knit by ethnic, social, and family bonds, they formed a recognizable group within the business community. Membership in the same temples and clubs, common philanthropic endeavors, and frequent marriages within the social set welded the group together, a fact which was important in their business dealings and led to frequent collaboration. Possessing excellent financial ties with banking interests in Europe—and especially in Germany—they were able to tap these sources for the U.S. market.

THE GARMENT INDUSTRY

New York's growing ready-made clothing industry was the main source of employment for the city's Jewish population. Its cutters, pressers, tailors, and seamstresses were largely Eastern European Jews, and its entrepreneurs were the more settled Jews of the earlier German immigration. In 1888, of 241 clothing manufacturers, 234 were Jewish and accounted for an annual product of $55,000,000.

The needle trade was fast becoming New York's most important industry. In 1870 the city's factories and shops produced men's clothes worth $34,456,884. In 1900 the value of goods they produced reached $103,220,201, and during the same period their work force rose from 17,084 to 30,272. The growth of the women's clothing branch of the industry was even more spectacular. The value of goods produced rose from $3,824,882 in 1870 to $102,711,604 in 1900. Where 3,663 workers were employed in 1870, 44,450 were employed in 1900. In 1913 the clothing industry as a whole numbered 16,552 factories and 312,245 employees.

East European Jews began streaming into the industry in the 1880s and by 1890 were the dominant element. They nearly completely displaced the German, Irish, and English craftsmen, as well as the German-Jewish manufacturers. One estimate made in 1912 calculated that approximately 85% of the employees in the needle trades were Jewish.

The immigrant Jews entered the apparel trade in such numbers because it was close at hand, required little training and allowed the congeniality of working with friends of similar background. The contracting system which became widespread in the industry by 1890 was responsible in large measure for these conditions. Contractors (middlemen) received cut goods from the merchant or manufacturer, rented shop-space (or used their own tenement flat), bought or hired sewing machines, and recruited a labor force. Generally about ten persons worked in these "outside shops" (in contrast to the larger "inside shops," where the manufacturer directly employed the work force, and where working conditions were better). The minute division of labor which prevailed permitted the employment of relatively unskilled labor. In the intensely competitive conditions of the time—compounded by the seasonal nature of the industry—hard-pressed contractors recurrently raised the "task" of garments for which payment was made. Under these circumstances the notorious sweatshops developed with their cramped quarters and long hours of work. In 1890 Jacob Riis wrote:

> The homes of the Hebrew quarter are its workshops also . . . You are made fully aware of [economic conditions] before you have

traveled the length of a single block in any of these East Side Streets, by the whir of a thousand sewing-machines, worked at high pressure from earliest dawn till mind and muscle give out altogether. Every member of the family, from the youngest to the oldest, bears a hand, shut in the qualmy rooms, where meals are cooked and clothing washed and dried besides, the livelong day. It is not unusual to find a dozen persons—men, women, and children—at work in a single small room.

Until the turn of the century a 70-hour week was not uncommon.

With all its abuses, the system of small shops which existed on the Lower East Side had its advantages for the new arrival. Old country ties often played a role in the operation of the system and softened harsh conditions with an element of familiarity. Manufacturers set up fellow townsmen *(landsleit)* as contractors; contractors hired *landsleit*. Bosses who were practicing Orthodox Jews made allowances for the religious requirements of their workers. The production system with its extreme specialization also had its advantages. The new immigrant could quickly master a subspecialty commensurate with his experience—or lack of it—and his physical stamina. Finally, the competitiveness of the industry provided opportunities and hope. The ascent from worker to contractor to small manufacturer beckoned to the enterprising and ambitious.

CLASS STRUCTURE

The compact Jewish neighborhoods had a broad working-class base. A survey of the most heavily populated Jewish wards of the Lower East Side, conducted by the Baron de Hirsch Fund in 1890, showed that 60% of those gainfully employed were shopworkers in the needle trades, 6.9% were shopworkers in other industries (approximately 20% of the cigarmakers in the city were Russian Jews), 8.2% were artisans (mainly painters, carpenters, and tinsmiths), and 23.5% were tradesmen (nearly half of these being peddlers).

The building boom in the city attracted Russian-Jewish builders who opened the way for their countrymen to enter the field as craftsmen. At first Jewish building activity was limited primarily to renovating old tenements, because of limited capital and the discriminatory practices of the craft unions. But in 1914, when the Jewish painters were finally accepted into the Brotherhood of Painters and Paperhangers, 5,000 joined

Lower East Side orange vendor, 1895 (left), and shoelace seller in N.Y. at Wall St. and Broadway, 1896 (right).

the union. An Inside Iron and Bronze Workers Union, organized in 1913 under the auspices of the United Hebrew Trades, had a membership of 2,000 in 1918.

Branches of the food-processing industry—like baking, and the slaughtering and dressing of meat—were "Jewish industries," owing to the ritual requirements of *kashrut*. One of the oldest labor unions in the Jewish quarter was the bakers' union, which numbered 2,500 by 1918.

By 1920, however, the occupational and class structure had changed considerably. The change was expressed in the decrease in number of blue-collar workers, the increase in number of college students, the rise of a professional group of notable size, the growth in magnitude and income of the mercantile class, and the consolidation of a wealthy stratum composed primarily of clothing manufacturers and real-estate entrepreneurs. The proportion of garment workers among the gainfully employed Jews in New York City dropped to 40%, and the total employed in all manual work stood at 50%.

By the turn of the century, a majority of the students at tuition-free City College was Jewish, and in 1918 the proportion of Jewish students was 78.7% of total enrollment. At the city's college for women, Hunter, the proportion was 38.7%.

In 1907, 200 physicians, 115 pharmacists, and 175 dentists served downtown's Jews. (The number of Jewish physicians in the borough of Manhattan rose from 450 in 1897 to 1,000 in 1907.) To this group of professionals should be added the growing number of lawyers. Evening law school—generally a two-year course of study—enabled the younger generation to prepare for a professional career while being self-supporting. The young lawyers had many avenues open to them: labor law, socialist organizations, Tammany politics, and Orthodox Jewish causes. (See Law, Chapter 5.)

JEWISH TRADE UNIONISM

The nearly all-Jewish needle-trade industry spawned the Jewish trade union movement whose successful organization of Jewish labor (1909–1916) coincided with the great drive by American trade unionism at large.

However, the fact that the trade-union struggle took place in New York City's garment industry made it a Jewish communal affair as well, and aided Jewish union development. Large clothing manufacturers were also leaders of the community; "downtown" social workers and "uptown" philanthropists were equally concerned with the good name of the community and the social integration of the newcomers.

In 1888 several small Jewish labor organizations had formed the United Hebrew Trades, which subsequently included a majority of the Jewish workers in the United States in its ranks. In general, however, the Jewish labor movement made little headway before 1900. This was due partly to ideological factionalism, and partly to the fact that the great majority of workers were employed in the garment industry which consisted of a virtually unorganizable mass of tiny workshops, in which employer and employee might be relatives and fellow townsmen, and in which the seasonal nature of employment was reflected in apathy among the workers.

In New York City the successful surge of trade unionism began with the tragic Triangle Shirtwaist fire of 1911, in which 146 Italian and Jewish workers, almost all girls, perished. It was followed by the bitter "revolt of the shirtwaist (blouse) makers," a six-week strike which aroused widespread public sympathy, but failed nevertheless. The most important event was the three-month strike of 60,000 cloakmakers (the largest sustained strike in the city's history up to that time) directed by the previously ineffectual International Ladies Garment Workers Union.

The strike encountered bitter employer resistance. (The main demand was for recognition of the International Garment Workers

Union as the exclusive bargaining agent for the workers. It was this point, rather than those which concerned wages, hours, and subcontracting, that the employers fought hardest.) Various Jewish community leaders, including Louis Marshall and Jacob Schiff, sought to mediate the dispute. However, the settlement was worked out by a young lawyer making his first appearance in Jewish public life, Louis D. Brandeis.

The resulting "protocol of permanent peace" provided for a system of joint employer-employee-public boards to deal with grievances, sanitation, etc. The contest over union recognition was settled by "the preferential shop"—i.e., preference in employment given to union members.

This strike was the critical event which turned the Jewish labor movement into an aggressive, responsible, and socially progressive force. It also greatly increased the stability and influence of general clothing industry trade unions. (See Chapter 5.)

COMMUNAL LIFE

GERMAN-REFORM BASE

In 1870 the New York Jewish community appeared to be well on its way to achieving homogeneity in form and content, directed by its Americanized element of German origin. For this group Jewish communal life expressed itself in membership in a Reform temple, and sponsorship of Jewish welfare institutions. Lay leaders of the established community found in these institutional forms a way to maintain their Jewish identity in a manner they considered compatible with American practice. Though they drew upon Jewish communal traditions, these leaders were profoundly affected by the model of American liberal Protestantism with its denominationalism, voluntarism, and moralistic rather than ritualistic emphasis.

By 1900 there were some 14 Reform synagogues in the city. In 1918, there were 16 Reform and 32 Conservative synagogues. These synagogues held services on weekends, sponsored one-day-a-week religious schools, and engaged university-trained rabbis whose most important function was delivering a weekly sermon. The leading newspapers regularly reported their discourses when reviewing the notable sermons delivered in the city's houses of worship.

The establishment of the Free Synagogue in 1907 as a pulpit for Stephen S. Wise was a novel religious development, for its services were conducted on Sunday mornings at Carnegie Hall, and it also embarked upon a wide-ranging program of social service. Wise and Judah L. Magnes represented a new type of Jewish minister. American-bred and American-trained, they were young, excellent orators, and forceful—even daring—in espousing their causes and attracting large followings in the community at large. Wise became best known for his attacks on municipal corruption and industrial conditions. Magnes' main efforts were directed toward cultural and social improvements within the Jewish community. He was president of the New York City Kehillah from 1908 until its demise in 1922 (see below).

"SCIENTIFIC" PHILANTHROPY

During the last third of the 19th century, the established community built, in addition to imposing temples, a number of large and progressive philanthropic institutions: general relief agencies, hospitals, old-age homes, orphan asylums, vocational training schools, and neighborhood centers. The outlook of these institutions reflected the receptivity of uptown's Jewish leaders to the social thought and patrician practices of

A Purim ball in New York, 1877.

the time. The emergence of scientific philanthropy, with its insistence on thorough investigation of the needy applicant, emphasis on economic and vocational rehabilitation, and espousal of the professionalization of welfare services, guided the policies of the older Jewish charities. So did the related sociological view of poverty which emphasized environmental factors, uplift, and "preventive work." (See Chapter 5.)

As late as 1885, the largest single group of applicants for aid from the United Hebrew Charities (formed in 1874 by a merger of six philanthropic societies) was of non-East European stock. By 1916, however, the vast majority were Russian-Jewish immigrants. An excerpt from a Yiddish article published in 1884 suggests the gulf which existed between the "professional methods" employed in the "uptown"-sponsored institutions, and the immigrant clients:

> In the philanthropic institutions of our aristocratic German Jews you see beautiful offices, desks, all decorated, but strict and angry faces. Every poor man is questioned like a criminal, is looked down upon; every unfortunate suffers self-degradation and shivers like a leaf, just as if he were standing before a Russian official.

In the field of child care, two of the leading institutions in the city were the Hebrew Orphan Asylum which in 1917 had a capacity of 1,250 children, and the Hebrew Sheltering Guardian Society. The latter moved to Pleasantville, New York, in 1912, where it introduced the "cottage plan," a model program. The largest institution sponsored by the uptown Jews was Mount Sinai Hospital which moved to its present site, Fifth Avenue and 100th Street, in 1904.

THE EDUCATIONAL ALLIANCE

The notion that philanthropic institutions should be nonsectarian carried weight with the leaders of Jewish philanthropy. Nonsectarianism, however, clashed with a second approach which urged the necessity of encouraging Jewish cultural and religious activity. Supporters of the latter position differed widely in their understanding of such a program, the debate bearing upon such fundamental issues as the meaning of Americanization, the legitimacy of preserving the Old World heritage and its secular offspring, and the nature of inter-group relationships within the New York Jewish community. These issues found their clearest institutional expression in the work of the Educational Alliance, the largest and most influential community center on the Lower East Side.

In 1889 a number of uptown societies sponsoring Jewish cultural activities on the Lower East Side amalgamated and formed the Hebrew Institute. Four years later, reorganization led to a change in name, which emphasized the nonsectarian stand by replacing Hebrew Institute with Educational Alliance. The institution's official scope was ". . . of an Americanizing, educational, social, and humanizing character." In 1897 the agency's president, Isidore Straus, explained that "our work may seem sectarian . . . [because] we have reached chiefly Jews, but this is due to the fact that the neighborhood . . . is inhabited principally by Jews."

Nevertheless, the Alliance did recognize the background of its constituents. The library and reading room were well stocked with Yiddish, Hebrew, and Russian books and periodicals. A synagogue and a religious school were established as well, though they were conducted in a manner which antagonized the Orthodox. In the early 1900s, the Friday evening lectures by Zvi H. Masliansky, the most eloquent and influential Yiddish preacher on the American scene, drew large crowds, as did guest appearances by such Yiddish literary figures as Shalom Aleichem. Orthodox Jewish leaders, however, still viewed the Alliance as a bastion of Reform Judaism, while the radical intelligentsia condemned it as an example of "uptown's" use of charity and Americanization to silence social protest.

Despite the opposition of these circles and the condescending approach of the lay leadership, the Jewish masses exploited the opportunities which the institution opened for them. English language classes and naturalization courses for adults, preschool instruction for newly arrived immigrant children, literary and civic clubs, music classes and a children's orchestra, drama circles and art exhibits, the Breadwinner's College, a physical education program, and a Free Library provided a rich fare. During the first decade of the 20th century as many as 37,000 persons went weekly to the main building and to the two branch centers.

EAST EUROPEAN COMMUNAL TRANSPLANTS

Important as uptown's welfare agencies were in aiding the immigrants, they at best complemented the communal order being created by the East European Jews themselves. Transplanted synagogues, *talmud torahs,*

Pupils at U.S. yeshivah, early 20th century.

"Chatham Square Cemetery among the Tenements," drawing by Lionel S. Reiss, early 20th century.

and traditional charities constituted a major part of that order. In addition, secular ideologies established a network of institutions, adding to the heterogeneity of Jewish life and enriching it intellectually.

In organizing their synagogues, the first and most typical communal undertaking, the immigrants mostly established congregations of *landsleit,* newcomers deriving from the same European town or province. In 1887 it was estimated there were 130 Orthodox congregations in New York City, by far the largest number on the Lower East Side. By 1902 the number of synagogues in the downtown quarter had reached 254, and by 1917, 418. A 1917 study estimated that 40% of 365 congregations located in the older sections of the Lower East Side sponsored traditional adult study groups, 45% had free loan societies, 33% sick benefit societies, and 91% cemetery plots. In addition, 50 to 70 "temporary" synagogues operated for the High Holidays on the East Side alone. In all of New York City there were 784 permanent and 343 temporary synagogues, in 90% of which Yiddish was the language of the sermon and of public announcements.

A few older synagogues gained stature as central institutions in the downtown community, transcending the localism of *landsmanschaft,* though they still retained a regional identity. These larger synagogues were also among the minority of congregations able to support rabbis. In 1887 there were three or four East European rabbis in New York; in 1917 the number may not have reached more than 50.

The comradeship of *landsleit* and the wish for family benefits in case of disability or death produced a vast network of mutual benefit societies, benevolent associations, and fraternal orders. Originally part of the congregations, they increasingly developed into separate organizations, offering some form of insurance, sick benefits, and interest-free loans, as well as cemetery rights. In 1917 there were about 1,000 such independent societies in New York with an aggregate membership of over 100,000; many of them found it financially advantageous to affiliate with a fraternal order. The largest order in New York City was the Independent Order Brith Abraham, which in 1917 had 90,000 members in 354 lodges.

Other *landsmanschaft* societies formed federations—of Polish, Galician, Rumanian, or Oriental (from the Ottoman Empire) Jews. These were loose groupings whose unifying factor was some joint effort at overseas aid and some major philanthropic undertaking.

ATTEMPTS AT UNIFICATION

The multiplicity of small synagogues and philanthropic agencies impeded their efficient operation and growth. Rivalries and vested interests compounded the situation and dogged all efforts at community collaboration in meeting larger issues.

In 1887 a number of Orthodox congregations federated for the purpose of creating a central religious authority to be headed by a chief rabbi. Rabbi Jacob Joseph of Vilna, a renowned European scholar, was installed in that post in 1888. The undertaking failed, however, chiefly because of the inability of the chief rabbi and his supporting organization to establish a communal regulation of *kashrut,* and the refusal of other rabbis to accept the chief rabbi's leadership. In 1902 Rabbi Jacob Joseph died in poverty.

Attempts at unification of the community were more successful in the field of welfare services: central institutions began to develop which came to be identified with the city's East European Jewish sub-community as a whole. One of the most respected community-wide bodies was the Hebrew Free Loan Society, established in 1892. Beth Israel Hospital was founded in 1890 to make kosher food available for Orthodox Jewish patients, and to provide employment for physicians of East European origin—neither service being available at Mount Sinai Hospital at that time. This downtown hospital in time achieved a status comparable to older community institutions.

The Hebrew Sheltering and Immigrant Aid Society (HIAS), formed by a merger of two older organizations in 1909, was the most prominent of the community-wide agencies. Responding to the needs of Jewish immigrants from Eastern Europe, the organization soon grew to national dimensions, providing help in legal entry, basic subsistence, employment, citizenship instruction, and locating of relatives for nearly half a million newcomers to the United States during its first decade of activity.

During the first decade of the century, influential leaders of the Jewish community became increasingly aware of the social costs of institutional parochialism, profusion, and confusion. The sharp rise in immigration following 1903 underscored the need for more rational use of the resources and communal wealth which the community did indeed possess. Uptown Jews, willy-nilly identified with the total Jewish community, sought better ways to stem the social disorganization and expedite the integra-

tion of the immigrants. Some downtown leaders recognized the ineffectu-
alness of their own institutions. In both sectors of the community the
alienation of the younger generation from Judaism and Jewish life was
viewed with alarm.

These concerns led to the establishment of the short-lived New York
Kehillah, a brave but unsuccessful attempt to create a united community
structure.

THE NEW YORK KEHILLAH

The immediate catalyst for the formation of the Kehillah was the accusation of police commissioner Theodore A. Bingham in 1908 that 50% of
the criminals in the city were Jews. (Though the figure was exaggerated,
crime in the Jewish quarter was a vexing problem.) Led by Judah L.
Magnes, a coalition of representative leaders established the Kehillah
as a federation of Jewish organizations in 1909.

Under Magnes' competent and spirited presidency, the Kehillah created
a number of bureaus—education, social morals (dealing with crime),
industry (concerned with labor relations), and philanthropy. In addition, it organized a rabbinical board and a school for training communal
workers. It sought to bring *kashrut* supervision under the purview of the
board, and use the resultant fees to finance neighborhood rabbinical
courts, support religious functionaries, and provide for religious education and other needs of the Orthodox community.

In 1909 a study of Jewish education had revealed that three-quarters
of the Jewish children of school age received no religious education at
all. Of those who did, 27% supplemented their public school sessions with
attendance in 468 improvised, ungraded, one-room private schools, the
ḥadarim. The level of instruction on the whole was poor; the *ḥadarim*
were beyond the reach of any form of communal supervision. About
20% of those receiving Jewish instruction attended the city's 24 *talmud
torahs.* Since these institutions were supported by independent associations and accepted children who could not pay the tuition fee, they were
in effect communal schools to whose support over 6,000 persons contributed small sums. The largest of these schools were generally superior
to the *ḥadarim.*

An auspicious endeavor to upgrade the *talmud torahs* was made by
the pioneering Bureau of Jewish Education of the Kehillah beginning

in 1910. Under the direction of Dr. Samson Benderly, attempts were made to modernize textbooks, provide a graded curriculum, improve pedagogical methods, and upgrade preparation and remuneration of teachers. Benderly encountered considerable opposition from Orthodox circles who feared the bureau's interfering with the independence of the *talmud torahs,* and mistrusted it because of the religious views of its lay supporters and staff. Nevertheless, the first seven years of the bureau's activities were auspicious ones. It recruited and trained a group of young educators, popularized the notion of communal responsibility for Jewish education, established model schools, and conducted educational research.

The Kehillah's productive years were brief. The Jewish community was too fragmentized; the struggle for a livelihood was too consuming; and the Old World rabbis in the local synagogues were ill-equipped to contribute the kind of leadership required for a community-wide undertaking. Moreover, Magnes' leadership was undermined by his pacifist convictions, his opposition to U.S. entry into World War I in 1917, and his activities in the peace movement during the war. In 1922 Magnes emigrated to Palestine where he helped found the Hebrew University, becoming its chancellor and first president. The New York Kehillah ceased to exist.

Though a number of the activities the Kehillah initiated proved to be of lasting significance—notably the Bureau of Jewish Education—no similar attempt at community organization has been made since.

FEDERATION OF JEWISH PHILANTHROPIES

The establishment in 1917 of a unified Federation for the Support of Jewish Philanthropies proved more lasting. As in other cities, the New York federation encompassed the larger welfare bodies of German-Jewish sponsorship, primarily interested in nonsectarian social welfare work.

There were signs, however, that the New York federation might develop into more than a central fundraising agency. Soon after its establishment, under the pressure of the group which had supported the Kehillah, the federation accepted five *talmud torahs* and the Kehillah's Bureau of Jewish Education as beneficiary agencies. This implied that the federation would concern itself not only with the relief of distress but also with the support of Jewish cultural endeavor. The federation also indicated in its first year of existence that it expected to become the spokesman of the entire community, and that it would solicit the support of the masses as well as of wealthy donors. But these statements remained little more than declarations of intention.

SECULAR IDEOLOGIES

During the period after 1900, Zionism and socialism played, with varying success, many-sided roles in the organizational and cultural life of the New York Jewish community. In institutional terms the Zionist achievements were minimal. The Federation of American Zionists, the Order Sons of Zion, Mizrachi, Po'alei Zion, the Jewish National Workers Alliance, Hadassah, and the Intercollegiate Zionist Association numbered in 1917 about 8,500 members who belonged to 95 loosely organized chapters. The influence of Zionism, however, went beyond membership figures. Much of the interest in the Hebrew language, Jewish education, and community planning stemmed from cultural Zionist circles.

Following the outbreak of World War I, Zionists of all shades vastly increased their influence in the community. During the war years, 125,000 Jews in New York City participated in the election of delegates to the newly formed American Jewish Congress which was to formulate a postwar program of the Jewish people. The 100 delegates elected to represent New York's Jews were overwhelmingly of East European origin, the majority of them sympathizers of Zionism.

The socialists, through the Workmen's Circle (Arbeiter Ring), possessed a stronger organizational framework than the Zionists. The order's 240 New York lodges and 25,000 members made it in 1917 the second-largest fraternal order in the city. Though the Workmen's Circle drew its membership from the Yiddish-speaking immigrant masses, it did not consciously identify itself with the Jewish community as a whole until World War I, when it began to participate in communal affairs and undertook direct support of cultural activities, such as Yiddish schools.

YIDDISH CULTURE

The Yiddish-speaking masses who settled in New York created a rich and varied cultural life. No less than the community's institutional structure, this life aided the newcomers in their adjustment to the great metropolis.

The very size of the immigrant community, its geographical compactness and social heterogeneity, and the impact of the new condition of freedom, encouraged a multiplicity of cultural undertakings. Between 1872 and 1917, for example, about 150 journals in Yiddish appeared, offering guidance, information, and entertainment, for a generation in the throes of accommodation to a strange civilization.

YIDDISH PRESS

The Yiddish-language daily press in particular served these ends. By the early 1900s four stable dailies had evolved: the Orthodox and Zionist *Tageblat;* the *Jewish Morning Journal,* Orthodox, conservative on social issues, and anti-Zionist; the radical and nationalistic *Warheit;* and the socialist *Forward.* In 1914 the *Tog,* pro-Zionist and liberal, was established; it absorbed the *Warheit* in 1919.

World War I marked the high point for the Yiddish press in the United States. Anxiety over the fate of relatives and of Jewish life in Eastern Europe sent the readership soaring. In the peak years of 1915–16, the circulation of the daily Yiddish press reached 500,000 in New York City (600,000 nationally). (See also Chapter 2.)

The Yiddish papers kept few reporters in the field, and relied for all but local news on the national and international wire services. At the same time they devoted much space to serious fiction by virtually every Yiddish author of note, to literary criticism, political essays, and articles on economics, history, and sociology. The *Forward* created the "Bintl Brief" column of personal woe and editorial advice, which had imitators in other papers. Slashing editorials frequently dealt with municipal problems and local Jewish affairs. The papers also provided information about employment, cultural activities, and community undertakings.

The functions of the Yiddish press made its publishers and editors major communal leaders, a fact which was recognized "uptown." Indeed, uptown circles were the initiators of the *Tog* in 1914, in an attempt to wean the Yiddish reader away from the political (socialist) and religious (Orthodox) extremism of the immigrant ghetto and hasten his Americanization.

The role of the Yiddish press found its fullest expression in the *Forward.* Its editor, Abraham Cahan, was a great innovator, and his apprenticeship as a reporter for the New York *Commercial Advertiser* under Lincoln Steffens served him well in turning the *Forward* into the leading Yiddish daily. The *Forward* was the focal center of the Jewish labor movement and a powerful cultural factor in the community.

Weekly and monthly periodicals reflected the broad range of ideas, movements, and professional interests of the New York community. The Yiddish journals and dailies drew to New York a significant colony of intellectuals, writers, poets, and critics whose work was read in the press and discussed in the lecture halls and coffeehouses of the East Side.

In addition to the Yiddish press, the Anglo-Jewish weekly *The American Hebrew* provided the older settlement with a résumé of Jewish news and social events in their circles; its circulation was less than 10,000. Catering to other small audiences were the Hebrew journals *Ha-Ivri* and *Ha-Toren,* and the Ladino *La America.*

The Yiddish press began its decline after the war. The restrictive Immigration Act of 1924 cut off the flow of Yiddish-speaking immigrants, so by 1939 the combined circulation of the Yiddish press had dropped to 400,000, while a study in 1945 showed a further decrease to 300,000 readers whose average age was 55. By 1970 the number was 100,000.

(Left) Ads from the N.Y. Yiddish newspaper, *Forward,* June 13, 1920.
(Right) Announcement of Yiddish plays in N.Y. on Rosh ha-Shanah, 1898.

YIDDISH THEATER

The Yiddish theater complemented the press. It has been called the "educator, dreammaker, chief agent of charity, social center, and recreation hub for the family." Melodramas and romantic musicals depicted historical and topical events which were drawn from the classic Jewish past, the "old home," immigrant life in the New World, and current American affairs. Nearly all weekday performances were benefits raising money for some charity, strike fund, or literary journal. In 1900, three theaters were devoted exclusively to Yiddish drama which, together with other houses giving occasional performances, drew about 25,000 patrons a week. By 1917 seven houses presented Yiddish theater.

POLITICS AND CIVIC AFFAIRS

For Jews, as for all minority groups, election to public office meant social recognition and acceptance into the body politic of the city. Prior to the 1900s the number of Jewish officeholders was small, their posts for the most part minor, their ethnic identity an insignificant factor, and their political careers brief. Three Jewish congressmen were elected in New York City between 1870 and 1899, and each served but one term. Considerably more Jews served in the state legislature. Among them was Joseph Blumenthal, who was a member of the Committee of Seventy which was responsible for the downfall of the Tweed Ring.

THE JEWISH VOTE

In the years following 1900, the densely populated Jewish neighborhoods and the rising political awareness of the immigrants carried increasing political weight. A number of assembly districts and several congressional districts had Jewish majorities or pluralities, and this was reflected in the ethnic origin of the candidates for public office, the particular issues raised, and the language of the campaigns. The number of Jewish voters was large enough to influence the outcome of city-wide elections. Though uptown Jews denied it, a Jewish vote existed. It was not prone to act *en bloc,* but it did respond to group interests and ethnic pride and was unafraid to demand its political due.

Jews came of age as a political force during the domination of the Tammany Hall political machine. Led by astute and, if need be, ruthless politicians, Tammany offered its constituents a host of services in return for their vote. Some of its leaders were attuned to the moods and needs of their Jewish constituents, and sensitive to ethnic ambitions. In 1900 Henry M. Goldfogle went to Congress as representative of the Lower East Side, serving until 1921 with the exception of two terms. By 1910 one or two Jews were entrenched as East Side assemblymen, and Jews received 5 to 8% of the mayor's top appointments.

ANTI-TAMMANY FORCES

Support of Tammany was not monolithic, particularly in mayoral and presidential campaigns. Anti-Tammany forces recognized this and, when mounting major reform campaigns, paid particular attention to the Jewish immigrant neighborhoods. In 1901, for example, the Fusion ticket flooded the Jewish districts with Yiddish circulars. Jacob A. Cantor, who had fought for tenement house reform as an assemblyman in the 1880s, was elected borough president of Manhattan as a Reform Democrat. The publisher William Randolph Hearst, in his effort to defeat the Tammany candidate for mayor in 1905, carried the Jewish East Side. His *New York American* featured stories of Russian barbarism and solicited funds for the relief of pogrom victims. Hearst even launched a Yiddish newspaper for a time.

Among the uptown Jews, a group of patrician "good-government" reformers emerged who helped finance repeated efforts to dislodge Tammany. Among them were Democrats like Nathan and Oscar Straus, and liberal Republicans like Jacob Schiff, Isaac N. Seligman, and Adolph Lewisohn. They assumed a particular responsibility for wooing their downtown brethren away from the "twin evils" of Tammany and socialism by supporting the reform candidates in their East Side campaigns.

THE SOCIALIST VOTE

Socialism was a significant political force in the Jewish immigrant districts. On the Lower East Side, the Socialists could count on a straight party vote of about 15%, and in some Jewish election districts in Brooklyn and the Bronx it may have been even higher. However, only when the party offered a candidate able and willing to appeal to the particular interest and ethnic sentiment of the East European Jew did it win at election time. In 1914 it sent Meyer London to Congress for the first of three terms, the first Socialist elected to the House of Representatives and the first elected Socialist for any office from New York City. London, a lawyer for a score of Jewish labor unions, lived in a Jewish neighborhood, and spoke the language of the immigrant. He eschewed party dogma.

Of special interest were the elections of 1917 in which Morris Hillquit, the outstanding figure in the Socialist Party, won 22% of the vote—twice that of the Republican candidate—in his unsuccessful bid for the mayoralty. That election sent ten Socialist assemblymen to Albany and seven aldermen to City Hall. One Socialist was elected municipal court judge. The vote reflected the strong anti-war sentiment among the East European Jews as much as it did Socialist Party sentiment.

ACCULTURATION

World War I expedited the social processes that molded a variegated and fragmented Jewish public into a more homogeneous ethnic community. The war confronted all Americans with the problem of their group identity—Americanized Jews of German origin no less than recently arrived East European Jews. By 1920 the Jews of New York saw themselves as a major group in the city.

But the war also brought prosperity which enabled families to leave overcrowded immigrant districts for a better, more "American" environment and so accelerated the process of acculturation.

THE LAST HALF CENTURY (FROM 1920)

DEMOGRAPHY

Following World War I, the Jewish population of New York grew moderately to 1,765,000 in 1927 and 2,035,000 in 1937. It tapered off to around 2,100,000 in 1950, and then slowly decreased as Jews moved to the suburbs. By 1960 the Jewish population of the city had declined to

1,936,000, while that of the metropolitan area increased to 2,401,600, owing to the large growth of the Jewish population in the suburban counties. The city's Jewish population, which fell further to 1,836,000 by 1968, was also an aging group as younger families moved to suburbs. The move to outlying areas by Jews and other middle-class whites in search of more comfortable residences and greener neighborhoods was intensified from the mid-1950s by negative factors which included the growing inadequacy of middle-class housing, the decline of municipal services and the public schools, and the increase of crime and racial tensions.

RESIDENTIAL PATTERNS

No less than during immigrant years, New York Jews preferred to dwell near each other. Thus, 676,000 of Brooklyn's 857,000 Jews in 1940 resided in areas where Jews formed 40% or more of the total population; in 1958, 388,000 of the Bronx's 493,000 Jews lived in neighborhoods of similar concentration. Anti-Jewish discrimination in the sale and rental of housing had been effectively quashed before 1950, except for isolated instances in opulent areas of Manhattan.

Within the city's five boroughs, Jewish population centers shifted as Jews abandoned highly congested Jewish areas. In 1918, 696,000 Jews (46% of the city's total Jewish population) lived in Manhattan, most of them on the Lower East Side and in Harlem. Masses of Jews left the Lower East Side as their economic situation improved, before the Depression of 1929. While 314,200 Jews lived on the Lower East Side in 1923, by 1940 only 73,700 remained. The number was much the same in 1960 when the Jews there lived mainly in cooperative housing projects sponsored by Jewish trade unions. In the 1920s Harlem became a Negro neighborhood; of the 177,000 Jews living there in 1923 fewer than 5,000 remained in 1930.

Many Jews from Manhattan and other areas moved north to the more recently settled Bronx. By 1927 about 420,000 Jews lived there, and by 1939 the Bronx Jewish population rose to 592,000, making that borough 44% Jewish. Following the general trend toward the suburbs, however, Jews began leaving the Bronx in the 1950s, so that by 1968 only 395,000 Jews remained.

From the 1920s the borough most heavily populated by Jews was

Brooklyn, where the number of Jews rose from 568,000 in 1918 to 975,000 in 1937. It then began to decrease, and was down to 760,000 in 1968. In contrast to Manhattan and the Bronx, Brooklyn tended to be a borough of well-defined neighborhood communities. Reputedly, Jewish religious life in Brooklyn was more active than in other boroughs. Williamsburg, across the East River from the borough of Manhattan, a community in which Jews numbered 140,000 in 1923, and only 33,400 in 1957, attained some celebrity, even as its population declined, as the site of a large ḥasidic colony of post-World War II immigrants from Hungary and Eastern Europe. Other Orthodox neighborhoods declined as areas in Brooklyn became Negro ghettoes. Bedford-Stuyvesant's 70,000 Jews in 1923 dwindled to fewer than 30,000 in 1957 and shrank further in the 1960s. In 1925 about 250,000 Jews lived in East New York-New Lots-Brownsville, where they comprised 82% of the population of the area. However, only 96,000 remained in 1957, and most of those

Drawing by Jacob Epstein, 1902.

left during the 1960s. On the other hand, Boro Park, long a center of Orthodox Judaism, increased in Jewish population and became strongly hasidic with the influx of Williamsburg *hasidim*. (See Chapter 4.)

The borough of Queens saw a sustained increase in its middle-to upper-middle class Jewish population, owing to its newness, relative remoteness from the center of the city, and rapid building of large apartment-house complexes. While only 23,000 Jews lived there in 1918, the Jewish population grew to 200,000 by 1950 and 420,000 by 1968.

About 5,000 Jews lived in the sparsely settled, isolated borough of Richmond (Staten Island) in 1918. Their number grew moderately, reaching approximately 11,000 in 1968. With the completion of the Verrazano-Narrows Bridge, an increase in the Jewish population was anticipated.

The Jewish population of Manhattan declined from the 1920s. In 1937 there were 351,000 Jews on the island, while only 250,000 remained in 1968. Nearly all Manhattan Jewish neighborhoods declined in the 1960s with the exception of the expensive, rebuilt Upper East Side, where Jews increased from 22,000 in 1940 to 42,000 in 1968.

TRADE UNIONISM

New York Jewry formed so large a proportion of the city's population that Jewish economic habits and aptitudes broadly influenced the city's economy. Jewish labor in the garment trades, the city's foremost industry, reached its peak at about 1920. Perhaps 200,000 Jews belonged to the trade unions of the garment industry. From this point the proportion of Jewish workers steadily declined in the clothing industry, dropping to 39% in the men's clothing branch in 1937; the new working group was largely composed of Italian women and, later, Puerto Ricans. The same process operated in the ladies' garment industry. One large local of the I.L.G.W.U. was still about three-quarters Jewish in the 1940s but declined to 44% in 1958. Jews remained in the garment industry at upper levels of skill as cutters and sample makers, and as entrepreneurs and salesmen.

The Jewish labor movement in New York was firmly established by 1920, and between 1920 and 1922 the unions successfully fought attempts to reestablish the open shop. However, they were beset during the 1920s by violent factional quarrels with Communists. The latter derived support from post-World War I Jewish immigrants who entered the garment industry and felt somewhat excluded by the established union leadership and ideology. Communist tacticians "boring from within" secured control of the New York Joint Board and led it into a series of disastrous strikes culminating in 1926. The union was left in ruins and did not reestablish itself until the New Deal period.

The Amalgamated Clothing Workers of America, led by Sidney Hillman, was more fortunate in maintaining its unity and power. A third garment union, the International Fur Workers' Union, succeeded in its trade-union objectives under Communist Party leadership, while the United Hat, Cap and Millinery Workers did likewise under liberal leaders.

During the 1920s the New York Jewish unions entered areas of activity never previously known to U.S. trade unions. They conducted large-scale adult education programs, health clinics, a bank, and summer resorts, built model urban housing, and generously subsidized struggling trade unions in the steel, coal, and textile industries. Except for their Communist wing, they became pioneers of liberal political action, thus preparing an eminent place for themselves in New Deal political and legislative affairs.

PATTERNS OF EMPLOYMENT

As late as 1950 the Jewish immigrant generation remained a workers' society. A survey indicates that 23% were "operatives and kindred" and that 16% were "craftsmen, foremen, and kindred." The 32% who were "managers, officials, and proprietors" included a mass of shopkeepers and small businessmen. Jewish retailers were especially heavily concentrated in such areas as candy and stationery stores, grocery stores, hardware stores, haberdashery stores, tailor shops, and delicatessens and small restaurants. The immigrants' children, however, shifted towards sales and clerical occupations and independent business: in 1950, 55% of immigrants' sons were in these groups, and only 22% remained in traditional working-class occupations.

One important channel of ascent was New York's excellent public school and college system. As early as 1915 Jews comprised 85% of the student body in the city's unique free municipal college system, a percentage which probably did not decrease before 1960; others attended college outside the city. This higher education helped launch thousands of young Jews in poor or very modest circumstances into independent business and the professions.

Areas of Jewish economic activity often were clearly demarcated. Thus, the port of New York, shipping and other transportation industries, large banks, insurance companies, and heavy industry hardly employed any Jews. Even after the removal of discriminatory employment policies in 1945, Jews remained few in these industries. Small, independent business, the garment trade, and light industry employed masses of Jews. Jewish entrepreneurs could be found in these fields as well as in real estate, building, and investment banking. By the 1930s, notwithstanding sharp anti-Jewish discrimination, over half the city's doctors, lawyers, dentists, and public school teachers were Jews.

After World War II, these tendencies continued, as the Jews became the city's mercantile and professional ethnic group, heavily represented in academic, scientific, and civil service organizations. Reflecting their occupational changes, they formed a large part of the membership and most of the leadership in trade unions of public employees.

DISCRIMINATORY PRACTICES

The most damaging and widespread form of discrimination against Jews, as well as Negroes, Italians, and others, was in the hiring practices of banks, insurance companies, large corporations, law firms, and department stores—some of which were owned by Jews. Several private universities and professional schools also imposed stringent admissions quotas against Jews and others, but the professional schools at the city's Catholic colleges enrolled a high proportion of Jews. Social discrimination against Jews was so firmly fixed that the most notable Jews could not belong to many of the city's leading business and social clubs—some of which their grandparents had helped to found.

Long-continued pressure, primarily from New York City and led by Jews, resulted in the passage of the state's Fair Employment Practice Act in 1945 prohibiting discrimination in employment, the first such law in the United States. By the time of its passage, however, its direct importance to Jews had already lessened, since employment discrimination decreased from the 1940s, in the wake of an expanding war economy.

A POLITICAL FACTOR

As the largest single ethnic group in the city, Jews were a highly important factor in its political life, which incorporated both rivalry and understanding among the various ethnic groups. As a religious body, the Jews, who were about 27% of the city's residents, were outnumbered only by the (predominantly Irish) Catholics, who were just over half the population. In no other city could Jews as a group weigh so heavily in politics, or were real or alleged Jewish political interests reckoned with so carefully.

Until the 1930s New York City was governed through the Manhattan organization of the Democratic Party, known as Tammany Hall, which held the support of most immigrants, including Jews. There were Jewish Republicans, and the preponderant ethnic element among Socialists and Communists was Jewish. Yet Jews generally followed the Democratic Party and some among them received the rewards of party loyalty—personal and business favors, municipal appointments, and judgeships.

The period from 1928 to 1945 witnessed far-reaching changes in New York City's political climate. Jews heavily supported Alfred E. Smith, liberal Tammany reformer of Irish stock, in his successful attempt for the presidency in 1928. The Depression in 1929 brought New York Jewry overwhelmingly behind the New Deal and the Democratic Party. Jewish support for Franklin D. Roosevelt during his presidential campaigns ran from 80% to 90%, higher than among any other group in the city. The urban liberalism of the New Deal had many of its seeds in the Jewish trade unions, East Side settlement houses, and Jewish philanthropists and social workers. Jews were enthusiastic for the New Deal Jewish Democrat Herbert H. Lehman, elected to the state governorship in 1932, 1934, 1936, and 1938, as well as for New Deal Senator Robert F. Wagner.

Of particular interest was the election of LaGuardia to the mayoralty of New York in 1933, by the votes of Italians, Jews mostly of middle-class reform sympathies, and upper-class good-government supporters. Of Italian stock, but partially Jewish in descent and fluent in Yiddish, LaGuardia was a nominal Republican whose mastery of ethnic politics succeeded in attracting the Jewish working class and left wing for his municipal version of the New Deal. During LaGuardia's incumbency from 1934 to 1946, Jews figured more prominently as city officials and political leaders.

As fervent supporters simultaneously of the Protestant aristocrat Roosevelt, the Jewish banker Lehman, and the Italian commoner LaGuardia, New York Jews indicated that they preferred liberal, reform-minded candidates and avoided Republicans unless they differed significantly from the generally conservative habits of that party. The American Labor Party (founded in 1936) and its successor the Liberal Party (organized in 1944) served their intended purpose of drawing voters of the left, especially Jews, to liberal or left-liberal candidates.

ETHNIC BALANCE

Following LaGuardia's tenure, the doctrine of "ethnic balance" became habitual in the city's politics. The major parties regarded it as necessary for victory on Election Day to nominate a Jew, an Irishman, and an Italian for the three city-wide electoral offices. The tripartite Catholic-Jew-Protestant division became accepted even in such spheres as the Board of Education, judicial nominations (where Jews may have exceeded this "quota"), and other foci of political power.

Under the Democratic mayoralties from 1945 to 1966, Jews remained firmly and prominently Democratic. During most of this period Jews were elected as city-wide controllers and presidents of various boroughs, and to the powerful position of county surrogates as well as to local judgeships. In 1965 the reigning Democrats for the first time nominated a Jew, Abraham D. Beame, for the mayoralty, but largely owing to a considerable Jewish defection from that party to the ranks of John V. Lindsay, the Republican reformer, the latter became mayor.

Readjustments of political power late in the 1960s to include Negroes and Puerto Ricans tended to reduce Jewish and other white influence, but Jews continued to be a major constituent in New York politics, sympathetic to liberal reform but protective of their status.

JEWISH COMMUNAL LEADERSHIP

In the years after World War I, New York retained its unchallenged position as the center of U.S. Jewish life. After the Union of American Hebrew Congregations moved to New York from Cincinnati in 1952,

B'nai B'rith was the only major nationwide Jewish organization that did not have its headquarters there. Indeed, the city became the capital of the entire Diaspora after World War II, as Zionist and other world Jewish movements established their offices in New York. Thus, it was habitual for New York Jews to preside over major Jewish organizations, or at least to conduct their daily affairs. A probable result was the weakening of the quality of local communal leadership, as many of the ablest men and women were drawn into the affairs of these national and world Jewish bodies. New York Jewry was intensely interested in worldwide Jewish affairs, and mass meetings on behalf of overseas Jewry sometimes brought out more than 100,000 persons.

After the ambitious attempt to coordinate communal life in the New York Kehillah ended in the early 1920s, no further attempt was made to establish a central Jewish community. New York Jewry had acculturated with such rapidity and formed so large a proportion of the city's ethnically and religiously diverse population that its minority-group consciousness was too tenuous to support such an undertaking. Jews who were leaders in politics, labor, business, and philanthropy, as well as rabbis, tended to exercise informally the functions of community leadership in limited spheres of New York Jewish life; weak Jewish community councils were founded during the 1940s in Brooklyn, Queens, and the Bronx.

Virtually every Jewish organization had chapters and members in the city, including *landsmanschaften,* lodges, cultural bodies, charitable groups, political causes, Zionist organizations, and synagogues, so that the total number of Jewish organizations probably exceeded 4,000 before the 1940s; with the disappearance of many lodges, benefit societies, and small immigrant synagogues there was probably a decrease thereafter. Altogether the city's Jews constituted an agglomeration of social classes, ideologies, clustered interests, and institutions, possessing Jewish identification in varying degrees of intensity.

A major sphere of community interest remained philanthropic, with the Federation of Jewish Philanthropies serving as its focal institution. The Federation served the poor and dependent; all of its affiliated hospitals and many other institutions associated with it were non-sectarian. Highly skillful direction came from social workers and executives supported by a wealthy, rather limited constituency, many of whom found fulfillment as Jews in this charitable effort alone. The federation's original 54 affiliates numbered 130 by 1968, and included hospitals, institutions for the aged and chronically ill, casework agencies, summer camps, Young Men's and Women's Hebrew Associations and neighborhood centers, and the Jewish Education Committee.

Service to the increasing number of aged and to troubled families (through the Jewish Family Service, successor to the United Hebrew Charities) replaced the earlier relief services. The Jewish hospitals, some of which were rated among the world's finest, totaled about 7,000 beds in 1968. The Federation's income was approximately 22 million dollars in the late 1960s. In addition, it conducted a successful 104 million dollar capital funds campaign during the late 1950s, three-quarters of which was devoted to hospitals and to care of the aged.

Except for some community centers, there was little linkage with the Jewish community at large. In 1970 New York's was the sole large U.S. Jewish philanthropic federation which did not combine its campaigns with those of the United Jewish Appeal.

YIDDISHISTS AND HEBRAISTS

An important aspect of New York City's Jewish life was the Yiddish-secularist culture typified by the Yiddish language daily *Forward,* the Workmen's Circle, Yiddish cultural societies and schools, the Jewish Labor Committee (after 1934), and the YIVO Institute for Jewish Research. The last sought to collect and preserve material mirroring Jewish life, to rescue Jewish folklore from oblivion, and to study various Jewish problems scientifically.

The early associations with Jewish trade unionism lessened as Yiddish secularism became a cultural and fraternal middle-class movement. Labor Zionists combined Yiddish with their Zionism, while Communist-oriented leftists maintained rival, parallel Yiddish institutions between the late 1920s and the 1950s.

Linguistic assimilation inevitably led to the decline of Yiddish from its peak during the 1920s. After 1950 the Yiddish sphere was limited to a dwindling group of veterans, a number of younger enthusiasts, and some post-World War II immigrants. The Yiddish press lost ground steadily in the years after World War II, and the Yiddish theatre which had staged hundreds of performances a month in the late '20s, presented only an occasional performance by the '60s.

A much smaller group of Hebraists was centered about the Histadrut

Ivrit, an organization devoted to encouraging the use of Hebrew and the knowledge of Hebrew culture, and the weekly Hebrew-language paper *Hadoar*. This group was composed largely of writers, Hebrew teachers, and rabbis, and was involved in Zionist and educational affairs. Its numbers shrank as the reality of the Hebrew renaissance in Israel drained interest in Hebrew literature in the United States.

RELIGIOUS PATTERNS

New York Jewry tended to be religiously active, but it was affiliated along lines which, until the 1950s, tended to be more social than theological. In several neighborhoods the Sabbath and Jewish holidays dominated the local atmosphere, as full synagogues, shut stores, and festively dressed residents were conspicuous. Large sectors of the garment industry and such kindred branches as rags and dry goods regularly closed on these days. The commerce and industry of the city as a whole came near to a standstill on Rosh Ha-Shanah and Yom Kippur. From the 1960s the public schools were officially shut on those days because Jews, who formed a majority of the teaching staff, absented themselves.

In 1967 there were 549 Orthodox, 184 Conservative, 93 Reform, and five unclassified synagogues in Greater New York; all but 163 of the total were within the city's boundaries. Actual synagogue affiliation tended to be low, however. A study of Brooklyn suggested that merely one-quarter of its Jews belonged to synagogues in 1945–46, a proportion which probably differed little in other boroughs. Many, however, habitually attended Orthodox synagogues without joining them, and vast numbers reserved seats on the High Holidays, the only days they attended religious services. The suburbs, on the other hand, appear to have had higher synagogue affiliation, with lower average attendance.

The Orthodox Jews were the least suburbanized segment in the city, with only 32 synagogues beyond the city limits in 1967. This factor, plus several hundred thousand committed members, lent New York Jewry a more Orthodox tone than any other community in the United States.

An undetermined number of prosperous, cultured Jews formed a large part of the membership of the Community Church, the Ethical Culture Society, and the small Jewish Science group.

JEWISH EDUCATION

Jewish education in New York followed nationwide trends in the slow disappearance of the *heder,* the rise and decline of communal *talmud torahs* and Yiddish schools in the period from 1915 to 1950, the continuance of the Sunday school, and the rapid growth of congregational schools, especially in Queens and the suburbs, after 1945.

Significant, distinctive local trends included the relatively smaller proportion of Jewish children who attended Sunday school and the higher proportion enrolled in *yeshivot,* all-day schools that combined Jewish and general studies in various proportions. The number of children attending a Jewish school rose from 65,000 in 1917, to 75,000 in 1935–36, then sharply to 202,000 in 1958. It declined to 136,000 in 1968–69. About 23.5% of all Jewish elementary school-age children were enrolled in Jewish schools in 1917; the proportion rose to 37% in 1959. About two-thirds attended weekday afternoon Hebrew schools. Yiddish school enrollment, about 6,900 pupils in 1935, declined to 3,200 in 1962.

About two-thirds of *yeshiva* enrollment in the entire United States was in New York; over 90% was under Orthodox auspices. Enrollment in *yeshivot* jumped from less than 2,000 in 1920 to 45,000 in 1968. The most striking development was that of Yeshivath Rabbi Isaac Elchanan and its high school (1920) into Yeshiva College, and then into Yeshiva University. In addition to several high schools, it included the college, graduate and professional schools, and a medical school. In addition to Yeshiva University, the city had numerous other *yeshivot* to which Orthodox young men came from many parts of the U.S. and abroad.

The Jewish Theological Seminary of America (Conservative), the Jewish Institute of Religion (Reform; combined in 1948 with Hebrew Union College, Cincinnati), and various divisions of Yeshiva University provided rabbinic training and attracted scholars of international standing to their faculties.

Columbia was the first university in the United States to offer instruction in every major area of Jewish studies at the highest level. The Jewish Division of the New York Public Library and the library of the Jewish Theological Seminary were two of the six or seven leading Jewish libraries in the world, and other local institutions possessed fine collections. The Seminary sponsored a Jewish Museum which housed outstanding collections of Jewish ceremonial art and Jewish coins and medals, in addition to its changing exhibits. New York's Jewish libraries, institutions of Jewish learning, and serious and learned Jewish periodicals made it a major Jewish cultural center by 1920, and the principal center in the Diaspora from the onset of the Nazi era.

No other city of the Diaspora offered such an abundance of Jewish scholars, books and manuscripts, and varied opportunities for study in a communal milieu which was profoundly Jewish.

INVOLVEMENT IN NEW YORK CULTURAL LIFE

The half-century following the end of World War I witnessed the entry of Jews in large numbers into every corner of New York artistic and cultural life. Since this period also marked New York City's growing domination of U.S. cultural life in general, and in some areas, such as theater, music, and publishing, its virtual monopolization, New York Jews prominent in these fields found themselves automatically at the center of national attention as well.

The role of New York Jews as consumers of the arts also grew im-

Dedication ceremony for the main building of Yeshiva University in Washington Heights, 1928 (left). The former Warburg mansion on Fifth Avenue in N.Y., now housing the Jewish Museum (right).

mensely during these years. It is safe to say that from the 1920s on Jews formed a disproportionately high percentage of New York's theatergoers, music listeners, book purchasers, and art collectors. (One rough estimate holds that Jews constituted 70% of the city's concert and theater audiences during the 1950s.) Similarly, Jews emerged in those years as major philanthropic patrons of the arts. After World War II, particularly, they played a prominent part in endowing and supporting local cultural and artistic institutions.

In effect, Jewish involvement in New York cultural life in the middle decades of the 20th century was virtually complete. Nor was this relationship one-sided. For if the Jews gave unstintingly of their experience, energies, and talents to New York, they received in return an education in urbanity and a degree of cosmopolitan sophistication unknown to any other Jewish community of the past.

Above all, when 20th-century New York Jews thought of the city they lived in, they did not simply consider it a great capital of civilization that had generously taken them in; rather, they thought of themselves—and with every justification—as joint builders of this greatness and one of its main continuing supports. It has been suggested that such a relationship marks a unique moment in Jewish history. Given current cultural and demographic trends both in the United States and the world at large, a similar relationship is not likely to occur again.

4

UNDERSTANDING THE JEWISH COMMUNITY

IS THERE AN AMERICAN JEWISH COMMUNITY?

American Jewry, numbering over half of all the Jews in the Diaspora, is unique among the Jewish communities of the world. A very large, fully modern society that was built from the start on individualistic principles, it is pluralistic in the full sense of the word. Settled by several significantly different waves of Jewish immigrants, it has lacked sufficient homogeneity to permit the emergence of a neat communal structure. Every effort to create even so much as a single nationwide address for United States Jewry has failed. Although there are one or two "umbrella" organizations concerned with Jewish defense and kindred matters, there is no central governing agent that serves as the point at which authority, responsibility, and power converge.

HISTORICAL PERSPECTIVE

In the earliest period of Jewish communal life in the United States, the small and relatively homogeneous Jewish population managed to achieve unity at the local level through a system of local congregations, but the wave of immigrants from Central Europe that arrived in the 19th century put an end to that kind of unity. A larger and more complex American Jewish community then experimented with a representative board. Whether it would have succeeded or not became a moot point when the mass migration from Eastern Europe created the largest and most diverse Jewish community in history, scattered over the largest area ever considered as embracing a single national group. Even local communities lost whatever features of unity they might have had under the impact of the new immigrants.

At the same time, the new immigrants brought with them, or stimulated by their arrival, the beginnings of a system of Jewish communal life which proved more suited to the American environment. Such a system had its origins in the closing years of the 19th century, but is essentially a 20th-century development.

At the end of the 19th century, the American Jewish community was largely composed of a proliferation of local synagogues and organizations, frequently formed along lines of national origin and often duplicating each other's efforts with little or no coordination between them. The first attempts at centralization began to appear on a local level at the turn of the century. However, the signal attempt to establish a community-wide *kehillah* in New York City under Judah L. Magnes's leadership lasted little more than one decade. The only successful community co-ordinating efforts have been in the form of a confederative framework in which local voluntary groups cooperate in certain joint ventures.

VOLUNTARY ASSOCIATIONS

The primary characteristic of Jewish communal life in the United States has been its voluntary nature, due, undoubtedly, to the virtual disappearance of legal and even social and cultural barriers to individual freedom of choice. Learning to give direction to and to function within this freedom has constituted a major challenge to the Jewish community and has been a key factor in determining the direction of Jewish life in the contemporary generation.

The American Jewish community is built entirely upon an associational base. Not only is there no unavoidable compulsion, external or internal, to affiliate with organized Jewry, but all connections with organized Jewish life are based on voluntary association with some particular organization or institution, whether in the form of synagogue membership, contribution to the local Jewish Welfare Fund (which is considered to be an act of joining as well as contributing), or affiliation with a B'nai B'rith lodge or Hadassah chapter. (Even such organic entities as the family have frequently taken on an association character in American Jewish life, in the form of the "family circle," a formal association of relatives.)

The usual pattern for affiliated Jews is one of multiple association, with memberships in different kinds of often overlapping groups reenforcing one another and creating a network of Jewish ties that binds the individual more firmly to the community. Without that associational base there would be no organized Jewish community at all; with it, the Jewish community attains the kind of social and even a certain legal status that enables it to fit well into the larger society.

The associational basis of American Jewish life is manifest in a wide variety of local and national organizations designed to suit every Jewish taste. While these organizations may be confined to specific localities or may reflect specific interests, classes, or types, the most successful ones develop both countrywide and local facets. Thus, the two most successful mass Jewish organizations in the United States, B'nai B'rith and Hadassah (see chapter 6), are both countrywide (the former is also international) organizations that emphasize the role of their local chapters or districts (which are often further divided into groups or lodges).

The key to their success is that they provide both an overall purpose attuned to the highest goals of Jewish life, and local attachments based on the immediate social needs of the individual Jew, so that one can become a member for either or both reasons.

All the large national Jewish organizations have found that their survival is contingent upon developing some sort of serious local dimension to accommodate the combination of American and Jewish penchants for organizational arrangements based on federal principles. In both civilizations, mobilization of human resources rests to a substantial degree on promoting the individual's sense of participation.

WHO REMAINS A JEW?

The new reality of voluntary choice regarding affiliation with the American Jewish community has encouraged a variety of options for Jewish identification, but has also given Jews greater freedom than ever before to decide whether they wish to identify as Jews or not.

ESTABLISHING JEWISH IDENTITY

"Who is a Jew?" The answers range from the clear definition provided by Jewish law (halakhah), namely, one who is born of a Jewish mother or who has undergone conversion according to halakhah, to the broad framework which includes all those who make an inner emotional choice to accept the label of "Jew" for themselves, or who are so labeled by the outside world.

The situation of world Jewry outside of Israel more nearly approximates the second definition of Jewish identity than the first.

Historically, membership in the Jewish community was never regarded merely as a matter of voluntary identification with a religious denomination. One's status as a Jew was not acquired through the profession of a particular creed. With the exception of converts, the privileges and responsibilities devolving upon a member of the People of the Covenant derived from the fact that he was born a Jew. However, significant elements of world Jewry in the modern era have defined Jewish identity as a community of history and destiny shared among those who still feel their involvement in this community, or whom others categorize as belonging to this community. Thus the term "Jew" covers a wide spread of degrees of religious beliefs and affiliations; but in practical terms it is understood by and acceptable to the people to whom it is applied.

INTERMARRIAGE

A crucial element in the preservation of Jewish community is the phenomenon of intermarriage with non-Jews. American Jews view intermarriage more as a threat than as an opportunity, although this attitude is not uniform throughout all sectors of the community. Incomplete and variable data indicate that the rate of intermarriage has been rising, now stands between 15 and 20% of all marriages involving Jews, and in some subcommunities may have climbed to 50%.

A number of methodological problems complicate the computation of intermarriage rates. A survey limited to the organized Jewish community yields, as might be expected, a significantly lower rate of intermarriage than one encompassing the total population of a locality. Surveys of the former type, sponsored by local Jewish organizations in the U.S. over the past 40 years, yielded an intermarriage rate of about 6%. By contrast, the Greater Washington survey which sampled the total population of the area yielded a rate of 13.2%. (A 1957 sample survey in the United States revealed that, compared to Catholics and Protestants, Jews are least likely to intermarry. It is believed, however, that the differential is no longer great in the 1970s.) Data on intermarriage must also be recognized as reflecting the religious diversity of marriage partners at the time of the poll, while ignoring any previous diversity that was overcome by a change of religion on the part of one of the partners. Finally, it has been recognized for some time that intermarriage rises in each generation. As a consequence, a cumulative rate of intermarriage is always considerably lower than a current rate. Thus the data at hand tend to underestimate the real extent of intermarriage in the United States.

It has been repeatedly observed that the rate of intermarriage reflects the density of a subgroup within the total population in a given locality. However, density becomes relevant only when the will for group survival has been weakened or abandoned. Once group cohesion is weakened, the factor of density operates in the expected manner; the smaller the proportion that Jews constitute of the total population in a given locality, the larger the intermarriage rate becomes. For example, in the United States, the intermarriage rate in the state of Indiana between 1960 and 1963 was 38.6% for the five large Jewish settlements, and 63.5% for those counties where there was only a scattering of Jewish families. This has been a factor in the eagerness of many Jews to concentrate their residence in specific neighborhoods and to establish their institutions within those locations.

Intermarriage is also likely to increase with increased length of Jewish settlement in the United States, as measured by generations, and in the absence of continued Jewish immigration. The Greater Washington survey found that intermarried families increased from 1.4% among the foreign-born, to 10.2% among the native-born of foreign parentage, to 17.9% among the native-born of native parentage.

Occupation and employment status are other factors significantly related to intermarriage. As long as occupational choice was limited by discriminatory practices, occupational homogeneity discouraged intermarriage. However, there is virtually unlimited freedom of occupational choice in the United States; and it has been observed that individuals who break away from traditional occupations are likely to have a high intermarriage rate. The growth of corporate capitalism is also likely to generate a higher rate of intermarriage. Since large corporations demand of their executive echelon considerable geographic and social mobility, ties of Jewish executives to the organized local Jewish communities have become attenuated.

Finally, intermarriage has been felt to be a function of education. Secular education in the Western world has two major functions. One is to ensure the continuity of cultural tradition and values, the acquisition of basic skills, and of occupational training. The other is to provide for cultural change, the production of new ideas, and technical innovation. The Greater Washington survey indicates that among the native-born of native parentage, the intermarriage rate of those who had enrolled in the first type of education was nearly one-third lower than of those who were products of the second type.

There is a widespread belief that Jewish education, including a *bar mitzvah* ceremony, helps to keep young men from marrying outside the Jewish faith. The Greater Washington survey showed that this belief is well founded as far as the native-born of native parentage (the third and subsequent generations) are concerned. Religious education halved the intermarriage rate among this group. Evidently, since the ethnic bond expressed in secular activities pursued jointly and in a common language had been virtually dissolved in the third generation of American Jews, exposure to religious instruction served as a check to intermarriage.

In a society where democracy and individualism are dominant values, intermarriage is bound to occur. In the democratic environment intermarriage also becomes a philosophical challenge, particularly to the educated Jew. As much as he may be opposed to it, it is nonetheless the logical culmination of his quest for full equality. Moreover, American Jewish life has been based on the belief that Jewish survival is possible in an open society. With the exception of certain Orthodox groups, American Jewry has contended that it is possible to achieve a meaningful Jewish identity together with full participation in the general society. Once it is conceded, however, that the intermarriage rate is high and seems to be increasing, it no longer seems so obvious that the twin goals of Jewish identity and of Jewish participation in the general society can be equally achieved.

Empirical observations have revealed that American Jewish communities are trying to keep the frequency of intermarriage low with the help of a "survival" formula consisting of a certain amount of voluntary segregation, residence in a high-status area, a modicum of Jewish education, and Jewish group consciousness in the form of identification with and support of the State of Israel.

CONVERSION

It is estimated that many thousands of conversions to Judaism take place every year, the largest number under Reform auspices. Reports from 785 congregational rabbis in 1954 showed that approximately 3,000 persons were then being converted annually. In 95% of the conversions, an impending or existing marriage to a Jew was involved; female converts outnumbered males five to one.

These converts, as well as non-converted partners of Jewish marriages, generally come into some relationship with the Jewish community, for American Jews do not, except for a very small group, intermarry in order to assimilate. Nor does the Jewish family tend to sever its relations with the intermarried member—although it may be deeply torn in its reactions to the marriage. In a positive sense this means that the Jewish community is not necessarily attenuated by each case of intermarriage-cum-conversion. However, these relationships have had an important negative effect on the function of the extended family as the natural group which reinforces Jewish identity through its joint celebrations and interactions. Because of intermarriage, non-Jews are now found in the majority of extended American Jewish families, and these can no longer serve as clearly distinguishable models of Jewish identity for the younger generation. (In addition, the strong family ties that have characterized the Jewish community are loosening, as better educated and economically more successful American Jews increasingly limit involvement with and obligations to immediate kin in favor of greater interaction with friends of a similar social and educational background.)

Whether the children of intermarriages will retain their Jewish identity amidst a Jewish environment that is increasingly watered down remains a question whose answer will be crucial for the future of the American Jewish community.

FAMILY STABILITY

It is difficult to assess the divorce rate of any religious or ethnic group in the United States, since the agencies which collect such data do not use religious or ethnic classifications. The only available sources of information are surveys of Jewish communities, or samples of population in which Jews are included. Studies made by Jewish social agencies in the early 20th century showed that desertion was not as prevalent among Jews as among other ethnic and religious groups. The scant data available point to an increase in divorce among the Jewish population during the current century—but local studies often provide contradictory data. Thus, according to a survey in 1958, only 4% of the Jewish respondents who had ever been married reported that they had been divorced, as compared with 8% of the Catholics and 16% of the Protestants. Figures from Baltimore, Philadelphia, Detroit, and other cities of large population all indicated that divorce, separation, and desertion were less prevalent among American Jews than among other groups. However, a study conducted in 1955 reported that the Jews in several cities had a higher divorce rate than Protestants.

JEWISH IDENTITY VS. AMERICANIZATION

The question of Jewish identity became a topic of community concern and consideration with the influx of masses of highly visible, ethnically identifiable Jews from Eastern Europe. The older Jewish community sought to mute the alien "Jewishness" of the newcomers, and it created a network of social agencies and institutions whose primary purpose was "Americanization."

There were two contesting philosophies which sought to bring the mass community of immigrant Jews into the larger American society of the 20th century. One view, espoused by such thinkers as Horace Kallen and Mordecai M. Kaplan, envisaged the American society of the future as one of cultural pluralism, in which the descendants of various European national traditions would retain substantial knowledge of and loyalty to their past. This meant that American Jews would exist as one of many separate communities within a pluralistic United States. Kallen, philosopher and educator, further affirmed that each ethnic and cultural group in the United States had a special contribution to make to the variety and richness of American culture. This provided a rationale for those Jews who wished to preserve their Jewish cultural identity within the American "melting pot." (Kallen also argued that the Jewish people needed a homeland in Palestine to protect them against persecution and to enhance their Jewish cultural heritage.) Rabbi Mordecai M. Kaplan, founder of the Reconstructionist movement (see below), viewed Judaism as an evolving religious civilization, and urged the development of Jewish community centers where all aspects of life could be enjoyed in a local Jewish setting and within the larger American society.

A counter theory was held by the dominant American Protestant cultural and political establishment. Their vision of America was on the model of a "melting pot." Upon arrival in the United States, the new immigrant was to undergo the process of Americanization as rapidly as possible, and was to surrender his foreignness and strive to live in imitation of the dominant social patterns. The older (German) American-Jewish community was overwhelmingly committed to the latter idea.

Among the second generation of native-born children of immigrant parents, some younger Jewish intellectuals tried to live in both the American and the Jewish culture. The overwhelming bulk of this generation, however, like their immigrant parents, simply tried to make their individual ways in the American society, restricting their strong personal Jewish emotions and commitments to their private lives.

The ideal of bi-cultural existence in America was attacked by some of the American-born children of East European-Jewish immigrants as a form of schizophrenia. Sociologist Jesse Bernard said that a child of immigrant parents "can never achieve complete oneness save he deliberately turn his back on one or the other (culture)," and advocated conscious and total assimilation. Social psychologist Kurt Lewin, a pioneer in group dynamics, was similarly concerned with what he called the "marginal man," living in two societies. His conclusion, however, was that "an early build-up of a clear and positive feeling of belongingness to the Jewish group is one of the few effective things that Jewish parents can do for the later happiness of their children. In this way parents can minimize the ambiguity and the tension inherent in the situation of the Jewish minority group, and thus counteract various forms of maladjustment resulting therefrom."

The American Jewish community followed neither prescription with avidity. Their choice was neither conscious assimilation, nor an active affirmation of Jewish self-identification. Until the mid-20th century, when external factors deeply affected it, the American Jewish community's sense of identification was more a reflection of its numerical growth and economic advancement than of a philosophical understanding of its needs or goals.

In terms of community affiliations, identification was based on membership in welfare organizations, Jewish defense organizations, and/or synagogue groups.

SOCIAL WELFARE SERVICES

At the height of 19th century liberalism in America, it was possible for some Jews to "pass" into the White Anglo-Saxon Protestant society without doing anything more than simply ceasing to function in any Jewish association of any kind. On the other hand, Jewish identity frequently persisted even after every vestige of religious faith and practice had evaporated. It was possible for Jews to feel a strong sense of Jewish identity on the basis of minimal or no association with a Jewish institution.

Increasingly, there arose Jewish organizations which accepted this situation. These were the prototype institutions of the voluntaristic Jewish community of the modern era. They regarded it as their task to serve any who claimed to be Jews, especially at moments of crisis or when such people needed social services. In the course of time, these associations to alleviate suffering developed into overarching Jewish organizations, approaching but not reaching the stage of an inclusive community structure.

The early success of these organizations lay in the noncontroversial nature of the services they rendered. There was general agreement about helping Jews in need, whatever their orientation to Jewish identity. (The obligation to help the needy is clearly spelled out in the Bible, and has been considered by the rabbis of all ages to be one of the cardinal practices of Judaism. Prophetic Judaism contributed the far-reaching concept of poverty and need being a function not of the poor themselves, but of the evils of the social order, and therefore rectifiable by the social order.)

THE CONCEPT OF VOLUNTARISM

The growth of the Jewish community in the United States was the scene of a great historic coincidence: the encounter of the European Jewish tradition of philanthropy with the American idea of voluntarism. Early observers of the American scene commented on a distinctive characteristic of Americans: that voluntary groups take into their hands the creation of organizations to meet their own needs. Jewish communal traditions of autonomy and mutual assistance found a favorable climate of growth in this American voluntarism.

Another factor impelling the development of the contemporary American Jewish community was the American impulse toward efficiency which, joined to the Jewish conviction of communal responsibility, coalesced disparate and often rival institutions into combined effort. The earliest example of this trend was the establishment of the first Jewish philanthropic federation in Boston in 1895. It was based on a simple concept: funds would be raised and disbursed jointly to meet the needs of the cooperating agencies. These included welfare services, hospitals, free loan agencies, settlement houses, and sundry social-aid groups. In the succeeding decades Jewish philanthropic federations were established in most Jewish communities. One of the last federations to be established (1917), and the largest, was in New York City.

The early federations also initiated rudimentary social planning for the Jewish community. They sought to explore which new services were needed, and which old ones could be dispensed with. The founding and expansion of federations occurred during the period in which social work was emerging as a new profession. The National Conference of Jewish Social Service (later, Social Welfare), was founded in 1899, and professional journals were published. During its brief existence (1927–36), the Graduate School for Jewish Social Work in New York City trained professional social workers specifically for service in the Jewish community.

COUNCIL OF JEWISH FEDERATIONS AND WELFARE FUNDS

The trend toward federalism culminated in the establishment of the Council of Jewish Federations and Welfare Funds in 1932. The Council was formed of a merger of several social welfare organizations that dated back to the early years of the century. It sought to provide statistical data and recommendations for social welfare planning for the American Jewish community.

The organization of the Council coincided with a watershed period in American philanthropic history. The magnitude of the impoverishment throughout the United States that followed the depression of the 1930s forced the federal government to undertake to provide material relief to the needy, and the voluntary agencies gave up this function. They then turned their attention to a wider scope of activities, which included coordinated fundraising efforts for European Jews.

By the 1940s most local federations had broadened their activities to include support for Jewish education, community relations activities, vocational services, and cooperation with national agencies that served the entire American Jewish community. The role of the Council of Jewish Federations and Welfare Funds expanded in importance to the point where it was widely recognized as "the organized Jewish community." (In 1970 it was estimated that local federations of community councils and welfare funds existed in one form or another in 300 cities, in 43 states in which at least 95% of the Jewish population was concentrated.) Increasingly there were debates on the proportion of funds to be divided between welfare institutions on the one hand, and educational and cultural services on the other. By 1968 the range of federation concerns included services for the individual and family, national programs designed to ensure the survival of Judaism in the United States, and international Jewish needs.

The dollar figures reflected the vast scope of these activities. In 1971 the annual campaigns of Jewish federations totaled 360 million dollars (197 million dollars in regular campaigns and 163 million dollars for the Israel Emergency Fund). Actually, the funds allocated by federations represented only a fraction of the money disbursed by the agencies which received them. These agencies' expenditures also derived from other sources of income—dues, tuition, fees, endowment and capital funds, and various governmental grants. The gross national Jewish philanthropic expenditure in 1971, inclusive of all these funds, was substantially in excess of one billion dollars.

NATIONAL COUNCIL OF JEWISH WOMEN

Women were active in all Jewish philanthropic endeavors, most frequently in "auxiliaries" to the main organization. And, following the American pattern of forming independent women's clubs, separate Jewish women's groups developed on the local and national level. The National Council of Jewish Women may serve as an example of the creative response of American Jewish women to the changing needs of the community.

The Council was founded in 1893 to provide broad services to immigrants. These ranged from organizing Sabbath schools and sponsoring vocational and industrial classes, to managing model tenements and offering free baths to slum dwellers. In 1904 it became the first organization to serve at Ellis Island, the immigrant admissions and screening center in New York harbor, through which hundreds of thousands of new arrivals passed before entering the United States. Council representatives in 250 cities and in European ports assisted single girls with immigration problems, and protected them from white slavery.

In 1909 the Council participated in President Taft's White House Conference on Child Welfare, and in 1911 it set forth its first complete program for social legislation, including regulation of child labor, slum clearance, mothers' pensions, public health programs, and food and drug regulations.

It geared its activities to refugee aid following both World Wars, and in the post-World War II period it brought educators and welfare workers from Israel and other Jewish communities abroad for advanced training in the United States, with the stipulation that they return to help rebuild Jewish welfare and educational institutions in their own communities. In the 1960s the National Council of Jewish Women, with more than 100,000 members, was a pioneer in the Head Start preschool program and in the establishment of Golden Age Clubs.

FOCUS BEYOND THE UNITED STATES

During the 1930s and 1940s the scope of organized American Jewish philanthropy expanded geographically. With the rise of Nazism the world Jewish emergency grew, and the desperate situation of European Jewry became the dominant focus for local federation campaigns. The formation of the United Jewish Appeal (see Chapter 6) provided a framework for a coordinated effort on behalf of overseas Jews. With the exception of New York, which maintained both a Federation of Welfare Funds and a separate United Jewish Appeal, the local federations cooperated in the raising and allocation of funds to be sent overseas, to Europe and to Palestine.

As the American Jewish community prospered it became a major, and finally the important, source of economic assistance for other Jewish communities throughout the world. In a certain sense, the bonds between American Jews and their co-religionists abroad provided a community of purpose and a compelling focus for the diffused American community.

COMMUNITY RELATIONS ORGANIZATIONS

The awareness of the American Jewish leadership that the needs of the community were not confined to philanthropic areas alone led to the formation of "defense" or "community relations" organizations.

AMERICAN JEWISH COMMITTEE

The oldest organization of this nature in the United States is the American Jewish Committee, established in 1906 to "prevent the infraction of the civil and religious rights of Jews in any part of the world." Its founders, who included Jacob Schiff, Mayer Sulzberger, Louis Marshall, Oscar Straus, and Cyrus Adler, represented the prominent German stratum within the Jewish community at that time. These were prominent figures in the business and professional world, who actively contributed to general civic and educational causes. But their sense of *noblesse oblige* also spurred them to philanthropic activities and diplomatic efforts on behalf of their fellow Jews. The formation of the American Jewish Committee was their response to what they saw as a dual threat; the wave of Russian pogroms that ravaged Eastern European Jewry at that time, and the rise of what they considered more "radical" Jewish organizations seeking to channel Jewish loyalties in the United States.

The plight of Russian Jewry before World War I prompted the American Jewish Committee to the strong defense of a liberal American immigration policy, and it helped defeat a literacy test requirement for immigrants. In 1911 it conducted a successful campaign for the abrogation of the Russo-American Treaty of 1832, on the grounds of Russian discrimination against American Jews who sought to enter Russia. With the outbreak of World War I, it sparked the organization of the American Jewish Relief Committee which set up a central relief fund for Jewish war victims.

The rise of Nazism led to intensified activities on two fronts. In an effort to ameliorate the plight of German Jewry, the American Jewish Committee applied pressure upon the Roosevelt administration, the Vatican, the League of Nations, and even individual German officials. When they failed to halt the Nazis by arousing public opinion, Committee members turned to plans of rescue and emigration for German Jews. The American Jewish Committee's original anti-Zionist policy was softened as it came to recognize the role of Palestine as a refuge for homeless Jews, and it cooperated with Zionist bodies in fundraising efforts.

In its battle against organized anti-Semitism in the United States, the American Jewish Committee, with Louis Marshall at its helm, fought the anti-Semitic charges disseminated in Henry Ford's *Dearborn Independent,* investigated the operations of the virulent hate groups of the 1930s and

1940s, and disclosed their connections with the Nazi regime. Discarding the traditionally apologetic Jewish reaction to anti-Semitism, the Committee asserted and demonstrated that anti-Semitism is a device to undermine the foundations of democratic society.

In the 1940s it took upon itself the strengthening of a pluralistic, democratic society, and the defense of the rights and liberties of non-Jews as well as Jews. In recent years, its focus on human relations has included new approaches to intergroup cooperation and intercultural education.

B'NAI B'RITH

Another approach to community relations has been undertaken by B'nai B'rith, the world's oldest and largest Jewish service organization. Its headquarters are in Washington, D.C., and it maintains lodges and chapters in 45 countries. Founded in 1843 with a program of mutual aid, social service, and philanthropy, it established orphanages, homes for the aged, and hospitals; it expressed the classic Jewish concern for local and overseas needs by extending aid to victims of the great Chicago fire (1871), and to cholera epidemic sufferers in Palestine (1865).

During the period of mass East European immigration B'nai B'rith sponsored Americanization classes, trade schools, and relief programs. The increase in anti-Semitism prior to World War I led it to found its Anti-Defamation League (ADL). Since 1913 ADL has sought to protect the status and rights of Jews, and to strengthen interrelations between ethnic groups.

In the 1920s B'nai B'rith established the Hillel Foundation, to serve the religious, cultural, and social needs of Jewish students on American campuses; and as the American Jewish community became increasingly child-focused, it formed the B'nai B'rith Youth Organization to conduct a program of cultural, religious, community service, social and athletic activities. In addition to departments of adult Jewish education and local community affairs, B'nai B'rith has been involved in Jewish affairs abroad through its lodges in Europe and Israel.

AMERICAN JEWISH CONGRESS

The third large national agency devoting itself to the highly political area of intergroup relations is the American Jewish Congress. Founded in 1918 and then reorganized in the 1920s by Stephen S. Wise, a Reform rabbi who was the spokesman for the mass of working and lower-middle-class urban Jews, the American Jewish Congress was designed to serve as a politically liberal, activist, pro-Zionist counterweight to the American Jewish Committee and other organizations of the elitist German-Jewish leaders.

The Congress set goals related to American Jewish affairs, as well as to Palestine and the world Jewish scene. In the 1930s it emerged as a leading force in the anti-Nazi movement, and sought to arouse American public opinion against anti-Semitic manifestations in America.

In 1945 the Congress embarked on a program that fundamentally altered its character. Proceeding from the premise that the well-being of Jews depended on a liberal political and social climate, it became increasingly involved in fighting racial and religious bigotry in the United States. It has been particularly active on behalf of Negro rights and against attempts to weaken the separation of church and state.

In 1944 the American Jewish Congress joined six national and twenty local Jewish agencies in the establishment of the National Community Relations Advisory Council (NCRAC), with the object of coordinating the member organizations' work and policies in the field of Jewish defense and community relations in the United States. The agencies exchange views and work together voluntarily, while retaining full autonomy. By 1968 the Council had expanded to include nine national organizations and 81 local community relations councils.

SYNAGOGUE MOVEMENTS

The synagogue is, historically, the most important institution in Judaism. As successor to the Temple in Jerusalem, it enabled the Jews in the Diaspora, throughout the centuries, to develop their religious faith and practices, and to retain their ethnic ties to the land of Israel and the Hebrew language. The synagogue has also had a decisive influence on organized religion as a whole. As has been pointed out (C. Toy, *Introduction to the History of Religions*, p. 546), "their [the Jews'] genius for the organization of public religion appears in the fact that the form of communal worship devised by them was adapted by Christianity and Islam, and in its general outlines still exists in the Christian and Moslem world."

The real custodians of Jewish affiliation in the United States since the end of World War II have been the three great synagogue movements,

Orthodox, Conservative, and Reform. These have been essentially confederations of very independent local congragations, linked by relatively undefined philosophical ties and a need for certain technical services. It is the combination of countrywide identification and essentially local attachments that has made the synagogue movement successful.

THE AMERICAN SYNAGOGUE

The American synagogue is focused upon Jewish survival. It has accepted even those Jews who are strongly secular in orientation and has been more concerned with transforming them into positive Jews than with erecting barriers to their admission. (This tendency was apparent as early as colonial times.)

There are no reliable nationwide statistics on synagogue affiliation; the most notable aspect of such affiliation is that it varies greatly with the size of the Jewish population of a particular community. In small Jewish communities the rate of affiliation is commonly well over 80%, despite the high intermarriage rates characteristic of such communities. In large Jewish communities the rate of affiliation is much lower, about 50% of the Jewish population. While no study is available of the Jewish population of New York City, it is generally agreed that the affiliation rate there is measurably lower than in any other large city.

Basically the decision to affiliate with a synagogue means making an affirmative decision regarding Jewish survival. Since the smaller the community, the clearer the threat of assimilation, the greater is the need to affiliate with the synagogue. The larger the community, the more remote the threat of assimilation, the greater the opportunities to become involved with an alternative Jewish organization, and the less symbolic is the decision to affiliate with a synagogue.

Despite synagogue affiliation, only a minority of American Jews attend religious services with any degree of regularity. Yet the increase in the number of synagogues and their general prosperity suggests that they fulfill a function beyond that of a house of prayer.

The synagogue has been the focus and center of Jewish religious life throughout the 2,500 years of its history. It has been a center not only for prayer and instruction, but a communal center as well. The last function was already noted in talmudic times, and under ghetto conditions it assumed much greater importance.

THE SYNAGOGUE CENTER

A further functional development of the synagogue took place in the United States, and in turn influenced the institution of the synagogue throughout the Western world. This was the formulation of the concept of the "synagogue center" by Rabbi Mordecai M. Kaplan.

Kaplan felt that if the synagogue were to continue to play its role in Jewish life it had to be more than a house of prayer and, in view of the disintegration of traditional Jewish values in the United States, more than a house of study. He therefore advocated that the synagogue become an all-embracing center of Jewish social and cultural activity, with the aim of encouraging the Jew to spend a great deal, if not most, of his leisure time within the confines of the synagogue which would seek to strengthen his Jewish identity. Such a building would no longer be a synagogue, but a "Jewish center" and "instead of the primary purpose of congregational organization being worship, it should be social togetherness. . . The history of the synagogue. . . is a striking illustration of the importance of creating new social agencies when new conditions arise that threaten the life of a people or of its religion." ("The Way I Have Come," *Mordecai M. Kaplan: An Evaluation,* p. 311.)

According to Kaplan, the synagogue center should contain a swimming pool, gymnasium, library, club rooms, public hall, and classrooms, in addition to facilities for worship. It should provide professional club leaders to supervise groups for adults and children and these should include activities of a Jewish nature, as well as clubs for photography, drama, music, sport, etc.

The synagogue center idea was, in fact, a reformulation and expansion in 20th century terms of what had always been the synagogue's role. The concept has been generally accepted, and, in varying degrees, most American synagogues provide such activities for their congregations.

JEWISH COMMUNITY CENTERS

The tendency of synagogues to act as Jewish centers sometimes brought them into rivalry with non-synagogal Jewish centers and Young Men's (and Women's) Hebrew Associations, which were professionally equipped for such work, and which constituted an option to affiliation with the synagogue. The community center does not require religious affiliation as a qualification for membership. In fact, one need not be Jewish to join a Jewish community center. In 1967 the proportion of non-Jewish membership on a nationwide basis was 9.5%, almost double what it had been a decade earlier; in some centers it exceeded 25%.

The Young Men's (Women's) Hebrew Association (YMHA–YWHA), or the Jewish community center, is an indigenous American institution. These centers arose in the last decades of the 19th century, primarily to help Americanize the masses of East European immigrants, but also, in part, to counteract the potential influence of Protestant missionizing efforts. They concentrated on providing educational, social, and recreational facilities for the younger generation of Jewish immigrants. As a native-born generation of Jews reached young adulthood, the center programs began to stress leisure-time activities, hobbies, and sports.

At the end of World War II, the community centers were confronted with a challenge to their ideological orientation and purpose. They had increasingly become nonsectarian agencies providing services to the neighborhood clientele, who were apt to be non-Jewish as a result of changing population patterns in the urban areas. The National Jewish Welfare Board commissioned a survey which resulted in the Janowsky Report (1948). The report called upon the community centers to reorient their outlook and activities toward a more explicitly Jewish program aimed at enhancing the Jewish identity of those they served. As a result Jewish cultural activities have assumed a somewhat greater role in the community center programs. Nursery schools have been established, summer camps under center sponsorship have multiplied, teen-age activities were stressed, and services to older persons have greatly increased. It is, however, difficult to determine the quality of the Jewish content of these programs, or the impact they have left on the participants' sense of Jewish identity.

In the mid-1960s Jewish community center membership stood at 729,000, scattered over more than 180 cities. New York City itself had 60 centers.

THE FUNCTION OF THE RABBI

As American synagogues developed into synagogue centers providing a variety of programs for their membership, the rabbi, who traditionally had been the spiritual leader, interpreter of Jewish law, and preacher of the congregation, tended more and more to become the senior Jewish professional in the community. He came to interpret the Jewish tradition not only to the members of his congregation, but also to their Christian neighbors. He had to assume responsibility for all aspects of Jewish education. National and international Jewish organizations looked to him for influence. He assumed the role of family counselor; both the Reform and Conservative rabbinical seminaries include courses in pastoral psychiatry.

In recent years, the modern rabbi has also played an increasing role in the general field of human relations or civil rights, and Jewish organizations dealing with these areas tend to have a rabbi as a senior staff member or elected head. One of the contributory reasons for this trend is that when Jewish organizations participate in government or communal affairs, the representatives of their counterpart organizations are likely to be Protestant or Catholic clergymen.

RABBINICAL SEMINARIES

The United States has rabbinical seminaries for all three groups in religious Jewry. The first to be established, the Hebrew Union College (Reform), was founded by Isaac Mayer Wise in Cincinnati in 1875. Wise was convinced that "Judaism would have no future in America unless. . . it would become reconciled with the spirit of the age" and the Jewish community found it possible to "educate American rabbis for the American pulpit."

In 1922 Stephen S. Wise founded the Jewish Institute of Religion (JIR)

Campus of Hebrew Union College, Cincinnati, Ohio.

in New York to provide training "for the Jewish ministry, research, and community service." Men of both Reform and traditional theological persuasion were to be encouraged at JIR. Housing JIR next to his Free Synagogue, Wise hoped that it would generate other Free Synagogues "animated by the same spirit of free inquiry, of warm Jewish feeling, and of devotion to the cause of social regeneration." In 1950 the JIR merged with the Hebrew Union College in Cincinnati. A Los Angeles branch of HUC–JIR was chartered in 1954, and a Jerusalem campus was opened in 1963. These campuses have trained Reform rabbis who hold pulpits or Jewish organizational positions throughout the world. In 1972 the first woman rabbi was ordained. HUC–JIR also offers bachelors degrees in Jewish education, sacred music, and Jewish communal service, and several doctoral programs in areas of Jewish scholarship.

The educational and spiritual center of the Conservative movement, The Jewish Theological Seminary of America, opened in 1887. The moving force behind its formation was Sabato Morais, rabbi of Congregation Mikveh Israel in Philadelphia, who sought to establish a school to train rabbis and teachers who would preserve traditional Jewish values and practices against the onslaught of "radical" reformers.

The Seminary foundered until, in 1902, it was reorganized under the

The Jewish Theological Seminary in N.Y.

leadership of Solomon Schechter, a noted scholar who was brought from Europe for this purpose. During Schechter's presidency, Jewish scholars were brought from all over the Jewish world to serve on the Seminary's faculty. Schechter also built an extensive library and founded a Teachers Institute.

To reach the rapidly growing Jewish community on the West Coast, a California branch of the Seminary, the University of Judaism, was opened in 1947. A student center is maintained in Jerusalem as well. The educational activities of the Seminary have also branched out over the years. From its origin as a school to train rabbis only, it now educates teachers, cantors, and synagogue administrators, and also offers courses in Judaica on a graduate level. From its first class of eight in 1887 (one of whom was Joseph H. Hertz, later Chief Rabbi of the British Empire), the Seminary expanded to a student enrollment of 800 in 1968.

American Orthodoxy is served by more than one rabbinical seminary, reflecting the various degrees of Orthodoxy within the community. These institutions include the Rabbi Isaac Elchanan Theological Seminary (later a unit of the Yeshiva University), established in 1897, the Talmudical College of Chicago (1922), and various smaller *yeshivot* which grant *semikhah* (Orthodox rabbinical ordination). Many of the latter were transferred from Eastern Europe during World War II, and have retained

The main building of Yeshiva University, N.Y., erected in 1929.

the traditional curriculum of talmudic studies. Since the middle of this century the most important of the European *yeshivot* have been relocated in the United States and in Israel.

At the turn of the century it became clear to Orthodox Jewry that only an orderly and organized religious education could serve as a protective barrier against the spread of general cultural trends and the new social movements of the time. As a result, just when the influence of traditional Judaism in the life of the individual and the community was being undermined, *yeshivah* education, which previously had been limited to the intellectual elite of Orthodox Jewry, began to be promoted as an accepted feature in the life of Orthodox young men in general. The first advanced *yeshivah* in the United States was the Rabbi Isaac Elchanan Theological Seminary, the nucleus around which Yeshiva University grew. (Yeshiva University actually dates its inception from 1886, when Yeshivat Etz Chaim, an elementary school, was founded. It later merged with the theological seminary.)

In 1908 some secular studies were introduced into the curriculum, and in 1916 an accredited high school was formed, which taught both talmudic and secular studies. In 1922 the theological seminary absorbed the Teachers Institute of the Mizrachi Organization of America, and in 1928 it opened a college division. The two undergraduate colleges (Yeshiva College for men, and Stern College for women) with a combined enrollment of 1,800 students in 1968, seek to achieve a "synthesis" of two intellectual worlds, the religious and the secular, so that the content from one area of study may shed light or direction on the other.

In 1945 the institution was elevated to university status. It includes specifically Jewish divisions and programs, such as a teachers college for women, a cantorial institute, and such secular, non-sectarian divisions as graduate schools of education, science, and social work, and the Albert Einstein College of Medicine with its affiliated hospital.

The youngest Jewish theological seminary in the United States is the Reconstructionist Rabbinical College, founded in 1967 in Philadelphia, to train leaders for the Reconstructionist movement within American Jewish life (see below). Students at this college are expected to complete a doctoral program in religious or cognate studies at neighboring institutions while preparing for rabbinic ordination.

Each of these rabbinical schools seeks to train community leaders who will educate congregational members in the philosophy of Judaism that it espouses. Each seminary has parallel rabbinic bodies and lay organizations which reflect its viewpoint to some extent in their functions and activities.

REFORM JUDAISM

Reform Judaism was the first of the modern interpretations of Judaism to emerge in response to the changed political and cultural conditions brought about by the emancipation of European Jewry in the late 18th century. True to its own inner dynamics, Reform Judaism's manifestations vary from place to place, and have undergone constant change in the course of time. Basic to Reform is the assertion of the legitimacy of change in Judaism, and the denial of eternal validity to any given formulation of Jewish belief or codification of Jewish law.

Numerically, the strongest constituent of Reform Judaism is the American branch which, because of its size and financial strength, has assumed the world leadership of the movement, even though outside the U.S. Reform Judaism tends to be far more traditionally observant than it is in the United States.

Reform (also known as Liberal or Progressive) Judaism had its origins in early 19th century Germany. The first reformers were laymen who were concerned with the large-scale defections from Judaism as the Jews were emancipated from the ghetto, and with the absence of Western standards of esthetics and decorum in the traditional Jewish service of worship. They set about making Jewish religious practices more attractive to the emancipated Jew by reforming the service: abbreviating the liturgy, providing a sermon in the vernacular, introducing singing with organ accompaniment, and supplementing the standard Hebrew prayers with prayers in the vernacular.

As German rabbis who had university education as well as traditional training began to show themselves sympathetic to the cause of Reform Judaism, considerations of dogma entered the picture. At first, the participating rabbis endeavored to remain within the mainstream of Judaism and refused to regard Reform as a separate sect. In contrast to American Reform Judaism, which developed somewhat later, German Reform Judaism always retained a pronounced traditionalist aspect, and preferred to call itself "Liberal" rather than "Reform."

The participation of rabbis in the Reform movement from the 1840s on led to the crystallization of two different theoretical positions associated with the names of the two German rabbis, Abraham Geiger and Samuel Holdheim.

Geiger held that Judaism was a constantly evolving organism, and that the modern age called for its further evolution in consonance with changed circumstances. But change in Judaism had always been organic, never revolutionary, and modern changes must similarly develop out of the past. While radical in his views, Geiger remained basically traditional in liturgy and in practice. He saw monotheism and the moral law as constant elements of Judaism, and viewed ceremonies as having the function of expressing those ideas in terms speaking to each era. Thus the latter were a changeable element in Judaism. The nature of the Jewish people was similarly subject to change. Though once a nation it was one no longer; the messianic hope was to be interpreted in universal terms rather than in terms of national restoration. Geiger's philosophy became basic to all future formulations of Reform doctrine.

For Holdheim, Reform was revolutionary, not evolutionary. The only eternally true religious elements in the Bible were monotheism and morality, and only they continued to have validity. All the rest of the Bible's contents, including *halakhah* (Jewish law), became invalid when the Temple and the State were destroyed in 70 C.E. Holdheim saw in the emancipation of the Jews the dawn of the messianic era of universal brotherhood, and called for the abolition of ceremonial barriers to that universalism.

In America, too, there was a division between moderate and radical Reform, but the radical position soon achieved dominance. It was expressed in the "Pittsburgh Platform" (1885) which contained statements such as the following: "We recognize in the Mosaic legislation a system of training the Jewish people for its mission during its national life in Palestine, and today we accept as binding only its moral laws, and maintain only such ceremonies as elevate and sanctify our lives, but reject all such as are not adapted to the views and habits of modern civilization... We hold that all such Mosaic and rabbinical laws as regulate diet, priestly purity, and dress originated in ages and under the influence of ideas entirely foreign to our present mental and spiritual state... Their observance in our days is apt rather to obstruct than to further modern spiritual elevation... We recognize the modern era of universal culture of heart and intellect, the approaching of the realization of Israel's great messianic hope for the establishment of the kingdom of truth, justice, and peace among all men. We consider ourselves no longer a nation, but a religious community, and therefore expect neither a return to Palestine, nor a sacrificial worship under the sons of Aaron, nor the restoration of any of the laws concerning the Jewish state..."

In keeping with its philosophy, Reform Judaism was not averse to change within its own ideological structure. When the easy optimism of the assimilationist 19th century American Jewish community (and particularly its elite of German origin) was upset by the harsh political and social realities of the 20th century, American Reform promulgated the "Columbus Platform" (1937). This statement of principles took a new look at traditional Jewish observance and recognized its role in Jewish survival: "The Torah, both written and oral, enshrines Israel's evergrowing consciousness of God and of the moral law. It preserves the historical precedents, sanctions and norms of Jewish life, and seeks to mould it in patterns of goodness and holiness." It defined Judaism as "the soul of which Israel is the body," and recognized "in the group-loyalty of the Jews who have become estranged from our religious tradition a bond which still unites them with us," and affirmed "the obligation of all Jewry to aid in [Palestine's] upbuilding as a Jewish homeland by endeavoring to make it not only a haven of refuge for the oppressed but also a center of Jewish culture and spiritual life." It stressed that "Judaism as a way of life requires, in addition to its moral and spiritual demands, the preservation of the Sabbath, festivals, and Holy Days, the retention and development of such customs, symbols, and ceremonies as possess inspirational value, the cultivation of distinctive forms of religious art and music and the use of Hebrew, together with the vernacular, in our worship and instruction."

Since the adoption of the "Columbus Platform," there has been a greater openness on the part of American Reform Jews to many traditional observances, and the study of Hebrew has returned to the curriculum of many schools. Some Reform congregations, particularly the older ones, have not shared this shift toward greater traditionalism. Anti-Zionism, at one time considered a mandate of "universalism," has given way to a large-scale support of the State of Israel. The Reform movement has a School of Biblical Archaeology in Jerusalem and requires its rabbinical students to spend a year of study there.

Aside from these practical changes, there has been a certain amount of theological rethinking since the Columbus Platform. First, the strong

Nelson Glueck, late president of
Hebrew Union College, on an
archaeological expedition in
Israel.

19th century religious liberalism, basically theistic in nature and stressing
the "rational" character of Judaism, has made its peace with Jewish
"symbols and ceremonies." A second school of thought, mainly confined
to the younger generation of the movement, has been engaged in the
rediscovery of traditional theological concepts such as covenant, revelation, and law. This group seeks to understand Reform Judaism as a link
in the unbroken chain of Jewish religious tradition. A third group, avowedly secularist and humanist, has turned away from traditional theism and
has called for the recognition of Reform Judaism as a new religion founded
in the 19th century. The Jews are primarily seen as a social grouping, and
tradition is considered of value only to the extent to which it furnishes
insights into human relations.

From the 1950s there was a gradual shift toward liberal social and political action as a major function and goal of Reform congregational activity. In the 1960s some objections were raised; Temple Emanu-El, the
oldest Reform congregation in New York City, resigned from the Union
of American Hebrew Congregations in protest at this emphasis.

Pulled simultaneously in opposite directions, Reform Judaism faces
the problem which has remained without solution since the movement's
beginning: what is to be the role of religious authority in a liberal religion.

One aspect of this problem periodically appears when the demand for a guide to religious observance is met with the repeated reply that the publication of such a guide would turn Reform Judaism into another orthodoxy, and must therefore be avoided. Yet such guides have already been issued by some congregations. It seems that any solution to the problem of authority will be on the local level. In the meantime, the leaders of Reform Judaism are concentrating on the strengthening of its organizational structures and institutions.

CONSERVATIVE JUDAISM

Conservative Judaism developed as another religious response to the situation in which Jews found themselves in the era of emancipation. Its philosophical approach developed in the middle of the 19th century both in Europe and in the United States; it was known then as "Historical Judaism." It was influenced in the early years by men who had received their education within the school of European historical Judaism, but as an organized movement it was an essentially autonomous American development.

Those who identified with Conservative Judaism affirmed the end of the ghettoization of the Jews and their emancipation, and the separation of church and state, as positive goods. They hailed the Westernization of Jews in manner, education, and culture. They knew, therefore, that some changes were inevitable in the modes of Jewish religious life, and they affirmed that these changes could be made validly in the light of biblical and rabbinic precedent, for they viewed the entire history of Judaism as a succession of creative responses to new challenges. At the same time, the founders of Conservative Judaism faced the contemporary age in the belief that the traditional forms and precepts of Judaism were valid and that changes in practice were to be made only with great reluctance.

This attitude was first represented in the States by Isaac Leeser, who had received both a talmudic and a secular education in his native Germany before he went to Richmond, Virginia, in 1824. Between 1829 and 1850 he was *ḥazzan* of the Sephardi congregation, Mikveh Israel, in Philadelphia, and he remained in that city until his death in 1868. Leeser pioneered in the introduction of the sermon in English and he proposed such changes as rearrangement of the service to remove unnecessary passages and the introduction of a few readings in English, but he was otherwise deeply devoted to the retention of the traditional liturgy. Leeser tried to cooperate with Isaac Mayer Wise, the leading Reformer, in organizing rabbinic and congregational unions in which all the various groups could cooperate in the creation of a unified American Jewish religious body, but such efforts failed repeatedly. The dominant tendency in American religious life was against compromise, and against the acceptance of the older restraints or the creation of a new authority. (This may have been a reflection of the nonconformist American Protestant religious situation.)

Leeser created a rabbinical school, Maimonides College, in 1867. Even though it disintegrated by 1873, it did graduate the first four men trained for the rabbinate in the United States, and it prepared the way for the later establishment of the Jewish Theological Seminary of America. Additional rabbis, of varying traditionalist postures, but none bound to Orthodoxy and all opposed to the more extreme Reform position, banded together cooperatively and Conservative Judaism in the United States began to crystallize its institutions, not in dissent from Orthodoxy, but in reaction to Reform. (In 1880 only 12 of the 200 synagogues then in America identified themselves as other than Reform!)

The true emergence of Conservative Judaism as a defined movement followed the Reform rabbinate's radical pronouncements in 1885 that the rituals of Judaism were dispensable, their elimination of Hebrew from the liturgy, their transfer of Sabbath worship from Saturday to Sunday, and their negation of the dietary laws and other halakhic practices. A group of traditionalist Jews, of West European birth and training, formed the Jewish Theological Seminary of America to "conserve" the knowledge and practice of historical Judaism as ordained in the law of Moses. They reaffirmed the continuing validity of *halakhah* in Jewish life, but did not discourage change as long as it flowed from a halakhic position and was effected through halakhic principles.

They were joined by such men as Jacob H. Schiff and Louis Marshall, themselves members of the Reform movement, who felt the need to provide an English-speaking, Westernized, but tradition-oriented clergy for the hundreds of thousands of East European Orthodox Jews who were being served by "foreign" immigrant rabbis. Attempts were made to bring the new immigrants into the Conservative ranks, but initially they were unsuccessful, for the East European brand of Orthodoxy was quite different from the West European traditionalism of historical Judaism. Inevitably, the group which had created the Jewish Theological Seminary had to define itself as Western traditionalist—but not Orthodox (at least in the East European sense). It was a "Conservative" movement.

From the beginning, the movement identified with Zionism as an expression of Jewish religious and cultural unity. Conservative Judaism was oriented toward the building of Jewish life both in America and in Palestine. (Since the 1960s the movement has had an Academic Center, several synagogues, and numerous youth and adult travel/study programs in Israel.) Its stance regarding *halakhah* was against convoking official assemblies to define the limits of permissible change in Jewish law and to enact (on the basis of valid precedent) those changes which were required. Rather, it held that halakhic change would develop naturally and spontaneously among those committed to the religious tradition.

Solomon Schechter, first president of the Jewish Theological Seminary, founded the United Synagogue of America, an association of synagogues sympathetic to the religious stance of the Seminary. There was internal opposition to this move on the grounds that such an organization would permanently close the door to the uniting of all the traditionalist forces, but Schechter prevailed. The founding assembly of the United Synagogue of America in 1913 announced the religious purpose of the organization to be "the maintenance of Jewish tradition in its historical continuity," and explained this purpose further by summarizing the main outlines of traditional Jewish practice. It was in the last sentence that the real purpose of the organization was made clear. The new body, "while not endorsing the innovations introduced by any of its constituent bodies," would "embrace all elements essentially loyal to traditional Judaism." The question remained unresolved as to whether it was the purpose of the United Synagogue to act as a pedagogic instrument to wean congregations from their nontraditionalist practices (mixed seating of men and women in the synagogue, organ music during services); whether it was willing to condone such deviations, tacitly; or whether these and other changes in practice would ultimately crystallize as the legitimate norm of Conservative Judaism. Subsequent decades indicated that the Conservative movement would accommodate itself to a wide spectrum of practices defined by the local rabbi as within the confines of halakhic Judaism.

In the 1930s and 1940s the members of the Rabbinical Assembly, the organization of alumni of the Jewish Theological Seminary and graduates

Louis Finkelstein, former chancellor of the Jewish Theological
Seminary.

of other institutions who shared the Conservative viewpoint, sought to
formulate a clear definition of outlook and practice for Conservative
Judaism, as avowedly differing from the Orthodox stance. This attempt
encountered strong opposition from the majority of the faculty of the
Seminary, as well as from some of the leaders of the rabbinate. The
question has continued to exercise the movement, and has assumed new
relevance since the 1960s, as elements within American Orthodoxy have
stressed a more "separationist" policy, and as the Conservative movement
has encountered negative attitudes on the part of the Orthodox establishment in Israel, which refuses to recognize the validity of divorces granted
by members of the Rabbinical Assembly.

The Rabbinical Assembly has increasingly tended toward assuming
a legal stance independent of the Seminary. In 1960 its Law Committee
permitted the use of electricity on the Sabbath, and endorsed, as a worthy
act, travel to the synagogue on Sabbath for the purpose of attending
services. (Both actions are forbidden in Orthodox Judaism.) The 1969
decision to permit individual congregations to abandon the second day
of all the Jewish festivals except Rosh Ha-Shanah, thus paralleling the

practice in Israel, evoked conflict with the traditionalists in the Rabbinical Assembly's own ranks.

In the period prior to and following World War II, Conservative Judaism rose rapidly in numbers. It became the religious movement which spoke to the American-born children of East European immigrants, reconciling their emotional attachment to the traditional practices of their youth, and their practical acculturation into American society. In their private lives congregational members observed substantially less of the tradition than was the norm of public and synagogue behavior, but only very few Conservative Jews showed a total disregard for Jewish tradition. In the 1950s, every poll of religious preference among the Jews in America showed that almost half regarded themselves as Conservative Jews. This degree of affiliation has lessened somewhat among the younger generation, which is to an increasing degree emotionally unidentified with any religious grouping.

The older generation of Conservative rabbis, most of whom had begun their careers or had been raised within Orthodoxy, has been supplanted by a majority of young rabbis trained in the Conservative movement. Faculty appointments to the Seminary have come almost entirely from within its own ranks.

The tensions inherent in Conservative Judaism from its very beginnings have continued to operate. Radical leadership emerged from Conservative ranks in the form of Mordecai M. Kaplan, the founder in 1918 of the Jewish Center in New York, the first American synagogue center. Kaplan's philosophy of Judaism, which became institutionalized as Reconstructionism (see below), exercised deep influence upon the shape of Conservative Judaism.

In 1943 the Rabbinical Assembly held its first joint session with the Central Conference of American Rabbis (Reform), and cooperation between these two bodies has been increasing, particularly as the Reform movement moves closer to a Conservative position with regard to traditional observances. The tendency within the Jewish Theological Seminary, however, has been toward a more Orthodox stance than existed in the previous generation. The Conservative movement has always prided itself upon its capacity for maintaining institutional unity amid ideological conflict. To continue such unity within ever greater diversity is the problem which it, perhaps more than either the Reform or the Orthodox movement, will have to face in the next generation.

RECONSTRUCTIONISM

Reconstructionism is an ideology and a movement completely indigenous to American Jewish life. Both the concept and the organization owe their inspiration to Mordecai Kaplan.

Kaplan argued that with the breakdown of certain traditional beliefs, Jewish identity had become attenuated. Jews remained loyal to their faith despite hardship and suffering because they believed that adherence to Judaism assured them of salvation in the next world. But, in Kaplan's view, this is no longer credible. Consequently, Judaism must help Jews to attain salvation in this world.

Belief in the possibility of this salvation is crucial to Kaplan's thought. It means the progressive improvement of the human personality and the establishment of a free, just, and cooperative social order. Kaplan defines God as the "power that makes for salvation." This notion of God conforms to our experience, since man senses a power beyond his own resources which orients him to this life and elicits from him the best of which he is able.

A more popular notion of Kaplan's was his definition of Judaism as an

Mordecai Kaplan, founder of the Reconstructionist movement.

"evolving religious civilization" whose standards of conduct are established by the Jewish people, and whose common denominator is neither beliefs, tenets, nor practices, but rather the continuous life of the Jewish people. The Jewish religion, said Kaplan, exists for the Jewish people, not the Jewish people for the Jewish religion. Judaism, like any other civilization, comprises a history, a language, a religion, a social organization, standards of conduct, and spiritual and social ideals.

Kaplan taught Jewish philosophy at the Jewish Theological Seminary for five decades, and influenced generations of Conservative rabbis, many of whom accepted his ideology, in whole or in part. His attraction lay in his emphasis on intellectual honesty in confronting the challenges posed by modern thought to traditional Jewish beliefs and practices, and in his combination of scholarship with the creative application of religious texts to contemporary problems. Tradition, he said, can guide, but must not dictate. Each Jew must solve life's perplexities for himself, while seeking to strike a balance between his own needs and those of the group. Jews must learn to live with and cherish diversity.

Many Jewish intellectuals were attracted to Kaplan's program for a Jewish life. He held that Jewish civilization expresses itself in clarifying the purposes and values of human existence, in wrestling with God (who is conceived in non-personal terms), and in the ritual of home, synagogue, and community. The secular elements of culture are essential to Jewish spirituality. They curb the tendency of religion toward rigidity, uniformity and worship of the past, and should be experienced within an "organic community."

The founding of the Reconstructionist movement may be dated from the establishment of the Society for the Advancement of Judaism (SAJ) in 1922. The society served both as a synagogue center and as a forum for Kaplan's ideas. A bi-weekly magazine, the *Reconstructionist*, has been appearing since 1935.

In 1945 the Reconstructionist *Sabbath Prayer Book* was published, which excised references to the Jews as a chosen people, and to such concepts as God's revelation of the Torah to Moses, and a personal Messiah. A Reconstructionist Rabbinical College was established in Philadelphia in 1967.

Although Kaplan left an indelible mark upon many of the leaders of the American Jewish community, his movement has been less successful in recruiting a mass following. In 1970 there were ten congregations and about nine *havurot* (small groups which met once every week or two for study and/or religious observance) affiliated with the Federation of Reconstructionist Congregations and Fellowships. The affiliates had a combined membership of about 2,300 families. Reconstructionist influence in American Jewish religious life, however, is far greater than these numbers might suggest.

ORTHODOX JUDAISM

Orthodox Judaism considers itself the authentic bearer of the religious Jewish tradition which, until the European ghetto walls began to fall in the late 18th century, held sway over almost the entire Jewish community. Its religious orientation stresses submission to the authority of *halakhah*, and holds that the revealed will of God rather than the values of any given age are the ultimate standard of human behavior. Thus it finds attempts to adjust Jewish beliefs or practices to the "spirit of the time" to be utterly incompatible with normative Judaism.

The Orthodox position is that the Masoretic text of the Torah represents an authentic record of divine revelation and the communication of the contents of this revelation to the Chosen People. The Oral Law (Talmud) in turn represents the application and extension of teachings that are ultimately grounded in and derive their sanction from direct divine revelation.

Orthodox leaders foresaw the perils to Jewish survival that would result from the breakdown of the ghetto walls in Europe. Some of them went so far as to urge the European Jewish communities to reject the political, social and economic opportunities offered them. Others, while willing to accept the benefits of political emancipation, were adamant in their insistence that there be no change in the policy of complete segregation from the social and cultural life of the non-Jewish environment.

Fear of assimilation was intensified by a number of alarming developments, ranging from numerous instances of conversion to Christianity, to the efforts of the Reform movement to transform the character of Judaism radically in order to facilitate the total integration of the Jew within modern society. The Orthodox reacted with an all-out effort to preserve the status quo. The slightest tampering with tradition was condemned.

Orthodoxy in this sense first developed in Germany and Hungary.

As its religious and political ideology crystallized, it emphasized both its opposition to those who advocated religious reform, and the essential differences in its outlook and way of life from that of the reformers. It refused to countenance any possibility of cooperation with those advocating differing viewpoints. Herein lay Orthodoxy's main impetus toward organizational separatism. It is this issue that has precipitated most of the internal conflict that has plagued Orthodoxy to this day.

In the United States, different varieties of Orthodoxy have coexisted. In 1898 the Union of Orthodox Jewish Congregations of America was founded, with the aim of accepting "the authoritative interpretation of our rabbis as contained in the Talmud and codes." The differences within American Orthodoxy, however, are evident in the existence of a variety of rabbinic bodies. Rabbis from Eastern Europe, representing traditional Orthodoxy, make up the Union of Orthodox Rabbis of the United States and Canada, while rabbis educated in America form the Rabbinical Council of America. Hasidic groups which became influential chiefly after World War II constitute a separate division within American Orthodoxy (see below). Rabbis, scholars, and heads of *yeshivot* who came after World War II and built *yeshivot* in the Lithuanian tradition have added their special quality to American Orthodoxy.

Paradoxically, the Orthodox community, which places so much emphasis upon the authority of the rabbis to interpret the revealed word of God, is the one that has been plagued most by conflicting claims of competing authorities. All efforts to establish some central authority have failed; the Orthodox camp has not even succeeded in evolving a loose organizational structure which would be representative of the various ideological shadings within the movement.

By the 1940s Orthodoxy had lost its intimate association with immigrant life and tended to be divided internally between modernists oriented to the problems of Orthodox Judaism in a secular, scientific, urban society, and others indifferent or hostile to such concerns and stressing intense piety, *yeshivah* study, and aloofness from non-Orthodox Judaism.

In recent years, this growing polarization within American Orthodoxy has threatened to split the movement. While much of the controversy seems to revolve around the question of membership in religious bodies containing non-Orthodox representation (such as the New York Board of Rabbis, or the Synagogue Council of America), the real issue goes far deeper. The so-called "modern Orthodox" element is under severe attack for allegedly condoning deviation from halakhic standards in order to attract non-observant Jews. On the other hand, there is mounting restlessness and impatience on the part of significant numbers of Orthodox Jews who are dismayed over the slowness with which Orthodoxy has responded to the upheavals of Jewish emancipation, the Enlightenment, and the establishment of the State of Israel. The charge has been made that instead of coming to grips with these events which have confronted the Jew with entirely new historic realities, Orthodoxy has been satisfied with voicing its disapproval of those who have reacted to them.

Some of the more "radical" thinkers see the need for a synthesis between Torah and culture, to meet contemporary needs. They stress the dynamic character inherent in the processes of the Oral Torah, and contend that as long as the domain of Torah remains completely insulated from the culture of a given age, the authorities of the *halakhah* cannot creatively apply the teachings of Judaism to ever-changing historic realities. They charge right-wing Orthodoxy with "moral isolationism" resulting from undue preoccupation with the minutiae of the Law. What is needed, they urge, is not merely the coexistence but the mutual interaction of the two domains of Jewish law and secular culture.

This view, of course, runs counter to the basic tenets of "right-wing" Orthodoxy, which frowns upon the intrusion of elements derived from secular culture as a distortion of the authentic teachings of the Torah. The exponents of the more radical positions of "modern Orthodoxy" are frequently charged with cloaking under the mantle of Orthodoxy what essentially amounts to a Conservative Jewish position. This argument, however, is countered by the claim that there is no thought of "updating" the *halakhah* in order to adjust it to the spirit of the time, but only of explicating it in the light of ever-changing historic conditions, in conformity with the proper procedures of halakhic reasoning.

Rabbi Joseph D. Soloveitchik of Boston has been accepted as a leader of enlightened Orthodoxy, although he has not identified himself with the view of the "progressive" wing. Yet his characterization of the "man of faith" in terms of the dialectical tension between a commitment to an eternal "covenantal community" and the responsibilities to fulfill socio-ethical tasks in a world of change, is widely hailed as an endorsement of the thesis that the Jewish religious ideal does not call for withdrawal from the world, but for the confrontation between human culture and the norms and values of the Torah. The observance of the *halakhah*, far

Joseph Dov Soloveitchik, talmudic scholar and Orthodox religious philosopher.

from exhausting the religious task of the Jew, is designed to make him
more sensitive and "open" to social and moral concerns.

As professor of Talmud and of Jewish philosophy at Yeshiva University, Rabbi Soloveitchik became the spiritual mentor of the majority of
the American-trained Orthodox rabbis. From 1952 he also exerted a
decisive influence on Orthodoxy in his capacity as chairman of the
Halakhah Commission of the Rabbinical Council of America. He
has expounded his method of talmudic study—insistence on incisive analysis, exact classification, and critical independence—in scholarly lectures and well-attended public discourses distinguished by the lecturer's unusual facility for explaining difficult technical problems.

The dilemma of modern Orthodoxy consists of its inability to formulate a systematic theology capable of integrating the findings of modern
science and historic scholarship. Nor has it developed a theory of revelation which would satisfy the demands of modern categories of thought.
Within Orthodoxy some widely recognized authorities unequivocally reject any approach which compromises in the slightest the doctrine that
divine revelation represents a direct supernatural communication from
God to man.

A more serious problem is the increasing resistance within the Jewish
community to the Orthodox emphasis on the authoritative nature of the
halakhah, which runs counter to the prevailing cultural emphasis upon
pluralism and the individual's free, subjective commitment, a freedom

which challenges acceptance of religious values or norms imposed upon the individual from without.

ḤASIDISM

Ḥasidic groups constitute a separate division within American Orthodoxy. Ḥasidism is a religious movement stressing a pattern of communal life and close-knit group cohesion. It is distinguished by the charismatic leadership of the *rebbe* or *ẓaddik* (religious leader and paramount authority within his community of followers).

Ḥasidism was introduced to the United States during the mass migration of 1880–1925, but the ḥasidim seemed to have been less successful than nonḥasidic immigrant Jews in transmitting their style of religious life to the next generation because, separated from their *ẓaddikim*, who had remained in Europe, they apparently felt a fatalistic impotence to perpetuate their philosophy and practices of Judaism.

After World War I several *ẓaddikim* came to the United States, gathered followers, but apparently lacked the means and sectarian fervor to establish a ḥasidic movement. This enervation ended with the arrival in 1940 of Rabbi Joseph Isaac Schneersohn, the *Lubavicher rebbe,* which coincided with the general revival of Orthodox Judaism in America at that time. A network of *yeshivot* and religious institutions was founded under the supervision of the *rebbe* and his successor, Rabbi Menahem Mendel Schneersohn.

The latter, the current *Lubavicher rebbe*, is probably the best-known and most influential of ḥasidic leaders in the world. From his headquarters in Brooklyn, New York, his influence has spread far beyond the community itself, penetrating the mainstream of Jewish life in the United States and in many parts of the world. The *rebbe* encourages his young followers to go out to Jewish communities everywhere to establish contact with the Jewish masses and bring them back to Orthodoxy. He is frequently consulted on Jewish problems and issues. It is estimated that the number of adherents to Lubavich ḥasidism is over 25,000.

Another influential figure in ḥasidism is Rabbi Joel Teitelbaum, the *Satmarer rebbe,* one of the most vigorous opponents of Zionism and Israel. According to Teitelbaum, Zionism and the establishment of the secular, non-halakhically governed State of Israel have delayed the coming of the Messiah and complete redemption, and resulted in all the troubles

Menahem Mendel Schneersohn, head of the Lubavich ḥasidic movement.

affecting the Jewish people in the 20th century. He also opposes the use of Hebrew as a spoken language, since this has secularized the holy tongue. Teitelbaum combines extreme fanaticism with a forceful personality and has gathered round his headquarters in Brooklyn, New York, a large ḥasidic community over which he exercises almost total authority.

Following World War II, additional Polish and Hungarian ḥasidim came to the United States and settled in self-segregated neighborhoods, mainly in New York City. A small community of followers of the *zaddik* of Skver established a suburban township of their own, "New Square," outside of New York City.

The emotional ties with the charismatic figure of the *rebbe*, the fervor and enthusiasm of ḥasidic prayer, the communal character of ḥasidic Sabbath and holiday observances, and the participation of members of the congregation in the services without the intermediary of salaried officiants, have proven attractive to numbers of young American Jews who have been searching for a more emotional content to religious observance. While not becoming formal adherents of the movement, they have borrowed much of the emotional content of ḥasidism and injected it into their own religious observances, on college compuses, in Jewish summer camps, and in *havurot* (fellowship groups of young Jews seeking to study and practice Judaism together).

SEPHARDIC JEWS

While not constituting a separate group in the ideological sense, Sephardic Jews, who may be affiliated with Orthodox, Conservative, or Reform congregations, do remain a separate ethnic element within American Judaism.

The first Jewish settlers in the United States were members of the Sephardi group within Jewry, descendants of Jews who lived in Spain or Portugal before the expulsion of 1492. They constituted about half of the estimated 2,000 Jews living in the original American colonies. With the increase in immigration of Jews from Eastern and Central Europe, however, the Sephardim assumed a smaller role in the life of the American Jewish community.

From 1900 onward greater numbers of oriental Sephardim migrated to the United States from the Balkans, Asia Minor, and Syria. The exodus was precipitated by natural disasters, the rise of nationalism among the Balkan peoples, and the general economic and political deterioration in the Ottoman Empire. In the period from the Young Turk Revolution in 1908 to the establishment of American immigration quotas in 1924, over 50,000 Sephardim arrived in the U.S. After World War II the Sephardi community was augmented by several thousand immigrants from Arab countries and Israel and, after 1959, by emigrés from Castro's Cuba. More than 30,000 settled in New York City, where they organized their own Jewish communal life. The remainder were scattered among half a dozen large cities throughout the country (those from Cuba largely settling in Miami).

La Vara, a Ladino weekly formerly published in N.Y. Front page of Dec. 7, 1923 issue.

The 20th century arrivals from the Levant were segregated from the mass of Yiddish-speaking East European Jews by linguistic, social, and cultural barriers. They also felt estranged from the indigenous Sephardim in the United States who constituted a social and economic elite. Moreover, they were further divided among themselves into three language groupings: Judeo-Spanish (Ladino), Greek, and Arabic.

Several unsuccessful attempts were made to unite the Sephardim. The Central Sephardic Jewish Community of America, founded in 1949, sought to coordinate the religious and educational activities of its constituent institutions. The most representative self-help organization, the Sephardic Jewish Brotherhood of America, has a membership of over 3,000 families. A singular loss to the Sephardic community and a severe blow to its continued vitality was the disappearance of the Ladino press, *La America* (1910–23) and *La Vara* (1922–49).

In 1971 there were some 33 loosely affiliated Sephardic synagogues situated in 15 cities. The larger congregations maintained afternoon Hebrew schools where an attempt was made to transmit Sephardic traditions, and two day-schools existed in Brooklyn. Since 1964 Yeshiva University has sponsored a Sephardic Studies Program to train leadership for the community.

BLACK JEWS

In recent years, due to the greater awareness of the problems and concerns of the Negro community in the United States, a certain amount of public attention has been focused on small groups of Black Jews which exist in several large cities. These groups, however, are more reflective of the religious cults among American Negroes than of any historical links to the Jewish religion.

In 17th-century colonial America, Jewish slaveholders, following ancient custom, often converted their slaves to Judaism. A number of Negro-Jewish congregations in the United States are made up, in part, of the descendants of these early proselytes; most of these congregations originated after World War I. One type of group was led primarily by West Indians who saw the sect as a politico-religious device for alleviating the general condition of the oppressed blacks. The second, led primarily by American Negroes from the South, emphasized the more emotional, affective, and purely religious elements common to the Christian sectarian pattern historically predominant among American Negroes. Their religious practices tended to be highly syncretistic, utilizing elements from both the Christian and Jewish traditions. Knowledge of Hebrew, ritual, and religious sources—other than the Bible—was rudimentary.

No reliable statistics exist regarding the number of Black Jewish congregations or their total membership, but estimates suggest a few dozen distinct groupings with a membership between two and six thousand. The largest Black Jewish group is believed to be the Commandment Keepers Congregation of the Living God, led by West Indian-born W.A. Matthew, and located in Harlem.

In the 1960s, a few young Black Jews began studying at Jewish institutions. Toward the goal of greater integration, a group called Hatza'ad Harishon (The First Step) was organized in 1965, to promote contact between Black Jews and the main Jewish community, and to expand Jewish educational opportunities among them.

It has been suggested that for many Black Jews (as for many Black Muslims), a primary motivation in their religious orientation was the search for a haven from the overwhelming rejection experienced at the hands of white society.

CURRENT TRENDS IN COMMUNITY ORGANIZATION

Jewish communal organization has undergone many changes in its long history, but none has been more significant than that of the post-World War II years. World War II marked the culmination of an era in modern times for all mankind. For the Jews, the Holocaust and the establishment of the State of Israel were decisive events that marked the crossing of the watershed into the "post-modern" world. In the process, the locus of Jewish life shifted radically, and virtually every organized Jewish community was reconstituted in some significant way.

The Jewish world that greeted the new State was a decimated group which had lost one-third of its numbers, whose physical survival was in grave jeopardy, and whose rate of loss from intermarriage and assimilation came close to equaling its birthrate. Moreover, the traditional strongholds of Jewish communal life in Europe, with their scholars and *yeshivot,* had been wiped out. At the end of the 1940s, the centers of

Jewish life had shifted decisively away from Europe, to Israel and North America. The American Jewish community became the primary source of financial and technical assistance for world Jewry. It was faced with the complex task of adapting its organizational structures to three new purposes: to assume the leadership responsibilities passed to it as a result of the destruction of European Jewry; to play a major role in assisting Israel; and to accommodate internal changes in its community. It has filled these three roles with varying success. The transfer of world Jewish power to the American Jewish community was paralleled by internal changes which included the disappearance of immigrant ideologies and associations, and the rise of a new generation of native-born, young leaders.

On the domestic scene, the concept of the needs of the American Jewish community has been changing, and the synagogues have begun to recognize that they must be responsive to these changes. They have slowly become aware of their responsibility to integrate formerly neglected constituencies into the framework of organized Jewish life. These marginal subgroups range from the "silent poor," to the vocal academic/intellectual community which has been disillusioned by the New Left. Synagogues are studying ways of providing alternative or simultaneous services and programs to a more varied group of members. In this they are extending the concept of the synagogue center that is so indigenously American.

Federations too are moving beyond the conventional social welfare needs that provided the original impetus for their creation. Some have sought to alleviate the alienation from Jewish life that is evident among Jewish youth in the New Left and other segments of the student population. However, such efforts have revealed that these agencies find it exceedingly difficult to deal with problems outside the realm of philanthropy. Alienation can only be countered by ideology, and the principle behind the existence of the federations has been non-ideological, that is, they stand only for those things that all Jews, regardless of ideology, can agree upon.

The urban crisis provides an even more striking illustration of another type of limitation inherent in the federation structure. One of the most significant local issues confronting the Jewish community is what should be done about families who live in changing, crime-ridden neighborhoods, about businessmen whose livelihood has been severely affected by the rise

Dignitaries at the 40th anniversary celebration of the Synagogue Council of America, 1966. Right to left: Seymour J. Cohen, president of the Council; Nelson Glueck, president of Hebrew Union College-Jewish Institute of Religion; Samuel Belkin, president of Yeshiva University; Arthur J. Goldberg, honorary chairman of the Council; Louis Finkelstein, chancellor of the Jewish Theological Seminary.

of the Black Power philosophy, and about the 900,000 American Jews (two-thirds of them elderly) who live close to the poverty line in New York City, Chicago, and Los Angeles. But the effect of the urban crisis cannot be mitigated solely by philanthropism. It requires political clout, and this has been outside the federations' scope.

At the political level, the organization of American Jewry has remained relatively unstructured, a reflection of the traditional reluctance, or perhaps inability, of the American Jewish community to identify itself as a distinct political bloc. In 1955, however, an umbrella group, the Conference of Presidents of Major American Jewish Organizations (the Presidents' Conference), was formed because of growing recognition of the need for unified action by major American Jewish organizations to help strengthen peace and stability in the Middle East.

The Presidents' Conference serves as a roof organization for 24 national Jewish bodies, both religious and secular, and has established contacts with world Jewish bodies to facilitate the exchange of information, opinions and ideas relative to ensuring the security of the Jewish people the world over. Its members represent the overwhelming majority of the

Jewish community of the United States, and the Conference thus comes closer than any other organization to wearing the mantle of an overall, countrywide body. It also serves as a central address for American Jewry, to which Jewish communities in other lands may turn with issues of mutual concern.

The weakness of the Conference lies in its consultative, rather than authoritative, nature. The power of the American Jewish community continues to reside in the constituent organizations of the Conference, which are tied together by intermeshing memberships, and shared purposes and interests.

5

INVESTMENT IN AMERICA

It would be difficult to find an area of American social, political, and economic life that has not been marked by contributions made by American Jews. The purpose of this chapter, however, is not to provide a list of "Jewish" scientists, "Jewish" politicians, and "Jewish" novelists. One can well question the specifically "Jewish" contribution of many of the well-known figures who would certainly find their place on such a list. Should they be judged "Jewish" by biological origin, by sociological identification, or by personal commitment and public action?

Rather, the general contribution of the Jewish community to certain areas of American life will be discussed in terms of its reflecting a specifically "Jewish" contribution that emerged from the sociological and/or religious tradition of that community.

POLITICS

Three facts stand out in connection with Jews in American politics. First, Jews have not been prominent as political office holders, political appointees, or party leaders. Perhaps the only time Jews held a disproportionately high number of political offices was during the 19th century, in those areas of the country where they constituted a very small proportion of the general population.

Second, support for liberal and left-of-center parties and candidates is proportionately higher among Jews than among any other group in the United States. A number of reasons have been advanced for the Jewish tendency to join such parties (see below).

Third, although a disproportionately large number of Jews go to the polls—they are better informed about politics than most other American groups and are among the large contributors to the funds of both major parties—they have never organized themselves for solely political purposes, and have not pressed expressly Jewish demands, except where they perceived an acute danger to the larger Jewish community outside the United States.

In such cases, Jewish politicians were frequently prepared to oppose government policies even in the face of the accusation of "dual loyalty." Jewish political leaders repeatedly pressed the government to take steps to stop anti-Semitic excesses in Central and Eastern Europe, and to help Jewish migration and settlement in Palestine. Later, Jews were also in the forefront of demands for the government to increase its assistance to Israel in the face of Arab threats. Domestically, however, Jewish voters and politicians have been at pains to deny the existence of a Jewish political interest, and have rarely organized themselves for solely political purposes.

There have been numerous cases of political candidates detached from the Jewish community who fervently sought to re-identify themselves before an election. The degree to which Jewish politicians canvassed Jewish issues often tended to reflect the political advantage to be gained by it. (Jewish political figures elected by a largely Jewish constituency usually fulfilled the voters' expectations that they would support Jewish causes, particularly Israel.) However, the American Jewish electorate tended to ignore excessive appeals to them to vote as Jews, as was evident in the case of contests for the New York City mayoralty in 1945 and 1965.

VOTING PATTERNS

In the first half of the 19th century, the small Jewish community in the United States tended to support the Democrats, the party of Jefferson. However, a disproportionate number of Jews, largely of German origin, switched to the Republican Party (the party of Lincoln), and continued to support it even when its candidate for president was Ulysses S. Grant who, as a general in the Union army, ordered the expulsion of all Jewish traders from an area under his command. Republicans controlled the presidency from 1860 to 1912, except for Cleveland's two terms, and solidified their Jewish support through efforts on behalf of Jews in Eastern Europe. (Nonetheless, in New York City the Democratic

Henry Morgenthau Sr. (left), financier and diplomat, and Henry Morgenthau Jr. (right), secretary of the U.S. Treasury.

Party boasted such prominent supporters as Henry Morgenthau and the Straus brothers; however, these men remained independent of Tammany Hall!)

The Republican hold over the Jewish vote was shaken in 1912, when that party's candidate, President Taft, showed himself unsympathetic to Jewish petitions to denounce the discriminatory Russo-American Passport Treaty. Jews were further attracted to the Democratic Party by the idealism and professorial background of Woodrow Wilson.

The Socialist Party also had strong supporters among the immigrants who comprised the vast majority of American Jewry in the early 20th century. It had a particularly strong following in New York City, where Jewish trade union leaders were influential, Jewish workers were class conscious, and the socialist Yiddish paper, the *Forward,* had a wide readership. However even in New York an attractive Democratic candidate with a liberal image, such as Alfred E. Smith, could cut heavily into the Socialist Party's Jewish vote. Such Jews as Gus Tyler, Max and Robert Delson, Sidney Hook, and J.B.S. Hardman were significant Socialist leaders during the 1930s. But between the American Socialist Party's pacifist and isolationist stance in the face of Nazism, and the drawing power of the New Deal, Jewish voters increasingly left the ranks of that party.

From 1930 on, Jews turned in ever greater numbers to the Democratic Party; three Democratic Jewish governors were elected in that year. After the Democratic Party assumed control at the national level in 1932, Jews became the most solidly Democratic (over 80%) voting group in the United States (with the possible exception of Negroes in more recent elections). Jews tended to support candidates whom they perceived as liberal in domestic affairs and internationalist in foreign politics, and such candidates generally ran on the Democratic ticket. Jewish labor leaders were instrumental in making the labor vote (generally Democratic) an important element in American political life, for they were staunch advocates of union members taking a partisan political stand.

Jewish support for Democratic candidates solidified during the presidency of Franklin D. Roosevelt, whom Jews perceived as especially sympathetic to the plight of European Jewry. (Posthumously published documents and correspondence indicated that their perception had been exaggerated.) On the domestic scene, Roosevelt appointed a number of Jews to important positions: Henry Morgenthau, Jr. was Secretary of the Treasury; Felix Frankfurter was appointed to the Supreme Court; men such as Samuel Rosenman, David Lilienthal, Bernard Baruch, and Sidney Hillman held Roosevelt's confidence, and served him in various official and unofficial capacities. All this further bolstered Jewish identification with the Democrats.

Unlike other minority groups, Jews continued to support Democratic candidates after Roosevelt's death. However, third-party candidate Henry Wallace drew a heavily disproportionate share of the Jewish vote in 1948, indicating once again that Jews were more attracted by a candidate's ideology or personality than by party orientation.

An estimated 75% of American Jews voted for Adlai Stevenson (Democrat) against Dwight Eisenhower in 1952. After initial suspicions, they were also attracted to John F. Kennedy.

In 1964 distrust of Barry Goldwater, as much as enthusiasm for Lyndon Johnson, brought Jewish support for the Democratic candidate up to 90%. In the 1968 presidential election, Hubert Humphrey, the Democratic candidate, received an estimated 81% of the Jewish vote, compared to 17% for the victor, Richard Nixon, and 1% for the right-wing third-party candidate, George Wallace.

Very few leaders of the Jewish community were associated with Richard Nixon, and in 1970 there was no Jew in the Cabinet or the Supreme Court. The leading Jewish figure in the Republican Party during the 1960s and early 1970s was New York Senator Jacob Javits.

It was a fact that in 1970, just as at the beginning of the 20th century, most American Jews were affiliated with the Democratic Party. Nonetheless, the 1972 elections saw a Jewish swing into the Republican camp, partially due to President Nixon's positive policy toward Israel. The urban crisis of the 1960s was also felt to have had an effect on Jewish voting patterns. There is some evidence that American Jews have become "conservatized." In New York City and other urban centers, Jewish voters expressed more interest in "public law and order" figures than in candidates who provided generalized moral statements. A significant number of Jewish intellectuals were "deradicalized" as they became disillusioned with the left-wing world-view.

A case in point is the Forest Hills incident (1971–72) which involved the proposed construction of a high-rise, low-income housing project in the heart of one of the largest middle-income Jewish communities in New York City. Local residents made known their opposition to this project. They feared that it would threaten the Jewish character of their neighborhood which housed a large number of communal, religious, and educational institutions. They also feared that a large influx of hard-core welfare cases would raise the crime and delinquency rate in the area. The organized Jewish community divided over the issue. A number of major Jewish organizations publicly supported the housing project, basing their stand on ultimate moral concepts. Other groups condemned it on practical grounds, in view of the negative consequences projected for the local Jewish community. Public demonstrations and heated controversy led to the formulation of a series of compromise proposals for the site.

LIBERAL TENDENCIES

Jews were prominent in the Reform clubs that developed after 1945 in New York, Chicago, and California in an effort to reorganize and reform the Republican and especially the Democratic Party. Jews have always been prominent in mildly leftist organizations such as the Americans for Democratic Action, and were founders and chief supporters of the New York State American Labor Party in 1936, and the anti-communist Liberal Party which split off from the A.L.P. in 1944. Jews were also prominent in the Communist-supported Progressive

Party whose candidate, Henry Wallace, ran for president in 1948. They have been among the supporters and leaders of the radical left.

Jewish support for liberal and leftist candidates is all the more striking and dramatic, given their high socioeconomic position. Among other ethnic and religious groups, a high socioeconomic position has always resulted in support for the Republican Party and center, or right-of-center, candidates. One study found that Jews voted 45% more Democratic than would be expected from their social and demographic characteristics. But, as has been indicated, it is not the Democratic Party which the Jews support, but rather political liberalism.

There are at least four theories which purport to explain Jewish orientation to left-of-center ideologies and parties. One theory explains Jewish liberalism on the basis of traditional Jewish values. Three values have been suggested as particularly relevant politically: the value of study and learning, which is translated into support for social planning; the value of communal responsibility for the welfare of others, which is translated into support for social justice and welfare policies; and a worldly, non-ascetic orientation, which is translated politically into a stress on the creation of a better life in the present rather than awaiting a heavenly reward. All these values presumably result in support for liberal rather than conservative candidates.

There are a number of difficulties with this theory.

1. Jewish religious values are not unambiguously liberal. There are elements within the religious tradition which are folk-oriented, ethnocentric, and even hostile to non-Jews and to secular education, rather than universalistic, cosmopolitan, and positive toward knowledge of all kinds. While Jewish liberals may find their source of values in the religious tradition, conservatives may do so as well. At the least, each group is choosing selectively.

2. It is not at all clear that theological values or beliefs are readily transferable to the arena of politics. Indeed, the evidence suggests that political behavior is not a direct consequence of a diffuse ideology, particularly an ideology derived from theology.

3. If the source of Jewish liberalism is the religious tradition, one would expect that the more religious a Jew was, the more liberal he would be. In fact, it would seem that Orthodox Jews are the least liberal politically. Certainly, Orthodox rabbinical organizations have been less liberal politically in their public posture than have Conservative rabbis,

and the latter less liberal than the Reform. One study, confined to members of a Conservative synagogue, found that those who were most religiously involved in Jewish life were no more likely to be politically liberal than those who were least religiously involved.

A second theory for Jewish liberalism is based on the purported status inferiority of Jews. According to this argument, Jews enjoy a social status far below what they might anticipate from their economic attainments. Consequently they are attracted to political ideologies which challenge the establishment and culture that disadvantage them. There are several difficulties with this theory.

First, it accounts for Jewish radicalism rather than liberalism. Secondly, it leaves unanswered the question why Jews should respond to society's image of them, rather than to their own self-image. Thirdly, it ignores the fact that since World War II Jews in America—certainly young American Jews—do not perceive themselves as suffering from status inferiority. Finally, while there is no empirical evidence in support of the theory, there is some to the contrary. A study of a small sample of Jews found an inverse relationship between political liberalism and feelings of ethnic subordination (i.e., the greater the feelings of ethnic subordination, the less political liberalism). (Ethnic subordination was defined as insecurity and defensiveness in social situations with gentiles, or concern about recriminations for conspicuous Jewish behavior, and thus seems very close to status inferiority.)

A third theory accounts for Jewish liberalism by historical factors, namely that the parties of the political right have associated themselves with the church, the establishment, and social tradition, three concepts with which Jews had no connection. Left-wing groups, committed to challenging the establishment and altering tradition, were more attractive to Jewish voters and prospective politicians alike.

More specifically, this theory points to the fact that, following the French Revolution, it was the left which adopted the view that citizenship should be extended to everyone, that the national state was secular, and that religious affiliation was irrelevant to political equality. The right associated citizenship with the nation's Christian traditions. Jews, therefore, were attracted to parties of the left, particularly the moderate left which was anti-conservative but also upheld law and order against plebian attacks and revolutionary capriciousness that often included anti-Semitic sentiments. Furthermore, the extreme left's political ideology, unlike that of the moderate left, comprised a total weltanschauung which left no room at all for Jewish allegiances.

Among the problems with the historical theory is that it relies too much on events that occurred many generations ago in an environment totally foreign to the American political tradition. (American Jews after the Civil War were predominantly Republican; among the immigrant community at the turn of the century, the Orthodox Yiddish press was Republican!) The historical theory fails to explain why, in the American context, Jews left the Republican Party.

The final theory suggests that Jewish liberalism, rather than stemming from the Jewish tradition, finds its source in the values of modern, estranged, partially assimilated Jews who seek a universalistic ethic to which they can adhere. Liberalism, they believe, will help integrate them into the broader community by destroying the barriers of cultural, religious, and political traditions separating them from non-Jews. The effect of liberalism, unlike radicalism, is that it leaves room for Judaism as a purely religious, narrowly defined aspect of life. Liberalism makes one's religio-ethnic-cultural identity politically irrelevant, and this is precisely what the emancipated and partially assimilated Jew desires. Indeed, the basic Jewish commitment according to this theory is less to liberalism than to "enlightenment," the optimistic faith that the application of human intellect can create a constantly progressing, universal, cosmopolitan society. Internationalism, civil libertarianism, and welfarism are merely consequences of this basic commitment. It is the image of the "enlightened" society and the "enlightenment" liberal that holds greatest resonance for the Jew.

To this extent political style may be more important than policy content. It is difficult to cite examples where Jews had to choose between an "enlightenment" candidate and one who was more liberal. One case may be the contest between Woodrow Wilson and Theodore Roosevelt for the 1912 presidency; another may be the race between Adlai Stevenson and Estes Kefauver for the 1956 Democratic nomination. In both cases Jews supported the "enlightenment"-style candidates, Wilson and Stevenson, over their opponents, who were more liberal politically. Generally, however, the "enlightenment" candidate is also the more liberal candidate.

The liberal-enlightenment ideology would seem to satisfy the basic desire of most American Jews on the one hand to be accepted in the society as individuals, with their Judaism a matter or irrelevance, and on the other hand to be free to live as the kind of Jews they wish to be. There is, however, no direct empirical evidence to support this theory.

SOCIAL PHILOSOPHY

Jews played little part in the brand of American socialism which derived from agrarian and populist discontent with the social order. Nor did they appear in the numerous short-lived utopian communities which sprang up early in the 20th century or in the proletarian-revolutionary-syndicalist Industrial Workers of the World which flourished from about 1908 to 1920. The role of Jews in American social philosophy lay within the urban, industrial environment from which the socialist movement drew its main strength, and whose ideology was more or less Marxist. Jews were most prominent in the American Socialist Party

Samuel Gompers, trade unionist.

from about 1915 to the 1930s, the period when ethnic minorities generally played a key role in the socialist movement.

Socialism developed among industrial workers and intellectuals during the 1880s, after the Socialist Labor Party was founded (1877) with one of its strongest bases in the largely Jewish membership of the International Cigar Makers Union. Two members of that union, Adolph Strasser and Samuel Gompers, were founders and leaders of the American Federation of Labor (1886), which they led away from socialist involvements and towards "pure and simple" trade unionism.

LABOR UNIONISM

As president of the American Federation of Labor for 38 years, Gompers exercised a formative influence upon the American labor movement. He argued for the strengthening of labor organizations which were to be independent of control by politicians, intellectuals, or any non-labor source. This viewpoint in effect acknowledged that organized labor lacked the political power to achieve its objectives through legislation, and that workers could not expect continuing support from the middle-class, since their objectives would inevitably conflict. Gompers maintained a vitriolic hostility to socialism almost throughout his presidency of the AFL. The socialists called for industrial unionism and political action, as opposed to his belief in craft unionism dedicated to the immediate interests of a relatively homogeneous membership. This position led Gompers, himself an immigrant, to demand the restriction of immigration to the United States, in order to protect the competitive position of workers in America!

After 1910 trade unionism, which was then overwhelmingly Jewish in membership and leadership, won control of labor conditions in the garment industry by means of a series of dramatic strikes. In all cases, negotiations ended with some form of recognition for the union, a preferential or union shop, a shorter work week (generally 50 hours!), a rise in wages, and arrangements for the continual arbitration of grievances. The last provision led to the creation of joint sanitation, grievance, and arbitration committees under "impartial chairmen" aided by professional staffs, which supervised the enforcement of the decisions. This constituted a striking innovation in labor relations which reflected a particularly Jewish group response.

N.Y. garment workers voting on strike action, 1913.

Great numbers of the East European immigrants who arrived in the United States between 1880 and 1925 had a European Socialist orientation. In America they helped organize the United Garment Workers of America (1891), and its spinoff organizations, the International Ladies' Garment Workers Union (1900), and the Amalgamated Clothing Workers of America (1914).

The socialist character of these unions was clear at the outset, but they tended to leave socialism behind with the passage of time, particularly when major breakthroughs were made in the needle trade unions' relations with management in the years immediately preceding World War I. The career of David Dubinsky, president of the ILGWU from 1932 to 1966, illustrates this process. When Dubinsky entered the United States in 1910, he had already been sentenced to a term in Siberia for having organized strikes in Lodz. He became an apprentice cutter and joined the ILGWU, rising in the ranks to assume a leadership position. During the 1930s Dubinsky dominated the ILGWU and was a powerful force in the American labor movement, making his organization a symbol of progressive unionism. He also helped found the Congress of Industrial Organizations (CIO) in 1935.

An influential figure in U.S. politics, Dubinsky helped create the American Labor Party in 1936; then, in 1944, when Communists began to dominate the A.L.P. he helped Alex Rose form the Liberal Party. After World War II he was one of the founders of the anti-Communist International Confederation of Free Trade Unions.

In an interesting development, rabbis early became active in labor mediation in the United States, serving on both general and Jewish mediation boards. The kehillah, the official community of New York City Jewry between 1908 and 1922, formed a "committee on conciliation," whose activities included the prevention of a threatened strike of poultry slaughterers in 1909, and the arbitration of complaints of Sabbath-observing cloakmakers against their union. Rabbi Morris Adler of Detroit served as chairman of the Public Review Board of the United Auto Workers from 1957 to 1966.

RADICAL MOVEMENTS

The years after World War II, with their combination of economic prosperity, cold war, and political conformism, witnessed the near total collapse of the socialist movement as a serious political force in the United States. Nevertheless, although socialist politics remained moribund in America for two decades after World War II, a community of influential socialist thinkers, many of them Jews, continued to exist and to sustain a tradition of radical political critique that served as an intellectual seedbed for the radical revival of the late 1960s. The individuals who composed this community held a wide divergence of views, ranging from the revolutionary Marxism of Herbert Marcuse to the anarchism of Paul Goodman and the social democratic humanism of Irving Howe. All joined in rejecting both Soviet communism and American capitalism as viable social models for the future, though most of them openly expressed their preference for the latter as the lesser of the two evils and more amenable to structural change. Academicians and writers, many of them Jewish, expressed their radical political viewpoints in the pages of such journals as *Dissent*, edited by Irving Howe, and *Partisan Review*, edited by Philip Rahv.

The participation of Jews in the radical movements was motivated by their perception that society was not living up to the promises of the middle-class revolutions, and that the only hope for real human equality was to uproot the past and to begin all over again.

Paradoxically, the allegiance of Jews to revolutionary movements represents both a conscious denial of a specifically Jewish identity, and an expression of certain aspects of that identity: the legacy of Jewish prophetic messianism, and of centuries of anti-Semitism.   Although creators and supporters of modern radical philosophies have tended to regard specifically Jewish issues as peripheral to broader social and economic problems, support for the State of Israel, both as a home for victims of the Holocaust, and as a legitimate expression of Jewish national aspirations, became a point of contention within their ranks, particularly after the Six-Day War.

SOCIAL WORK AND PHILANTHROPY

The moral imperative of alleviating the suffering of the needy, which is basic to Jewish law and tradition, has operated within the American Jewish community since its formation, as has been traced in the preceding chapters. Inevitably Jews turned beyond specific concern for their own community to the concerns of the general society.

Lillian Wald may be cited as the prototype of the social worker and liberal reformer of the early 20th century. Born to an upper-middle-class German Jewish immigrant family in Cincinnati (1867), she turned her attention to the needs of the era without sectarian impulse. She demanded that social reform proceed from fact and sound argument, not sympathy, and she argued that charity could make no dent in social

Lillian Wald, social worker.

problems, since it left both the individual and the environment unchanged. Instead, the state must take the responsibility for creating the proper conditions for a decent and humane society. Thus she campaigned for the end of child labor, supported trade unions, and was an important member of most of the leading social reform organizations of the day. In 1895 she established the Nurses (later Henry Street) Settlement House on New York's Lower East Side. The institution provided nursing services and hygienic instruction to the needy, campaigned for improved sanitation, pure milk, and the control of tuberculosis, and offered a full range of educational, recreational, and personal services.

When social work began to develop as a profession in its own right, the American Jewish community was among the first to recognize its value and adopt its methods. Jewish welfare agencies began to utilize professionals in the fields of social work, medicine, public relations, and other areas, for its own programs. This practice, in addition to the sophisticated concepts of fundraising developed by the American Jewish community, have been copied by general social work agencies. The federated fundraising idea was another distinctive Jewish contribution to American philanthropy, and served as a model for the nationwide Red Feather–Community Chest campaigns.

LAW

References to Jewish law appear in the official records of the American colonies from the earliest times. The founders of the original colonies looked upon English common law with distrust. (Even in England, the common law was not universally appreciated nor popularly accepted in the 18th century. It was too technical, and reflected too much of the feudalism and tyranny of the Middle Ages.) The Puritans deliberately attempted to establish a theocratic government, in a sense modeled after that of the ancient Hebrew state. It has been said that they considered Moses as their law-giver, the Pentateuch their code, and Israel under the Judges their ideal of popular government.

An order of the General Court of Massachusetts (1636) and the *General Lawes* of Plymouth Colony (1658), for example, both decreed that the divines and magistrates (who were laymen familiar with Hebrew and Hebraic learning) were to decide cases as near the law of God or of Moses as possible. Litigations were often decided by reference to the Scriptures, particularly in matters of inheritance, maintenance of churches and schools, and in criminal cases. The arguments in those early court cases frequently depended more on the authority of the Mosaic Code or the wisdom expounded by the Prophets, than upon the decisions of the Lord High Chancellor of England.

The first American law book, *Body of Liberties,* officially enacted in 1641, directs the magistrates to be guided by "the word of God" rather than the common law, when the law was silent on a particular situation. Similar directives appear in the fundamental orders of the colonies of Connecticut, Rhode Island, and Massachusetts.

One of the most significant Jewish contributions to law is the concept of a compact between the government and the people, with the purpose of protecting their basic liberties. Justice Hugo L. Black of the U.S. Supreme Court traced the idea of the American Constitution's Bill of Rights back to the Puritan dissenters of 17th century England who had revived the biblical concept of the covenant between God and Abraham, and later between the people and David. This was refined into the idea of a covenant between the government and the people. The American Bill of Rights was established in the form of an inviolable compact or formal agreement of the people; it was a fundamental law of the land, superior to any act of the national legislature.

The meager number of Jews in the legal profession in the United States during its early history has already been alluded to. In the 19th century, however, their numbers began to grow, and the 20th century saw a dramatic increase in Jewish lawyers. Still, for many years, Jewish lawyers in the United States found advancement difficult, since many were foreign-born, could not attend the best colleges, and did not have the financial backing to open their own firms. In 1939 it was estimated that over half the lawyers practicing in New York City were Jews, but that annual income on the average was less than their non-Jewish counterparts. The same situation was true in other American cities.

Few of the large law firms had Jewish members and, with the notable exception of Felix Frankfurter, Jews did not become law professors at leading universities. Discrimination also existed in appointments to the bench. Even in New York, where the majority of the Jewish legal profession was congregated, only two Jews had been appointed to the New York Court of Appeals before World War II.

A gradual improvement in the status and condition of Jewish lawyers took place after World War II. To some extent, Jews found it easier to be admitted to large law firms, although surveys in the late 1960s indicated that discrimination still existed there. By then 20% of America's 350,000 lawyers were Jewish; in 1969 Bernard Segal became the first Jewish president of the American Bar Association.

Four Supreme Court justices: Benjamin Cardozo (upper left), Louis D. Brandeis (upper right), Felix Frankfurter (lower left), and Arthur J. Goldberg (lower right).

Despite these difficulties, a number of Jews achieved national distinction in the legal profession. Louis Brandeis, Benjamin Cardozo, and Felix Frankfurter were successively appointed to the U.S. Supreme Court and established a tradition of the "Jewish seat" on the Court bench. Two Jews were appointed to the Supreme Court after World War II: Arthur Goldberg, appointed by President Kennedy in 1962, and Abe Fortas, appointed by President Johnson in 1965. This tradition was broken during President Nixon's period of appointing judges; by 1970 there was no Jewish judge on the Supreme Court.

THE SUPREME COURT

Brandeis, Cardozo, and Frankfurter have been recognized as among the greatest judges ever to sit on the Supreme Court of the United States. Brandeis, the first Jew to occupy a seat there, was born in Louisville, Kentucky (1856), of immigrant parents. He devoted himself to public causes and to the representation of interests that had not previously enjoyed powerful advocacy—the interests of consumers, investors, shareholders, and taxpayers. He became known in Boston as the "People's Attorney."

When Woodrow Wilson was elected President in 1912, he turned to Brandeis for counsel in translating political and social reform ideology into the framework of legal institutions. In 1916, after a lengthy contest over confirmation by the Senate, Brandeis was named to the Supreme Court.

In his judicial career Brandeis was preeminently a teacher and moralist. At a time when a majority of the Court was striking down new social legislation, Brandeis, together with Justice Holmes, powerfully insisted that the U.S. Constitution did not embody any single economic creed, and that to curtail experimentation in the social sciences, no less than in the natural sciences, was a fearful responsibility. He voted to sustain such measures as minimum wage laws, price control laws, and legislation protecting trade unions against injunctions in labor disputes.

Another notable category of cases in which Brandeis interested himself concerned the distribution of governmental powers between the federal government and the states. He upheld the prerogative of the state to promulgate new legislation, unless Congress itself had plainly exercised authority over the subject matter.

Brandeis was a foremost champion of freedom of thought and expression. He believed that "the greatest menace to freedom is an inert people; . . . that order cannot be secured merely through fear of punishment for its infraction; that it is hazardous to discourage thought, hope, and imagination; that fear breeds repression; that repression breeds hate; that hate menaces stable government; that the path of safety lies in the opportunity to discuss freely supposed grievances and proposed remedies; and that the fitting remedy for evil counsels is good ones" (*Whitney v. California,* 1927).

Brandeis's active interest in Jewish affairs and in Zionism will be detailed later in this book.

Benjamin Nathan Cardozo was appointed by President Hoover to the Supreme Court in 1932. Born (1870) in New York City, where his family had settled before the American Revolution, he was known as a "lawyer's lawyer." Quiet, gentle, and reserved, Cardozo was deemed "a paragon of moral insight on the American bench" by legal philosopher Edmond Cahn. Dean Roscoe Pound of Harvard Law School ranked him as one of the ten foremost judges in American judicial history. He is still recognized as the great interpreter of the common law.

Cardozo wrote several books on sociological jurisprudence, and emphasized that a judge had to look beyond the legal authorities to meet his responsibility to those seeking justice. He had to be cognizant of, and acquaint himself with, the latest developments in the fields of economics and psychology.

On the bench he was a bulwark in defense of New Deal legislation, finding constitutional such important social programs as social security and old-age pensions. He justified searching the language of the Constitution for a grant of power to the national government to improve the well-being of the nation by providing for needs which are "critical or urgent."

Felix Frankfurter's life is an example of the archetypal Jewish immigrant success story. Viennese-born (1882), he was brought up on the Lower East Side of New York where his father, scion of a long line of rabbis, was a modest tradesman. He graduated Harvard Law School as the leading student in his class and was invited to become assistant to Henry L. Stimson, U.S. Attorney in New York. Thereafter, his professional life was divided between public service and teaching at Harvard Law School. The association with Stimson was one of the most significant experiences in Frankfurter's life, constituting living proof that the effective enforcement of the criminal law did not compromise the guarantee of due process of law.

Frankfurter had a strong attachment to the values of the Anglo-American system of government-under-law, and a deep love of the United States, derived from his experience of seeing the vistas of opportunity opened to a gifted immigrant boy.

He was concerned for the integrity of the law's processes and procedures, and earned a reputation as a radical reformer because of his defense of various victims of legal injustice. The most bitter experience in his life was his involvement in the Sacco-Vanzetti murder case in Boston, in which he fought unsuccessfully to have the death verdict set aside on grounds of prejudicial conduct by the trial judge and the prosecuting attorney. He was one of the founders of the American Civil Liberties Union, legal adviser to the NAACP, and counsel to the National Consumers' League.

In 1939 President Roosevelt appointed Frankfurter to the Supreme Court where he served alongside Justice Brandeis. As a judge, Frankfurter rejected the claims of absolutism for even the most cherished liberties of speech, assembly, and religious belief, maintaining that they must be weighed against the legitimate concerns of society expressed through government. Yet when those concerns could be satisfied in a less intrusive way, he contended that the liberty of the individual must prevail. Thus, he upheld the sanctity of the university classroom against the threat of state domination, and condemned released-time religious instruction in the public schools. Yet, he wrote the dissenting opinion in a case of Jehovah's Witnesses resisting compulsory flag-salute in the public school, concluding that the government had not gone beyond permissible bounds in seeking to inculcate loyalty and national pride in schoolchildren by requiring a salute to the flag. His dissenting opinion begins with a most explicit and deeply felt statement of his judicial philosophy in the troubled area of individual freedom:

> One who belongs to the most vilified and persecuted minority in history is not likely to be insensible to the freedom guaranteed by our Constitution. Were my purely personal attitude relevant I should wholeheartedly associate myself with the general libertarian views in the Court's opinion, representing as they do the thought and action of a lifetime.

But as judges we are neither Jew nor gentile, neither Catholic nor agnostic. We owe equal attachment to the Constitution and are equally bound by our judicial obligations whether we derive our citizenship from the earliest or the latest immigrants to these shores. As a member of this Court I am not justified in writing my private notions of policy into the Constitution, no matter how deeply I may cherish them or how mischievous I may deem their disregard ... The only opinion of our own even looking in that direction that is material, is our opinion whether legislators could in reason have enacted such a law.

Frankfurter was closely associated with Louis D. Brandeis in the Zionist movement.

CIVIL LIBERTIES

One of the most significant aspects of Jewish participation in American law in the 20th century has been the extensive interest of Jewish lawyers and judges in upholding and extending civil liberties, and the profound influence they have exerted on major constitutional doctrines affecting race relations, the administration of criminal justice, and the operation of the political process. This interest undoubtedly reflects their recognition of their own group's historical disabilities, and the traditional liberalism and concern for civil rights that has long characterized the U.S. Jewish community. Among the prominent trial lawyers whose careers have been in large measure dedicated to civil liberties cases are Samuel Leibowitz and Walter Pollack, who cooperated in fighting and winning the world-famous "Scottsboro Boys" rape case in Alabama in the 1930s. Jack Greenberg and Anthony Amsterdam defended white and Negro civil rights workers in the South during the 1960s, the latter as chief legal counsel of the NAACP. Leonard Boudin and William Kunstler were active as defense counsels in the political trials of prominent Communists and radicals, the latter gaining national fame in 1970 as chief attorney for the militant Black Panthers.

ACADEMIC LIFE

Judaism has always emphasized education—the Torah imposes a duty on the father to educate his child, and if he is unable to do so, this duty becomes incumbent upon the Jewish community. Judaism's traditional respect for the educated man has been evident in the development of the American Jewish community. The immigrant to America had an almost single-minded ambition to see his children educated through the college level; the native-born generation turned to academic careers as soon as these were opened to Jews.

In medicine, the 1930s were a watershed decade during which the mainstream of Jewish medical activity was diverted from Europe to America; coincidentally American medicine began to advance in relation to medical science in Europe. The influx of European doctors after the rise of the Nazi Party, whether they escaped the Holocaust in time, or survived it and arrived in the United States after the war, came at a propitious time. The 1930s and 1940s marked the beginning of the golden age of scientific medicine, ushered in by the discovery of antibiotics and cortisone, and advances in molecular biology and medical technology. The hub of new medical activity was in the United States, and the country's medical establishment was receptive to new talent among the immigrants.

Immigrant doctors, and children of immigrants who studied medicine in the United States, have brought the number of Jewish physicians in the United States up to approximately 27,000, about 9% of all the physicians in the country. Jewish physicians in the United States greatly outnumber those in other countries, including Israel! (In New York State alone there are about 7,500 practicing Jewish doctors, as compared with 5,500 in Israel.) Their distribution is heaviest in internal medicine (20%) and in psychiatry (30%). Indeed, the practice of psychiatry and the application of psychoanalytic theory in medical care in the United States dates from the transplantation of psychoanalytic centers and practitioners (to a large extent Jewish) from Europe. The most influential figure in introducing psychoanalysis and the practice of psychiatry into the United States was A. A. Brill, who translated Freud's writings into English, and founded the New York Psychoanalytical Society.

Jewish immigrants from Germany and Austria also enriched the development of American psychology. Jews currently make up a disproportionate number of American psychologists and psychiatrists. It has been suggested that these fields attracted Jewish professionals because they presented an opportunity for intellectual advancement that was denied in some of the better established academic and professional fields.

There has also been extensive Jewish participation in medical research and education. Bela Schick (diphtheria), Selman Waksman (streptomycin and neomycin), Jonas Salk and Albert Sabin (poliomyelitis) broke new ground in immunology, and have lent their names to popular medical terminology.

The single most influential force in changing American education may be considered to have been Abraham Flexner, whose wide-ranging reports on American colleges and universities severely criticized their functionalism, and contained suggestions for the reform of secondary and higher education. His survey of medical schools brought about a fundamental reform in all aspects of medical education in America. Flexner also founded and directed the Institute for Advanced Study in Princeton.

A survey of faculty members in American universities reflects a sizeable proportion of Jews in the fields of mathematics and sciences; these areas in particular have attracted a number of Orthodox Jews, possibly because they do not impinge upon areas of doctrinal belief.

An interesting phenomenon in contemporary American academic life is the disproportionate number of Jews in the departments of social sciences, particularly in sociology. It is a moot question whether the interest of Jewish intellectuals in this area stems (as the philosopher Martin Buber suggested) from a long and deep-rooted proclivity of the Jewish mind to think in relations rather than in stances, or whether it reflects the opportunity offered by the social sciences to assume a frankly critical stance toward the existing social order and to suggest means of improving it. Whatever the incentive may have been, Jews were prominent both among the founding fathers of academic sociology in Europe, and among the spokesmen of the social science viewpoint which sprang from the socialist movement.

American Jews came late to the field of sociology. In the 1930s only two Jewish sociologists of some importance were on the American scene: Samuel Joseph, later chairman of the department of sociology at the (predominantly Jewish) City College of New York, and Louis Wirth who was to rise to prominence at the oldest and most prestigious department of sociology in the country, the University of Chicago. Wirth's intense concern with the maintenance and development of democratic institutions and the furtherance of social justice led to his interest in the elimination of discrimination against minorities, in systematic socio-economic planning, and in a workable theory of public opinion and mass communication. He was also deeply interested in the sociology of the Jews as part of his general interest in the incorporation of minorities into the democratic society.

This late start may be a reflection of a negative reaction in academic circles to entrusting "foreigners" with the teaching of such sensitive topics as American history and sociology. Among older American sociologists, "progressives" like Henry Pratt Fairchild reminded immigrants that as "guests" they must adapt themselves to their "hosts" if they wished to be "accepted" as equals.

The field of anthropology provides an instructive contrast. The founding father of cultural anthropology in the United States undoubtedly was Franz Boas, a German-Jewish immigrant who was appointed professor of anthropology at Columbia University in 1899, and whose students have been instrumental in the development of the research parameters and academic disciplines of both anthropology and, later, sociology. It has been suggested that the analysis of remote cultures may have been considered less dangerous to entrust to "foreign" hands!

The integration of cultural anthropology and psychology has been undertaken by several Jewish psychoanalysts, including Theodor Reik, Erich Fromm, and Abram Kardiner. They have sought to analyze the relation of the individual to his culture from a psychological point of view, and to relate psychology to current problems of religion and ethics.

Jewish prominence in American sociology is reflected in the fact that in 1967–68 about 25% of the members of the editorial boards of the two best-known sociological journals in the United States were of Jewish origin. That same year fully 50% of the officers and committee chairmen of the Society for the Study of Social Problems were Jews. The emphasis of the S.S.S.P. is on the application and implementation of the findings of sociological research, a purpose which apparently attracts many Jewish academicians.

American sociological literature includes studies focusing on the image of the Jew and other Jewish topics. A subject of extended controversy among American Jewish sociologists is the image of the Jew as the "marginal man" who hovers in psychological uncertainty between two or more social worlds, reflecting within himself the discords and harmonies of these worlds. In this vein, Louis Wirth has analyzed the ghetto not merely as a physical abode, but as a state of mind marked by marginality. The outward pull of the larger society, and discriminatory rejection by that society, correspond to flight from the narrow restrictions of the ghetto, and longing for its sheltering intimacy.

An analysis of papers published in three leading sociological journals between 1929 and 1964 showed that 74 of the published papers dealt with topics referring to intergroup relations (acculturation, assimilation, intermarriage, prejudice, discrimination, anti-Semitism, etc.), while 51 papers dealt with predominantly, although not exclusively, internal topics of Jewish life.

Several American Jewish sociologists have made their mark in race and intercultural relations studies, partly because the field explicitly or implicitly includes Jewish topics, but chiefly because, for a variety of reasons, the problems of the American Negro and other minorities have appealed to them. Other sociologists have been concerned mainly with Jewish themes: demography, the analysis of Jewish institutional life, and changing factors in Jewish identification.

By and large, Jewish contributors to U.S. cultural life, at least until the middle 1960s, were not rebels or path breakers, but excelled and advanced in the established forms. Their general orientation continued to be the liberal left, with echoes of earlier radicalism. To the Jewish community, however, its "Jewish intellectuals" were a source of concern: could they be made to demonstrate positive interest in established U.S. Judaism, and why did most of them shy away? A symposium on "Jewishness and the Younger Intellectuals," published in *Commentary* in May 1961, strongly suggested that under the cultural consensus and religiosity of the 1950s lay the alienated restlessness of many of the highly acculturated, talented young.

LITERATURE

American Jews were late in making their presence known in the world of American literature, but once they felt sufficiently secure in the language to venture upon the literary scene, they quickly began to live up to their reputation as the "people of the book." American literature in the post-World War II decades brought the American Jewish community to the forefront of national attention, and erased some of the alien quality of the Jew in the eyes of non-Jewish fellow citizens.

It was only in the 19th century that Jews first came upon the American literary scene, as authors and as fictional characters. Curiously, during this period it was only in the writings of non-Jews that Jewish characters appeared. The works of the early 19th-century Jewish playwrights Mordecai Manuel Noah, Isaac Harby, and Jonas B. Phillips were conventional melodramas, conspicuously devoid of Jewish subject matter, despite the active involvement of Noah and Harby in Jewish community life. Perhaps they felt that Jewish life was too insubstantial to provide the working basis for a dramatic theme; or perhaps they wished to vie with their contemporaries on more universal ground. On the other hand, as drama critic of the New York *Evening Post,* Harby attacked the anti-Semitic stereotype of Shylock in Shakespeare's *Merchant of Venice.*

In contrast to these playwrights, the legendary American actress Adah Isaacs Menken, whose romantic personality won her friends among the American and European literati of the 19th century, wrote poetry of a specifically Jewish character. Her first poems, largely on Jewish national themes, were published by Isaac M. Wise in the *Israelite.*

THE IMAGE OF THE JEW

In contrast to the generally sympathetic treatment of Jews as a collective entity in early American journalism and political writing, the relatively few portraits of Jewish characters in fiction and drama tended to draw heavily on the negative stereotypes of Jews that predominated in British literary tradition, on which American authors were greatly dependent. Perhaps the first such Jewish character to appear in American literature was in Susanna Haswell Rowson's *Slaves in Algeria* (1794), a drama about piracy along the Barbary Coast in which a central role was played by a rapacious Jewish miser and swindler. A similar character appeared in James Ellison's *The American Captive* (1812). In fiction, George Lippard's Gothic novel *The Quaker City* presented a minor Jewish character named Gabriel von Gelt as a misshapen incarnation of greed.

In the middle of the 19th century, Jewish characters began to make their appearance in serious works of American fiction. Significantly, their entry occurred at the time of the first large increase of the American Jewish population, which was created by the arrival of German Jews in the wake of the European upheavals of 1848. The critic John J. Appel has observed that in Hawthorne's well-known story *Ethan Brand* (1851), "the German-Jewish peddler reflected American awareness of the growing numbers of German-Jewish immigrants who traveled the backwoods with their moveable stocks of goods." These peddlers also appear in the correspondence of Emily Dickinson and may be the source of some odd images in her poems, such as one in which she describes her orchard "sparkling like a Jew!"

In contrast, Longfellow's moving poem "The Jewish Cemetery at Newport," which was written in 1852, delineates Jewish martyrdom and anti-Semitic persecutions throughout the ages with the most profound sympathy for the victims. Yet its concluding stanza is hardly calculated to inspire any hope or nurse illusions in the heart of its Jewish readers:

> But ah! What once has been shall be no more!
> The groaning earth in travail and in pain
> Brings forth its races, but does not restore,
> And the dead nations never rise again.

This dispiriting ending prompted a protest by Emma Lazarus—the author of the sonnet "The New Colossus," which is inscribed on the base of the Statue of Liberty—who pointed out that it was hardly consonant with the facts.

Walt Whitman's voracious curiosity about the inhabitants of the city of New York led him to consider the Jews. Long before the appearance of *Leaves of Grass,* he had published two sizable articles in a newspaper he was editing at the time, recording his impressions of the customs of the Sabbath service that he had witnessed at the Crosby Street Synagogue. The philo-Semitic temper of the time is nowhere more evident than in the writings of William Cullen Bryant, who was not only a distinguished American poet but also, for almost 50 years, the influential editor of New York's *Evening Post,* a newspaper that enjoyed the greatest prestige in mid-19th-century America. Commenting on a performance by the Shakespearean actor Edwin Booth in the role of Shylock, Bryant took the opportunity to find fault with Shakespeare for his repulsive caricature of the Jew and paid eloquent tribute to that superiority of intellect which has survived all persecutions, and which, soaring above the prejudice of the hour, has filled us with reluctant admiration on finding how many of the great events which work the progress of the age or minister to its improvement or elevate its past may be traced to the wonderful workings of the soul of the Hebrew and the supremacy of that spiritual nature which gave to mankind its noblest religion, its noblest laws, and some of its noblest poetry and music.

The mass immigration to the United States of East European Jews that began in the 1880s totally transformed both the character and the size of the American Jewish community, and, concomitantly, the attitudes of American intellectuals toward it. On the whole, the first reactions echo the generous sentiments of an earlier age. William Dean Howells wrote with great insight and compassion about the Jewish immigrants on New York's Lower East Side in his *Impressions and Experiences* (1896). Howells's friend, Mark Twain, expressed himself equally strongly on the subject of Jewish immigration. The Jew's "contributions to the world's list of great names in literature, science, art, music, finance, medicine, and abstruse learning," he wrote in an article in *Harper's* in 1899, "are . . . out of proportion to the weakness of his numbers . . . [the Jew] is now what he always was, exhibiting no decadence, no infirmities of age, no weakening of his parts, no slowing of his energies, no dulling of his alert and aggressive mind . . ."

It is difficult to pinpoint with any precision the exact moment when far-reaching historical changes first began to challenge this hitherto predominant image of the Jew in American literature. The new attitudes of the 20th century were already anticipated by Henry James in his novel *The American Scene* (1907), in which he speaks of his impressions of New York's Lower East Side, of "a Jewry that had burst all bounds . . . The children swarmed above all—here was multiplication with a vengeance . . . There is no swarming like that of Israel when once Israel has got a start." In a similar vein, some years later in his novel *The Beautiful and Damned* (1922), F. Scott Fitzgerald described a trip down the length of the island of Manhattan:

Down in a tall busy street he read a dozen Jewish names on a line of stores: in the door of each stood a dark little man watching the passers from intent eyes—eyes gleaming with suspicion, with pride, with clarity, with cupidity, with comprehension. New York—he could not dissociate it now from the slow, upward creep of this people—the little stores, growing, expanding, consolidating, moving, watched over with hawk's eyes and a bee's attention to detail—they slathered out on all sides. It was impressive—in perspective, it was tremendous.

Even the normally sympathetic Mark Twain commented wryly on the enormous increase of Jewish numbers in America:

> When I read [in the Encyclopaedia Britannica] that the Jewish population of the United States was 250,000, I wrote the editor and explained to him that I was personally acquainted with more Jews than that in my country, and that his figures were without a doubt a misprint for 25,000,000.

The same impression is communicated humorlessly in the correspondence of Theodore Dreiser, who was inclined to assume the existence of a sinister conspiracy on the part of official agencies to minimize Jewish population statistics in the United States. Dreiser's anti-Semitism, which was unusual at the time for one who held radical left-wing opinions, surfaced so unmistakably during the depression following the financial crash of 1929, and especially after the accession of the Nazis to power in Germany, that he was publicly taken to task for it by his Communist comrade Michael Gold, the author of *Jews Without Money* (1930).

During the first four decades of the 20th century, it became almost fashionable for many American writers of distinction—especially among the expatriates—to express anti-Semitism. It was sometimes present in the writings of Edith Wharton, who once described Fitzgerald's gangster-villain Wolfsheim in *The Great Gatsby* (1925) as the "perfect Jew," Henry James, T. S. Eliot, Ezra Pound, Ernest Hemingway, e. e. cummings, and others. It is strong in those of German ancestry like Dreiser, H. L. Mencken, and Thomas Wolfe; and it even touches a writer like Gertrude Stein, who was herself, as Wyndham Lewis described her, "a brilliant Jewish lady."

Among those who wrote about urban Jewry was Damon Runyon, whose *Guys and Dolls* (1932) and other short story collections teem with amiable Jewish gangsters and Broadway characters.

In the late 1930s, the pendulum began to swing back again, as the emerging barbarism of the Nazis had an inhibiting effect upon intellectual anti-Semitism in America. A number of American writers, including Thomas Wolfe, T. S. Eliot, and F. Scott Fitzgerald, whose sentiments concerning the Jews had hitherto been less than friendly, now gave signs of regretting that their own position might be confused with or lend comfort to that of the Hitler regime. After being lionized by the Nazis on his visit to Germany in the mid-1930s, Wolfe returned to the United States to write a report on what he had seen, which promptly resulted in the suppression of all his books in the Third Reich. World War II and its aftermath once again generated a new wave of philo-Semitic sympathies in American intellectual life.

PALESTINE AND ISRAEL AS LITERARY SUBJECTS

American writers who visited Palestine in the 19th century found the land both inviting and forbidding. Herman Melville's *Journal* pictured the writer's impression of the desolation in Jerusalem (1857): "In the emptiness of the lifeless antiquity of Jerusalem, the emigrant Jews are like flies that have taken up their abode in a skull." All Judea seemed an accumulation of stones, rubbish, and the "mere refuse of creation." Almost twenty years later he published the two-volume *Clarel: A Poem and Pilgrimage in the Holy Land,* which was inspired by this visit to Jerusalem.

Mark Twain's impressions of Palestine ("It is sacred to poetry and tradition—it is dreamland . . .") in *The Innocents Abroad* (1869) brought the Holy Land to the attention of American travelers.

Works by Jewish authors about the Holy Land have ranged from the early prose poems by Jessie Sampter (*The Emek,* 1927), portraying the first pioneers in the Valley of Jezreel, to the most recent, highly popular novels, *Exodus* by Leon Uris and *The Source* by James Michener. The latter works introduced to a mass audience the ideas of Zionist philosophy, the fight for Israel's independence, and the historical significance of the Land of Israel and its continuing relevance to the Jews.

THE JEWISH AMERICAN GENRE

One of the first writers to realize that the growth of a Jewish audience provided the conditions for the evolution of a distinctive American-

Jewish literary school was a non-Jew, Henry Harland, who, under the pseudonym of Sidney Luska, wrote a number of popular novels during the 1880s on subjects of Jewish concern. One of them, *The Yoke of the Thora* (1887), dealt with the tragic difficulties of intermarriage more than 40 years before Ludwig Lewisohn's eloquent treatment of the same subject in *The Island Within* (1928).

Before 1880 the most significant Jewish writing had been in the form of biographical documents, such as those collected by Jacob Marcus in the three volumes of his *Memoirs of American Jews, 1755–1865* (1955–56). Few literary productions by American Jews concerning Jewish life at the turn of the century in the immigrant ghettos or elsewhere are as interesting and significant as such memoir-type works as Mary Antin's *The Promised Land* (1912), Ludwig Lewisohn's *Up Stream* (1922) and *Channel* (1929), Charles Reznikoff's *Early History of a Sewing-Machine Operator* (1936) and *Family Chronicle* (1963), Anzia Yezierska's *Red Ribbon on a White Horse* (1950), Morris Raphael Cohen's *Dreamer's Journey* (1949), Jacob Epstein's autobiography *Let There Be Sculpture* (1940), S. N. Behrman's *The Worcester Account* (1954), and Meyer Levin's *In Search* (1950).

Abraham Cahan was the first American Jewish writer of considerable power to attempt the ascent from memoir and journalism. (For the better part of his career he led the dual life of English novelist and editor of the Yiddish *Jewish Daily Forward*.) Cahan's magnum opus, *The Rise of David Levinsky* (1917), continues to reap the praise of literary critics. Although the novel is, among other things, a scathing indictment of the American "success story," the dream of so many millions of immigrants, it is also representative of the first generation of Jewish immigrants to America after 1880 in its refusal to make any sweeping rejection of American life as such. Although nearly all Jewish immigrant writers were critical to a degree of the American realities that confronted them, such as poverty or social discrimination, they were nevertheless grateful to America and could never forget the contrast between the freedom and opportunity they found there and the repressiveness and narrowness of the old world. None of them could ever have written, as did native-born Michael Gold in his "proletarian" novel about Jewish immigrant life in New York, *Jews Without Money* (1930), "America has grown so rich and fat because she has eaten the tragedies of millions of immigrants." Such an attitude arose from a depth of alienation, hostility, and resentment that they simply never experienced.

The 1920s and 1930s witnessed a series of "proletarian" Jewish novels by second-generation American Jews, expressing indignation over the social injustices of American life. One feels, however, that the predatory capitalists, venal and reactionary schoolteachers, corrupt rabbis, and sentimentalized workers who populate the pages of these Jewish-American novels sprang more from some economic or political textbook of socialist theory than from their authors' actual observations of the life around them. The lessons of moderation, patience, and fortitude that were learned by the first generation of immigrants through hard experience seem to have been lost upon their rebellious offspring, whose psychological experience of American reality may have been even harsher because of the higher level of expectation with which they, as native sons, were raised. It was the paradoxical contradiction so often evident in American life between limitless promise and limited performance that turned so many of them to social and political extremes.

The best literary work of this second, native generation of Jewish Americans, was done by writers who, while they were by no means oblivious to social ills and may even have been, for a time, sympathetic to their more "activist" fellow authors, were more esthetically oriented, and more apt to look upon the art that they created as an end in itself. Charles Reznikoff's *By the Waters of Manhattan* (1930) and Henry Roth's *Call It Sleep* (1934) pictured the New York immigrant slum, and evoked a Jewish childhood there. (Earlier, in 1926, F. Scott Fitzgerald had predicted the coming of a "novel off the Jewish tenement-block, festooned with wreaths out of *Ulysses* and the later Gertrude Stein.")

An anomaly among Jewish novelists of the 1930s was Nathanael West, whose small output included *Miss Lonelyhearts*, considered a minor American classic. Though West avoided writing about Jews (characteristically, he changed his own name from Weinstein), in a sense he was, more than any other figure of his age, a precursor of the great flowering of American-Jewish writing that took place in the years after World War II. Whereas nearly all of his contemporaries wrote naturalistic fiction, West was inclined to fantasy; whereas his contemporaries cultivated a tone of dramatic seriousness, West's preference was for comedy; and whereas his contemporaries were for the most part concerned with the problems of immigrant life and/or the great depression, his own interest lay in that psychological alienation of the individual in modern, atomized, American industrial society that, in the final analysis, had little to do with either poverty or wealth. In all of these respects, West foreshadowed tendencies that were to be fully and exuberantly developed in the American-Jewish literature of the later 1940s, 1950s, and 1960s.

THE PSYCHOLOGICAL BURDEN OF
AMERICAN JEWISH LITERATURE

The quarter of a century of American literary life that followed the end of World War II witnessed a conspicuous emergence of Jewish talent and activity that reached its peak in the late 1950s and early 1960s, which were on occasion even referred to by critics as American literature's "Jewish decade" and as a period of "Jewish renaissance." I. Malin and I. Stark wrote in their anthology *Breakthrough: A Treasury of Contemporary American-Jewish Literature* (1964): "For the first time in history a large and impressively gifted group of serious American-Jewish writers has broken through the psychic barriers of the past to become an important, possibly a major reformative influence in American life and letters." While there is perhaps an element of hyperbole in such phrases, it is well worth considering why this phenomenon came into existence and what its defining characteristics were.

The period after World War II marked the coming of age of a third generation in American-Jewish life, dating back to the great East European immigration of the turn of the century. Three main features distinguished this generation from its predecessor: American-born itself, it was for the most part raised by parents who were either native-born or who had broken away physically and culturally from the immigrant ghetto; unlike these parents, most of whom grew up in relative poverty, it was largely the product of middle- or lower-middle-class homes, where physical want was unknown; and unlike its parents again, it was overwhelmingly college-educated. Forming a more thoroughly acculturated, economically secure, and better educated group than its parents, it was only natural that third-generation American Jewry should have included a higher percentage of academicians, artists, intellectuals, and writers.

At the same time, the salient fact about this third-generation intelligentsia, at least to judge by the literature that it produced, was an unmistakable sense of estrangement not only from the generation that raised it but in a subtler sense from American culture as a whole.

The former reaction is perhaps the easier to understand. In a sense, the conflict between the third generation of American Jews that reached intellectual maturity after World War II and the preceding generation was more intense and exacerbated than the conflict between the second and the original immigrant generation. Whereas the earlier struggle was a clear-cut one between the desire to preserve certain old-world values and the urge to "Americanize" at any cost, the later one was between two conflicting versions of "Americanism" itself. It was precisely what the second generation looked upon as its successful adaptation to American life that was repeatedly excoriated and satirized in "third-generation literature" as vulgar materialism.

It is more difficult to explain the definite sense of not being entirely at home in the general American landscape. This may be regarded as the surfacing of a residual Jewish unease that continued to exist beneath the accomplishments of Americanization. It may also be a reaction to the overall complacency and thinly veiled anti-intellectualism of a great deal of American life in the 1940s and 1950s, which made adjustment difficult for many non-Jewish intellectuals as well. In any case, whatever its roots, what is significant about this feeling of estrangement is that time after time it is deliberately expressed in openly Jewish terms, as in Delmore Schwartz's poem "Abraham":

> ... It has never been otherwise:
> Exiled, wandering, dumbfounded by riches,
> Estranged among strangers, dismayed by the infinite sky,
> An alien to myself until at the last caste of the last alienation,
> The angel of death comes to make the alienated and
> indestructible one a part of his famous and democratic society.

In a remark which might be applied to the work of numerous Jewish writers of these years, Schwartz commented how ". . . the fact of being a Jew became available to me as a central symbol of alienation . . . and certain other characteristics which are the peculiar marks of modern life, and as I think now, the essential ones."

These words help to explain why Jewish writing played the crucial role that it did in America during this period. For if the theme of social and spiritual alienation seemed immemorially Jewish to the Jewish author, it was fast becoming basic to American intellectual life in general in an age when the individual was increasingly being viewed as a helpless pawn of the manipulations of big business, big government, mass communications, and modern technology.

The result of this overlap was, paradoxically, that at the very historical moment that American-Jewish writers were feeling sufficiently confident of their position in American life to express their sense of estrangement from it, non-Jewish readers and intellectuals were prepared for the first time to see in the figure of the "alien Jew" a genuine American culture hero of the times—or, more precisely, an anti-hero, since the treatment of alienation in the American-Jewish writing of these years was a self-directed irony, by means of which the predicament of the alienated character was simultaneously intensified and mocked. This attitude owed much, it would appear, to traditional East European Jewish humor and is an excellent example of how fragments of immigrant folk culture survived among American Jews to be eventually transmuted into serious art.

THE JEWISH ANTI-HERO

If one takes, for example, the three postwar Jewish novelists whose work has aroused the greatest interest among the serious reading public in America, one finds that the most representative characters of all three share much with the traditional Jewish folk-humor figure of the *shlemiel*. For all the differences between these characters and the authors who created them, Saul Bellow's Herzog (*Herzog,* 1964), Bernard Malamud's Levin (*A New Life,* 1962) and Fidelman (*Pictures of Fidelman,* 1969), and Philip Roth's Portnoy (*Portnoy's Complaint,* 1969) share a common private war against a society to which they cannot adjust and against which their only retaliation is to play the comic buffoon. The harder each tries, the more miserably each fails, yet none is ultimately defeated, for in terms of a highly Jewish paradox, to win such battles is to lose; to lose is to win. In the words of Ivan Gold, another Jewish novelist who made his debut in the 1950s with a long comic story *(Taub East)* about Jewish servicemen in Japan: "There must be an outgroup. This is the divine order of things. If lucky enough to be one, rejoice!"

This association of the Jew with the eternal outsider—less by virtue

Four writers: Saul Bellow (upper left), Bernard Malamud (upper right), Philip Roth (lower left), and Norman Mailer (lower right).

of any sustained social prejudice directed against him than of his own ingrained sensitivities, which make it impossible for him to integrate successfully into the aggressive, competitive fabric of American life— occurs as a unifying theme in much Jewish fiction of the 1950s and 1960s, despite the wide variety of backgrounds and environments invoked. One finds it in the Kafkaesque stories of Isaac Rosenfeld; in Wallace Markfeld's recollections of boyhood in Jewish Brooklyn; in Herbert Gold's short stories about life in Jewish suburbia; in Leslie Fiedler's fiction about Jewish intellectuals on the campus; in Edward Wallant's urban novels; in the Glass family stories of J. D. Salinger; and in the writings of many other Jewish novelists and short-story writers of the period. Hardly any of the central characters created by such authors have an active sense of identification with the Jewish community or Jewish tradition as such. In fact, nearly all are more alienated from the organized Jewish life of the communities in which they live than from their surroundings in general, yet almost all are obsessed with the moral implications of being Jewish and the sometimes bewildering problematics of dealing with them. Norman Mailer has been by far the most radical among major American Jewish novelists in his indictment of American society. His prose virtuosity and intellectual boldness have made him, for many readers, the most exciting American novelist and essayist of his time. On the whole, Mailer studiously avoided Jewish characters and concerns in his work, a fact that is itself of some critical interest, and that constitutes the exception rather than the rule among his Jewish contemporaries.

Mailer moved from novels which explored the individual who intellectually, morally, or physically feels compelled to drive himself to extremes beyond the norms of human conduct in order to experience his own individuality, to essays which dealt with political issues of the day, and expressed his "radical conservatism" and generalized hostility toward the regimentation and mechanization of modern life.

It is debatable to what extent the emergence in the 1960s of the so-called "novel of the absurd," with a wide range of grotesquely comic situations reflecting the meaninglessness of contemporary existence, was indebted in part to the surfacing in American life of a traditional mode of Jewish humor. It is a matter of record that among the earliest practitioners of "black humor" as a tool of social criticism were such stand-up Jewish comedians as Lennie Bruce and Mort Sahl. (The former, in particular, acquired a devoted avant-garde audience before his early death.) This same sensibility appears as a defining stylistic element in the works of a number of prominent Jewish novelists of the 1960s, such as Bruce Jay Friedman and Joseph Heller. Heller's morbidly comic novel of army life during World War II, *Catch-22* (1961), became practically a Bible for a generation of young Americans who came to political consciousness at the time of the Vietnam War and for whom it epitomized the struggle of the individual to survive in a mindlessly bureaucratic world.

THE AMERICAN JEW IN POETRY

American Jewish poets of the modern period have also, for the most part, drawn freely on their experience as Jews. Many would no doubt agree with Muriel Rukeyser when she writes that

> To be a Jew in the twentieth century
> Is to be offered a gift. If you refuse,
> Wishing to be invisible, you choose
> Death of the spirit, the stone insanity

—or with Hyam Plutzik's lines in "The Priest Eskranath," in which the Jew is portrayed as the eternal outsider, the compulsive intellectual critic who can never be at rest:

> Listen, you nations:
> They will lure you from your spontaneous ecstasies,
> And positive possessions, and with themselves,
> Carry you forth on arduous pilgrimages,
> Whose only triumph can be a bitter knowledge.

If one were to compile a list of leading American Jewish poets of the post-World War II years—Charles Reznikoff, Louis Zukofsky, Karl Shapiro, Howard Nemerov, Delmore Schwartz, David Ignatow, Irving Feldman, Babette Deutsch, Denise Levertov, John Hollander, Kenneth Koch—one would find that almost all have availed themselves at times of the wealth of symbolic and allusive material that the Jewish heritage provides, though few have actually made this heritage the theme of an entire volume, as did Karl Shapiro in his *Poems of a Jew* (1958).

Unique among American Jewish poets in his impact upon both the American and the international world of poetry has been Allen Ginsberg, whose long free-verse poem "Howl" was a landmark in the development of contemporary American prosody and one of the first poetic trumpet blasts of the "beat generation" and of the profound cultural transformation that began to affect American life in the 1960s. Ginsberg has used Jewish motifs, as in his poem "Kaddish" (1961), and his mystical inclinations have led him to take an interest in the symbolism of Hasidism and the Kabbalah.

In the years after World War II, the 92nd St. YMHA in New York City served as a major center for readings of modern American poetry and for the introduction of a number of young contemporary poets to a wide public.

LITERARY CRITICISM

The activity of American Jews in the creative literary field was paralleled by their increasing prominence as literary critics in the post-war period. Susan Sontag was among the leading exponents of the new "form" criticism which insisted on regarding the literary work in isolation, to be analyzed only in its own internal terms. Philip Rahv, Alfred Kazin, Irving Howe, Lionel Trilling, and Leslie Fiedler all rejected form criticism and expressed interest in the study of literature for the sake of its wider cultural, political, and psychological ramifications.

Also noteworthy in the 1950s and 1960s was the key role played in American literary life by cultural and critical publications edited by Jews: *Partisan Review* (Philip Rahv); *New American Review* (Theodore Solotaroff); *New York Review of Books* (Robert Silvers and Barbara W. Epstein); and *Commentary* (Norman Podhoretz). A certain amount of resentment was expressed within the literary world over "Jewish domination." Truman Capote complained about "a clique of New York-oriented writers and critics who control much of the literary scene through the influence of Jewish-dominated quarterlies and influential magazines."

Commentary, published by the American Jewish Committee, was one of the most widely read and influential journals of opinion in the United States. It had always printed articles of specifically Jewish nature in addition to those of general political and cultural interest. Early in the 1970s, however, *Commentary* and its editorial staff began to turn more and more from generally humanistic concerns in its editorial pages, to a more "survivalist-preservationist" attitude toward Jewish problems and identity.

PUBLISHING

A large number of American Jews have been involved in the production and distribution of books. Three publishing developments during the first half of the 20th century greatly expanded the market for books, and American Jews were prominent in all three. These were book clubs, low-price reprints (paperbacks), and low-cost children's book publishing.

(The basic idea of membership in a club for the publication and distribution of books was not new. The Jewish Publication Society of America (1888) was the successor to at least two earlier membership projects. The paperback book industry had issued and distributed small paperbound books through the mail since 1889, for as little as five cents a copy.)

From the 1920s on, Jews played a major role in the New York publishing industry (Alfred A. Knopf, Random House, Boni and Liveright, Simon and Schuster, Viking Press, Farrar, Straus, and Giroux and numerous other publishing houses were established by Jews or had Jews in leading managerial positions.) Several smaller publishers specialized in a largely or wholly Jewish line of books for which they found an adequate market.

JOURNALISM

Although the overall number of Jews engaged in American journalism has been small, the significance of their contributions is readily apparent. Of the 1800 dailies published in the United States, about 50 are owned by Jews. Among them are the influential *New York Times, Washington Post, Philadelphia Inquirer,* and *New York Post.* In the history of American journalism, the names of Adolph S. Ochs, Arthur Hays Sulzberger, Joseph Pulitzer, and Samuel Newhouse occupy key positions.

Joseph Pulitzer purchased the *New York World* in 1883 and built it up to the largest daily circulation of any newspaper in the United States: 250,000. Pulitzer was an ardent believer in professional training, and provided a large endowment for a school of journalism at Columbia University. He also established the major prizes in journalism which bear his name. Pulitzer and William Randolph Hearst *(Morning Journal)* vied with each other in sensational news reportage; their rivalry gave rise to the expression "yellow journalism."

Adolph Ochs recognized that New York was beginning to tire of sensationalism, and pledged his paper to "give the news impartially, without fear or favor, regardless of any party, sect or interest involved. . . ." He thought of the *New York Times,* which he owned, as a public institution of which he had only temporary charge.

Jews have been prominent in two special areas of American journalism: commentary on current affairs, and the "gossip" column. In the first area, Walter Lippmann, Arthur Krock, and David Lawrence have commented on domestic and foreign affairs in the nation's most important journals. As gossip columnists, Walter Winchell, Leonard Lyons, and Sidney Skolsky attracted a wide readership by their reporting on the lives of entertainment personalities, government officials, and public figures.

JEWISH BEST-SELLERS

No discussion of the Jews and American literature in the 20th century would be complete without mention of the unique phenomenon of the Jewish "best-seller"—the popular book or novel on a Jewish subject whose sales ran into the hundreds of thousands, or millions, frequently leading all other contenders on national "best-seller" lists. Among the most popular of them were Herman Wouk's *Marjorie Morningstar,* Leon Uris' *Exodus,* Harry Golden's *Only in America,* Harry Kemelman's *Friday the Rabbi Slept Late,* Chaim Potok's *The Chosen,* John Hersey's *The Wall,* and James Michener's *The Source* (the last two by non-Jewish authors). Since one may assume that such books were in large measure purchased, or at least promoted, by Jewish readers, the dimensions of their success reveal the extraordinary impact of Jewish readership on the American book market in general.

Characteristic of the Jewish "best-seller" was the fact that unlike most of the more serious American-Jewish novels mentioned previously (some of which, however, were also highly successful commercially), it tended to portray Jewish life in America and elsewhere in highly flattering and often sentimental terms. Of generally slight literary value, such books will nonetheless interest future historians for the picture they give of how the majority of American-Jewish readers during these years preferred to view themselves and their tradition.

ARTS, ENTERTAINMENT, AND MASS MEDIA

THE ART WORLD

As opposed to the literary tradition, it has become increasingly difficult to establish whether a particular artist is a Jew or not. The subject matter of modern art generally does not provide any clue to the artist's background, as from 1945 onward the visual arts have been predominantly abstract and increasingly universal, with little distinction of national or ethnic character.

This reality stands in contrast to the older generation of representational artists in the United States. During the 1920s, Raphael, Moses and Isaac Soyer, and Chaim Gross were prominent in the social-realistic "Fourteenth Street School" of art that flourished in Greenwich Village.

Ben Shahn and Jack Levine were among the many Jewish artists whose early careers were associated with the programs of the Works Projects Administration that provided public funds for art projects during the Depression years.

ARCHITECTURE

The recent prevalence of abstract or near-abstract art made it possible for the synagogue to become an important patron of the arts. (Jewish tradition has retained the ban on portraying the human figure in a religious context, as an extension of the injunction against idol worship.) Such nationally recognized architects as Louis I. Kahn, Richard J. Neutra, Percival Goodman, Eric Mendelsohn and Albert Kahn have created pioneering synagogue designs.

The founder of this tradition was German-born Leopold Eidlitz, who began his career in America shortly after the middle of the 19th century. He built a number of churches (his Christ Church Cathedral in St. Louis has been called "the most churchly church in America") and the former Temple Emanu-El, one of the most notable buildings in old New York.

Albert Kahn, creator of the Ford automobile works outside Detroit, has been described as the most influential industrial architect of modern times. Dankmar Adler (with Louis Sullivan) was largely responsible

"Transients," a study of the unemployed during the depression of the thirties, by Raphael Soyer.

"Horse," etching by Jack
Levine.

"Sacco and Vanzetti," drawing by Ben Shahn.

for the evolution of the American skyscraper. Some other important names in 20th century American architecture include Louis I. Kahn, who has been called a major form-maker; Max Abramovitz, designer of the Philharmonic Hall in Lincoln Center in New York; Victor Gruen, who may be said to have invented the suburban shopping center; and Albert Mayer and Percival Goodman, city planners.

MUSIC

Since World War I, the musical world in the United States has been heavily Jewish, and since the 1930s, when there was a sizable migration of Jewish composers and musicians to America, Jews have occupied most of the chairs in the New York Philharmonic Symphony Orchestra, the Metropolitan Opera Orchestra, and other major musical ensembles throughout the country. They have also been prominent in opera, as symphony conductors, instrumentalists, and jazz musicians. From the 1930s on, the New York Musicians' Union has been over 70% Jewish!

The outstanding example of an American musician who successfully assimilated the Jewish tradition into his personal musical expression is Leonard Bernstein. The first American-born musician to be appointed conductor of the prestigious New York Philharmonic Orchestra, Bernstein also composed scores for the theater, and orchestral works. Among the latter are the *Jeremiah Symphony,* with a vocal solo to the Hebrew text of the Bible; *Kaddish,* a Hebrew oratorio; and *Chichester Psalms* for orchestra and chorus (in Hebrew).

THEATER

The high proportion of Jewish participation in the American theater undoubtedly had its origin in the rich world of the Yiddish theater which provided a varied training ground for actors, such as Paul Muni and Al Jolson, who later made their mark on Broadway and in Hollywood. Boris Aronson, one of America's best-known stage designers, also began his career in the Yiddish theater.

There has been no aspect of the theater that has not numbered Jews among its outstanding contributors: comedy—the Marx and Ritz brothers, Danny Kaye, and Zero Mostel; directors-producers—Florenz Ziegfield, the Shubert brothers, Lee Strassberg, and Mike Nichols; theatrical composers—Irving Berlin, who composed more than 1,000 songs and whose "God Bless America" was a nationwide patriotic melody during World War II, Jerome Kern, George Gershwin, and Richard Rodgers; lyricists—Oscar Hammerstein II, George S. Kaufman, and Lorenz Hart.

The golden age of the Broadway musical drama was dominated by Jewish composers and librettists. During the 1930s and 1940s these men presented a series of musical plays that mirrored the reality of American life: *Of Thee I Sing*, a satire on American politics; *Porgy and Bess*, which dealt with American Negro life; *Pins and Needles*, an amateur revue presented by the International Ladies' Garment Workers Union, which became a Broadway hit; *Pal Joey*, one of the first "adult" musicals; and *Lady in the Dark*, which dealt with psychoanalysis. American musical theater reached a new level of maturity in the 1940s with the production of *Oklahoma, Carousel, South Pacific, Guys and Dolls, My Fair Lady*, and *West Side Story*, all of them the work of American Jews.

In the area of serious drama, Arthur Miller was widely regarded throughout the 1950s as the leading American playwright of the period. His reputation faded somewhat in the 1960s with the decline of realistic theater in general, but his *Death of a Salesman* remains a classic of the American repertoire.

The experimental theater of the 1960s presented the works of Jack Gelber, Arthur Koppitt, and Israel Horovitz. The Living Theater, headed by Julian Beck and Judith Malina, was an avant-garde company that pioneered in the creation of "total" or "action" theater, emphasizing improvisation, audience involvement, and radical social and political content. (It spent much of the 1960s in political exile.)

Throughout the years, the Broadway theater has been extensively patronized by Jewish audiences. This fact, plus the general interest in all things Jewish during the 1950s and 1960s, led to the production of a number of Broadway shows on Jewish themes. The most successful by far was *Fiddler on the Roof*, based on the Yiddish stories of Shalom Aleichem, the longest running show ever to appear on Broadway.

RADIO

Jews played a major role in the development of the American radio industry. They have been well represented in all its executive and technical aspects, as well as among its performers.

One factor encouraging Jewish participation in radio was its development during a period when discrimination blocked opportunity for Jews in many other fields. Broadcasting was a new field without fixed traditions and prejudices. It had room for those with individual ability, original ideas, and initiative.

Jewish inventors and promoters played significant roles in the early days of broadcasting. As early as 1877, Emile Berliner, an immigrant from Germany, patented a telephone receiver which produced a clear sound and extended the range of communications. This was the forerunner of the microphone and was purchased by the Bell Telephone Company which engaged Berliner as its chief instrument inspector. Berliner also invented the flat disc gramophone record which developed into the Victor Talking Machine.

Jews held key positions in the emergence and shaping of the three major U.S. radio networks. David Sarnoff started the National Broadcasting Company; C.B.S. was founded by William S. Paley; and Leonard H. Goldenson became president of A.B.C.

Such stars as Al Jolson, Ed Wynn, Eddie Cantor, Jack Benny, Groucho Marx, Milton Berle, and Sid Caesar were household names as radio (and later television) stars. "The Goldbergs," a situation comedy based on American Jewish life, was one of the most popular radio programs for many years.

As the television industry developed it employed many American Jews who were active in the worlds of radio and theater.

MOTION PICTURES

The development of motion pictures as a form of mass entertainment in the United States was largely the doing of Jewish producers and entrepreneurs who made Hollywood the world's film capital after 1920.

The motion picture was created at a time when the Jews were seeking entry into the economic and cultural life of the United States. Jewish involvement with motion pictures was due to a number of factors: the industry had not developed a tradition of its own and had no vested interests to defend; participation in it did not require a good knowledge of English; and motion pictures were initially regarded as a low-grade form of entertainment, suitable for the immigrant or the uneducated masses. Recent arrivals, therefore, found it relatively easy to enter the field. Jewish immigrants helped transform movies from a marginal branch of entertainment into a worldwide, multi-million-dollar industry.

Most of the Jews connected with the film industry at the beginning of the 20th century were film exhibitors or distributors. They owned shabby, little movie theaters, expecially in the poor immigrant neighborhoods where the new form of entertainment enjoyed great popularity, for silent-films provided mass entertainment without any language problems.

The first Jewish film producer was Max Anderson (Aronson), who was also an actor, scriptwriter, and director. He played the lead in *The Great Train Robbery* (1903), the first genuine American feature film, and initiated the "Bronco Billy" series of Westerns, producing 375 films in a seven-year period. The first talking film, *The Jazz Singer* (1926), starred Al Jolson, and was produced by Warner Brothers (Sam, Jack, Albert, and Harry).

All the large Hollywood companies, with the exception of United Artists, were founded and controlled by Jews. The largest of such film companies was Paramount, founded and managed by Adolph Zukor who, together with Daniel Frohman, a theatrical agent, imported a prestigious European film, *Queen Elizabeth* (1912), starring Sarah Bernhardt. The film was shown in legitimate theaters and enabled Zukor to claim that the motion picture was a legitimate art form. Under the slogan "Famous Players in Famous Plays," Zukor produced films based on literary and dramatic works, with casts of legitimate actors. He also initiated the practice of advertising "star" actors; the first "star" he promoted was Mary Pickford.

Many of the best-known names in the film industry over the years have been those of Jews: Irving Thalberg of M.G.M., the "wunderkind" of Hollywood in the 1930s; David O. Selznick, who produced *Gone With the Wind, David Copperfield, King Kong, Spellbound,* and *Rebecca*; Hal Roach, one of the most prolific producers of comedies, who was responsible for part of the Harold Lloyd series and for the Laurel and Hardy films during the 1920s and 1930s; and Sam Spiegel and

Stanley Kramer, who produced some of the best films to come out of Hollywood in the 1940s and 1950s. A large number of Jewish directors came to Hollywood after beginning their careers in Germany: Ernst Lubitsch, Erich von Stroheim, William Wyler, and Billy Wilder. The number of well-known actors, scriptwriters, and songwriters who have worked for the films is too lengthy to be listed.

ADVERTISING

Finally, let us consider that area of American life which has paid for so much of the country's mass entertainment, and which has uniquely reflected American society and presented it to the world beyond the country's borders: advertising.

America's position as world leader in the use of mass media carries over into the advertising industry. And here, too, American Jews have played an influential role. It has been suggested that they have been responsible for the form and broad scope of the modern advertising agency.

It was Albert D. Lasker, often called the father of modern advertising, who realized in the closing years of the 19th century that by providing first-rate copywriters who were creative, imaginative artists, the advertising agency could be of far greater help to the client than by offering the limited service of selling space for his advertisements, as was the case previously. He initiated the modern system of advertising based on creating a demand for a product before introducing it to a market.

William Bernbach was one of the leaders of the "creative revolution" that swept Madison Avenue, the New York center of American advertising. He began to use a low-keyed, even self-deprecating formula of advertising. It was Bernbach who introduced the term "the soft-sell" into the American vocabulary, and added a new dimension to a uniquely American field of business.

6

INTERACTING WITH WORLD JEWRY

THE CONCEPT OF MUTUAL RESPONSIBILITY

"All Israel is responsible for one another." This dictum, established by the sages of the Talmud, has been assimilated into the innermost value system and psychology of the Jewish community in every country and in every period of history. The term *kelal yisrael,* meaning the kinship of all members of the Jewish community, describes the common responsibility and destiny of Jews wherever they may live.

The American Jewish community has always felt itself part of *kelal yisrael,* and it has always been receptive to the needs of Jews in other parts of the world. Even in early colonial times, aid was forthcoming for needy Jews living in the Holy Land. During the 19th century, officials of Jewish organizations in Palestine began to travel with regularity to the United States, to enlist support for their institutions. As the American Jewish community grew and prospered, it assumed an ever greater role in providing economic assistance for other Jewish groups in the world.

In a certain sense, the bonds between American and overseas Jews provided a community of interest and purpose to the various groups of American Jewry, and enabled them to give expression to their Jewish identity. As the process of assimilation into the general American culture progressed, and the common Jewish cultural concerns waned, the "foreign aid" policy of American Jews provided them with a much-needed psychological satisfaction, and helped to maintain their sense of self-identity.

PHILANTHROPIC ACTIVITIES

The main thrust of mutual concern for Jewish communities the world over was expressed in the philanthropic area. The large-scale movement of Jewish populations in the 19th century from areas of scarcity (Eastern and Central Europe) to countries of plenty (the United States and Western Europe) made it more possible for the Jewish "haves" to provide financial aid to the "have-nots," whether the latter wished to join their more fortunate brethren, or to remain in their countries of residence. The Hebrew Immigrant Aid Society (HIAS) offered a variety of services to Jewish newcomers.

The Baron de Hirsch Fund (1891) also sought to aid immigrants and teach them trades. In 1901, when immigration was at its height, B'nai B'rith joined with the Baron de Hirsch Fund to help settle Jews in various parts of the United States, away from the crowded eastern seaboard region. They set up an "Industrial Removal Office" which, before it closed its doors in 1916, dispersed 100,000 Jews into every state of the Union. The Jewish Colonization Association (ICA) tried, apart from its more successful activities in providing credit facilities for immigrants, to establish agricultural colonies in the United States and Canada as well as Argentina and Brazil.

Many of the immigrants were imbued with the ideal of the nobility of farm labor as the most honest of occupations; but few had had experience as farmers in Eastern Europe. It was hoped, however, that philan-

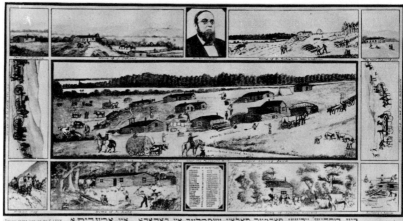

THE RUSSIAN JEWISH FARMER SETTLEMENT WECHSLER
BURLEIGH COUNTY DAKOTA TERRITORY.

A pictorial record of the attempt to establish the Wechsler Russian Jewish Farmer Settlement in North Dakota at the end of the 19th century.

thropy combined with high motivation would help the newcomers acclimate themselves in a rural setting. A score of farm colonies were established from Louisiana to Kansas, the Dakotas, and Oregon, but within a few years all failed. In the East, however, the farm settlements in New Jersey survived into the 20th century, and were able to absorb a newer wave of Jewish refugees from Germany in the 1930s and 1940s. (At the end of World War II, there were about 20,000 Jewish farm families in the United States. By the late 1960s the number had been halved, mainly because of the decline of American agriculture generally.)

THE ROLE OF INDIVIDUAL COMMUNITY LEADERS

Concern for the broader Jewish polity included intercession on behalf of Jewish groups abroad whose rights were endangered by the governments under whose jurisdictions they lived.

Through the personal influence of a few outstanding communal leaders, the American Jewish community was able to convince key American political figures to intercede on behalf of Jewish interests throughout the world. This quiet diplomacy was made possible by the existence of American democratic traditions, and by the potential political power of Jewish voters. Among the outstanding American Jewish community figures whose help was crucial to Jewish interests in the 19th and early 20th centuries were Louis Marshall, Jacob Schiff, and Henry Morgenthau.

Louis Marshall (1856-1929) was the chief spokesman for the German Jewish elite in the United States at the turn of the 20th century. He achieved national prominence in 1911 when he and Jacob Schiff successfully led a campaign for the unilateral abrogation of the Russo-American Treaty of 1832 because of the refusal of Czarist Russia to issue visas to American Jews, and its mistreatment of those who did receive them. They argued that tacit acceptance of this situation by the American government constituted a slur on the full citizenship rights of American Jews. To Marshall, Congress's abrogation of the treaty symbolized "the removal of the last civil disabilities to which the Jews of this country have been subjected." The following year Marshall became president of the American Jewish Committee, a post he held until 1929.

Marshall's concern for the protection of Jewish rights, expressed in his campaign against Henry Ford's anti-Semitic publications, the battle against restrictive immigration legislation, and against the quota system in universities, was extended to other groups as well. Believing in the indivisibility of civil rights, Marshall was a consistent champion of other minorities. He was active in the National Association for the Advancement of Colored People, and fought major legal battles on behalf of Negroes.

Jacob Schiff (1847–1920), a leading figure in the financial world at the turn of the century (he reorganized the Union Pacific Railroad, and together with Edward H. Harriman formed the most powerful and successful railway combination the country had ever known), made substantial contributions to major American cultural and social institutions, as well as to Jewish community agencies.

Schiff also used his financial leverage to promote the welfare of Jews throughout the world. Schiff was prominently involved in floating loans to the American government and to foreign nations at the turn of the 20th century. Perhaps the most spectacular of his financial dealings involved the support of a 200 million dollar bond issue for Japan at the time of the Russo-Japanese War in 1904–5. Deeply angered by the anti-Semitic policies of the czarist regime in Russia, Schiff was delighted to support its enemy's war effort. He consistently refused to participate in loans on behalf of Russia, and used his influence to prevent other firms from underwriting Russian loans. At the same time, he provided financial support for Russian-Jewish self-defense groups.

Henry Morgenthau, Sr. (1856–1946) served as American ambassador to Turkey from 1913 to 1916, where his diplomatic duties were largely concerned with the protection of Christian missionaries, Armenians, and Jews in the Ottoman Empire. He was able to be of particular assistance to Jews in Palestine who suffered acutely from food shortages during the war years.

In 1919 Morgenthau was named by President Wilson to head a U.S. commission investigating the treatment of Jews in Poland. A series of pogroms following World War I had aroused lively concern and stormy demonstrations among Jewish communities throughout the world. These assumed political form in the creation of the commission of inquiry. The commission spent two months noting facts and seeking to uncover their causes and to offer proposals for improving the situation.

Because of his delicate position as a Jew, Morgenthau made a point of appearing objective, and was inclined to justify the Poles as much as possible. Thus, the commission's report minimized the outbreak of violence, and merely recommended that in the future the Polish government should ensure the equality of all its citizens, without any distinctions in their rights or obligations. At the same time, it was recommended that an effort was to be made to introduce changes in the lives of the Jews by diversifying the branches of the economy in which they were engaged.

Morgenthau also extended his concern for human welfare to groups beyond the Jewish framework. He was one of the organizers of the International Red Cross, and of the Near East Relief, Inc.

REORGANIZATION FOR 20TH CENTURY NEEDS

Political developments throughout the world, from the mid-19th century onward, called for unprecedented Jewish philanthropic efforts on an international scale. The 19th century informal alliance of American Jewish "aristocrats" who had taken upon themselves the defense of Jewish interests and the protection of the rights of individual Jews was no longer adequate to handle the problems of the world which emerged in the wake of World War I. A reorganization of international Jewish philanthropic endeavors more appropriate to the 20th century was needed.

AMERICAN JEWISH JOINT DISTRIBUTION COMMITTEE

A first step in the direction of a reorganization of financial aid to needy Jewish communities was made during World War I, with the foundation of the American Jewish Joint Distribution Committee (JDC) a non-political organization seeking to help Jews wherever they might be, and, initially, those who had suffered as a result of the war. It was known popularly as the "Joint," because three separate commissions for assistance, which represented three major currents in American Jewry at the time, joined together to found it.

During World War I, the JDC spent almost 15 million dollars to aid Jews in Turkish-controlled Palestine, and sent relief to Jews in Russian- and German-held areas of Europe. In the post-war years it sent a staff of social workers to set up health and child-care institutions for

Founders of the Joint Distribution Committee, photographed in 1918. In the foreground, Felix Warburg (left) and Jacob Schiff (right).

Jewish refugees of East European pogroms. Additional millions of dollars were expended in the provision of medical, financial and vocational training to war refugees.

In the 1920s it was anticipated that the JDC would no longer have to provide help to needy Jewish communities. But this pious hope proved to be an illusion. In the subsequent decade, as the conditions in Eastern Europe deteriorated, the JDC continued to provide free loans, health and child-care programs, and educational and religious services to Jews living in that region. The 1920s and 1930s were marked by severe disputes between pro-Zionist advocates of higher allocations to Palestine, and the dominant non- or anti-Zionists in the JDC who provided most of the funds and who sought to syphon them primarily to European relief and to Jewish projects in Soviet Russia.

During the depression years, JDC income declined and its work was reduced to a minimum, but the ruthless Nazi campaigns against the Jews in 1933–1939 increased American Jewish readiness to give funds to help the victims wherever possible. The JDC office in Paris became the center of non-political action to help German Jewry, through relief funds, and through various rescue projects. After 1941, as the need to save Jewish lives became even more acute, the JDC began to borrow money against a promise of post-war repayment; during the war it became a major factor in the rescue of Jews from Nazi-dominated Europe.

THE PARIS PEACE CONFERENCE

The strength of American Jewry was also manifest when American Jewish organizations made their voice heard at the Peace Conference in Paris in 1919. There, the American Jewish Congress presented a program of Jewish demands to the delegates. The national minority rights secured for Jews in the newly created states in Central and Eastern Europe were largely the result of the work of three American Jews on the delegation, Julian Mack, Louis Marshall, and Cyrus Adler. Louis Marshall had already achieved national prominence through his public activities on behalf of Jewish rights. Judge Mack served as president of the first American Jewish Congress in 1918 and as chairman of the Comité des délégations juives at the 1919 Peace Conference. On the domestic scene, he was active in child welfare organizations and the area of juvenile delinquency. Cyrus Adler, second president of the Jewish Theological Seminary of America, bridged the difficult gap between the world of scholarship and government, and was able to interpret the needs of traditional-minded Jews to the men of wealth in American Jewry.

ANTI-NAZI BOYCOTT

Concern for Jewish communities abroad assumed a new expression in the United States as protest began to spread against the anti-Jewish activities in Germany. Jews throughout the world held mass rallies, marches, and initiated a spontaneous, and later organized, anti-German boycott. This program was most fully developed in the United States, where it was initiated by the Jewish War Veterans in March 1933. Three months later the American Jewish Congress created a Boycott Committee which was joined by non-Jewish groups, such as the American Federation of Labor. It then changed its name to the Non-Sectarian Anti-Nazi League to Champion Human Rights.

Work was begun to consolidate the boycott on an international level. The World Jewish Congress meeting of 1936 reaffirmed a worldwide boycott resolution, and channels were created to help the boycotting businessmen find substitutes for former German sources of supply. Eventually, even the largest department store chains in the United States gave in to continued boycott pressure.

Pickets outside a N.Y. five-and-ten-cent store urging a boycott of Nazi goods, November 1937.

The boycott was continued until the United States entered World War II in 1941. There is evidence that the Nazis, at least during the first two years of their regime, suffered from this boycott. A memorandum prepared for Hitler by the Economic Policy Department of the Reich in late 1938 cited the following comparative figures, which it attributed partly to the boycott:

Year	1929/1932	1937
Imports from the U.S.	1,790,592	282
Exports to the U.S.	991,281	209

(Figures in millions of Reichsmarks.)

WORLD JEWISH CONGRESS

Developments within the American and European Jewish communities during and after World War I led to the formation of the World Jewish Congress which, after three preparatory conferences, convened in Switzerland in 1936. There Rabbi Stephen S. Wise was a major figure, leading 280 delegates representing the Jews of 32 countries.

The history of the World Jewish Congress is closely identified with the most tragic period of contemporary Jewish life. The organization played a central role in the creation of Jewish policies with regard to the peace treaties following World War II, the prosecution and trial of Nazi war criminals, the adoption of a scheme of indemnification and reparations for Jewish victims of the Holocaust, and the rehabilitation of Jewish life in the years after the war.

Various departments within the World Jewish Congress coordinate action on behalf of Jewish communities exposed to particular dangers, handle relations with non-Jewish religious bodies, spur the fight against anti-Semitism, represent Jews before international organizations, and seek to preserve the identity of Jewish communities through the encouragement of creative Jewish social and cultural life. The World Jewish Congress maintains a branch of its executive in the United States.

WARTIME ACTIVITIES

The intelligence services of the Allied Powers were well informed of the mass murder of the Jews of Central and Eastern Europe prior to and during World War II. Jewish sources, in turn, were active in disseminating this information to the public. Jews in the United States and other free countries tried to prod their governments to action, but the general attitude of the Allies was that only a general victory could save the Jews. Thus the extermination camps, for example, were never bombed, although Allied bombers were active in the immediate vicinity. Nor were restrictive immigration policies softened to admit refugees in any large numbers.

The efforts of American Jews toward saving the lives of their coreligionists in Europe were limited to the sphere of financial aid, whether directly to those in need, or in the form of bribes which would help them leave the countries of mass murder.

After the war, the activity of the American Jewish Joint Distribution Committee reached a peak. The sum of 342 million dollars was spent on the feeding, clothing, and rehabilitation of 250,000 displaced persons left in the concentration camps and in the remnants of the Jewish communities of Europe. The JDC also financed social welfare work in the Cyprus detention camps which held some 50,000 "illegal" immigrants who had been seized by the British government as they attempted to enter Palestine. In addition, it financed social service and educational institutions in Israel, North Africa, Iran and France.

In 1949 JDC work was suspended in Eastern Europe. It resumed in 1957, but again had to cease operations in communist countries (with the exception of Rumania) after the anti-Zionist and anti-Israel propaganda drives of 1967 in the Soviet bloc.

UNITED HIAS SERVICE

During the 1930s and 1940s HIAS, which had been formed earlier to aid the absorption of Jewish immigrants from Eastern Europe, devoted its efforts toward financing and assisting emigration from Nazi Germany. It also sought homes for refugees in Western Europe and South America, and carried on a campaign to influence Western governments to open their gates wider to Jewish war refugees.

In 1954 HIAS merged with the United Service for New Americans, and the JDC Migration Department, into the United HIAS Service, a single international agency which has helped thousands of East European and North African emigrants—especially following the Hungarian revolt of 1956 and the Middle East crises of 1956 and 1967—to find new homes, mainly in Western Europe, the United States, and South America.

UNITED JEWISH APPEAL

The greatest voluntary fundraising organization ever known, the United Jewish Appeal, arose in response to the desperate plight of European Jewish communities during the years of the Holocaust, and has continued its activities on behalf of the settlement of immigrants in Israel.

The United Jewish Appeal was founded in 1939 with the American Jewish Joint Distribution Committee and the United Palestine Appeal as principal partners, and with the National Refugee Service as a beneficiary. Since that time it has been the major vehicle for providing American Jewish support to Jews throughout the world. In the period between 1939 and 1971, the UJA raised an estimated total of around 2.6 billion dollars, largely through allocations from combined campaigns in local Jewish communities throughout the United States. There

Israel Defense Minister Moshe Dayan addressing the National Conference of the United Jewish Appeal in N. Y., 1971.

was a peak year of contributions in 1948, in response to the needs of Jews in the newly created State of Israel and in the displaced persons camps in Europe, and another crest of giving at the time of the Six-Day War in 1967.

Funds provided by the United Jewish Appeal also helped make possible the settlement of 370,000 Jews in the United States, Canada, and France. In addition, economic, social, and cultural aid was provided to post-war European communities and individuals, and to Jews in North Africa. The division of funds is based upon an agreement by the contracting agencies. As more Jews have emigrated from Europe, Asia, and Africa to Israel, the proportion of UJA funds available for activities of the United Israel Appeal has increased, while the American Jewish Joint Distribution Committee proportion has decreased.

There is no question but that the partial rehabilitation of the Jewish communities in many countries of Europe would have been impossible without the well-established Jewish community of the United States. It had the organization and the financial strength to shoulder the major burden of relief during the war years, and in the post-war period of reconstruction of Jewish communities in Europe and in Israel.

WAR REFUGEE BOARD

Another plan to provide relief to European Jewry was the brain-child of an American Jewish public figure, Henry Morgenthau, Jr. As Secretary of the Treasury under President Franklin D. Roosevelt, Morgenthau initiated national and international monetary policies in the 1930s aimed at stabilizing the economy.

In 1943 Morgenthau successfully intervened with Secretary of State Cordell Hull to obtain State Department approval of a World Jewish Congress plan to transfer private funds of U.S. citizens to Europe, in order to rescue French and Rumanian Jews.

Then, in January 1944, Morgenthau, together with John W. Pehle and Randolph Paul, the general counsel of the U.S. Treasury, submitted a personal report accusing the State Department not only of having failed to use American government machinery for rescue purposes, but of having used it to *prevent* the rescue of victims of Nazism. A week later, at Morgenthau's suggestion, President Roosevelt established the War Refugee Board. The board was charged with the responsibility of implementing the government policy of rescuing war victims, and with facilitating their transportation, maintenance, and relief. At a rather late hour indeed, the WRB made many efforts to provide help to the victims of the Holocaust, working with private organizations, state agencies, and representatives of foreign governments.

ZIONISM AS A SOLUTION TO THE REFUGEE PROBLEM

The decimation of European Jewry during the 1930s and 1940s brought renewed awareness of Jewish identity to American Jewry and other Jewish communities who felt themselves lucky to have been spared the Holocaust of Europe. This awareness was expressed in support of the Zionist settlement of Palestine, which most Jews throughout the world recognized as the only place that could provide a refuge for the homeless, and a normal framework in which they might be rehabilitated. American Jewry recognized that the Zionist movement, with its philosophy of returning Jews to the land, required the concerted support of Jewish communities throughout the world, and it threw its strength and numbers behind the efforts to create a political reality of a Jewish homeland.

ZIONISM

The root of the term "Zionism" is the word "Zion" which, very early in Jewish history, became a synonym for Jerusalem. As far back as the destruction of the First Temple, "Zion" expressed the yearning of the Jewish people for its homeland. The concept of the return to Zion is found in the Psalms, in the traditional prayers, and in the Jewish religious and secular literature that developed throughout the centuries.

Zionism in the modern, political sense appeared at the close of the 19th century. The Basle Program, formulated in 1897 at the First Zionist Congress, spelled out the objectives and program of the modern Zionist movement. It defined Zionism as seeking to establish a home for the Jewish people in Palestine, secured under public law. This was to be accomplished by the promotion of settlement in Palestine by Jewish farmers, artisans, and manufacturers. World Jewry was to be organized behind this effort, and Jewish national consciousness . was to be strengthened. Where necessary, the Zionist movement would seek governmental consent to realize its goals.

Theodor Herzl, the father of political Zionism, and founder of the World Zionist Organization, had long been sensitive to the problem of anti-Semitism, and to the stereotype prevalent in Europe of the money-oriented, cosmopolitan Jew. Assimilation, conversion, and socialist revolution had all been suggested as solutions to these problems, but Herzl rejected them as answers. It was after attending the Dreyfus trial as a newspaper correspondent that he became convinced that the only solution to the Jewish problem was the mass exodus of the Jews from areas infested by anti-Semitism, and their resettlement in a territory of their own where they could "normalize" their existence in their own homeland, emancipate themselves, and build new healthy lives reflecting the dignity of physical labor and the spirit of social equality.

EARLY ZIONIST ORGANIZATIONS

The Zionist movement in the United States was not a 20th century phenomenon. Jewish immigrants who came from Eastern Europe had brought the ideals of the Ḥibbat Zion (Love of Zion) movement with them, and by 1890 organizations affiliated with that movement existed in several large Jewish communities.

Other American Zionist organizations appeared in the months preceding the First Zionist Congress. They met opposition led by upperclass Jews and Reform rabbis. The Central Conference of American Rabbis (of the Reform movement) passed a resolution in July 1897 denouncing Zionism in sharp terms as being antagonistic to "Israel's mission which, from the narrow political and national field, has been expanded to the promotion among the whole human race of the broad and universalistic religion first proclaimed by the Jewish prophets."

By 1898, however, two major Zionist organizations had developed in New York City. Shortly thereafter they established the Federation of American Zionists (FAZ) on the national level. In keeping with American patterns of pluralism, the FAZ encountered great organizational difficulties as the various independent Zionist organizations, many of them based on *landsmanschaften,* refused to recognize its authority. Another obstacle to the growth of the FAZ was the opposition to Zionism expressed by immigrants who belonged to socialist organizations and regarded socialism and trade unionism as ultimately providing the solutions to Jewish problems. Difficulties were increased by the reluctance of the organization's membership, primarily from Eastern Europe, to accept the leadership of German Jews.

The leaders of the Federation of American Zionists were divided in their philosophical attitudes toward Zionism. Some were "political Zionists" who saw the establishment of a Jewish homeland as the greatest imperative of the movement. Others were "cultural Zionists" who were more concerned with the content of the Zionist ideology, and tried to adapt Zionism to the American scene where it would serve as a check on assimilation and would spark a renaissance of traditional Jewish values. Although they viewed Palestine as a cultural center for all Jews, they did not negate the importance of the Diaspora.

Some of the Orthodox elements banded together in a religious Zionist movement, Mizrachi, whose aim was expressed in its motto: "The Land of Israel for the people of Israel according to the Torah of Israel." It sought to work for the return of the Jews to the land of their forefathers and for the perpetuation of Jewish national life in the spirit of Jewish tradition and in accordance with the observance of the commandments of the Torah. To this end it also enrolled youth and women in affiliated organizations.

Po'alei Zion (Labor Zionist movement) recognized both the dominant role of the Jewish proletariat in modern Jewish history, and the endemic nature of anti-Semitism in the Diaspora. It concluded that the abnormal situation of the Jewish working class ruled out a Diaspora solution to the Jewish question, and thus it supported the establishment of a Jewish homeland in which Jews could develop normal working patterns. Its platform was a dual one: the Zionist goal of a Jewish homeland in Palestine, and a social philosophy dedicated to the establishment of a new political and economic order based on respect for labor and equality among all classes within the Jewish society.

Not unexpectedly, in its initial stages, Po'alei Zion was rejected by the socialists, and regarded with suspicion by the Zionists! Its ancillary Jewish National Workers Alliance—Farband—was established as a benevolent organization in 1910, in part to attract members from the ranks of the socialist Workmen's Circle, which was anti-Zionist. A sister-group, Pioneer Women, was founded to bring women into active participation in Zionist projects.

In 1911 a new FAZ administration of mostly East European origin was elected; gradually the various independent Zionist organizations affiliated with it. In 1917, the FAZ was reorganized along territorial district lines into the Zionist Organization of America (ZOA).

LOUIS D. BRANDEIS

With the outbreak of World War I, various European Zionist leaders came to the United States, which then became the center for much of international Zionist activity. A Provisional Committee for General Zionist Affairs (PZC) was established, and Louis D. Brandeis, then an outstanding lawyer and soon to become the first Jew to be named to the Supreme Court, accepted its chairmanship.

Brandeis's involvement in Jewish affairs began only a few years before his appointment to the Supreme Court in 1916. He later was to say that his interest in Judaism was stirred by two experiences. One was his service as mediator in the New York garment workers' strike. He felt a strong sense of kinship with the striking Jewish workers who, he found, were remarkable not only for their exceptional intelligence, but above all for a rare capacity to see the issues from the other side's point of view.

The other experience was a meeting with Jacob De Haas, then editor of the *Jewish Advocate* in Boston, who had served as Theodor Herzl's secretary in London. De Haas awakened Brandeis's interest in Jewish history and particularly in the Zionist movement. Brandeis became convinced that, far from constituting a threat of divided loyalties, American and Zionist ideals reinforced each other. In his own words:

> My approach to Zionism was through Americanism. In time, practical experience and observation convinced me that Jews were by reason of their traditions and their character peculiarly fitted for the attainment of American ideals. Gradually it became clear to me that to be good Americans we must be better Jews, and to be better Jews we must become Zionists. Jewish life cannot be preserved and developed, assimilation cannot be averted, unless there be established in the fatherland a center from which the Jewish spirit may radiate and give to the Jews scattered throughout the world that inspiration which springs from the memories of a great past and the hope of a great future.

Brandeis took up his role with great energy, and under his able leadership the financial situation of the Federation of American Zionists improved and its membership and political influence increased. He drew to the Zionist movement other public figures previously unassociated with the Zionist ideology, who agreed that Americanism and Zionism were compatible in the United States where different cultures were blended into a unique nation based on cultural pluralism.

After Brandeis's elevation to the Supreme Court in June 1916, he resigned as active chairman of the FAZ, but remained in contact with the organization through his associates. His close relationship with President Wilson and high administrative officials in Washington played an important part in securing American support for the Balfour Declaration in 1917, and later for the creation of the British Mandate over Palestine.

Among the public figures who followed Brandeis into the Zionist ranks was Felix Frankfurter, lawyer and later also Supreme Court judge. Frankfurter went with the Zionist delegation to the Peace Conference in Paris, and through T. E. Lawrence he met Emir Feisal, head of the Arab delegation to the conference. In consequence of their talks Frankfurter received from Feisal a historic letter, dated March 1, 1919, stating that the Arab delegation regarded the Zionist proposal as "moderate and proper," that they "will wish the Jews a most hearty welcome home," and that the "two movements complete one another," and "neither can be a real success without the other."

A turning point in Brandeis's leadership of the Zionist movement developed out of a conflict of views with Chaim Weizmann, the leader of the World Zionist Organization who was later to be named the first President of the State of Israel. After the war, Brandeis had visited Palestine and formed plans to build its future on the basis of large-scale investment and centrally-controlled public corporations. He wanted the Zionist Organization of America to collect funds for specific economic projects. Weizmann was at first attracted to the plan, because of the new strength which he felt it would give to the movement. However, when he found his old colleagues from Eastern Europe offended because they had been excluded from the executive body which would oversee the economic development of Palestine, he expressed his misgivings. The Weizmann group suggested founding a general fund, to be known as the Keren Hayesod, to support the economy, improve settlement methods, and establish educational institutions in Palestine.

Letter to Felix Frankfurter from Emir Feisal, head of the Arab delegation to the Paris Peace Conference, 1919. Feisal, in support of the Zionist movement, wishes the Jews "a most hearty welcome home."

Brandeis and his group refused to accept the decision of the World Zionist Organization to back Weizmann's position, and the issues were debated at the Cleveland convention of the Zionist Organization of America in 1921. A majority of the delegates to that conference rejected Brandeis's views, and he and his close associates then seceded from the mainstream of Zionist activity in the United States. Louis Lipsky, a veteran Zionist who had founded the first English-language Zionist periodical in the United States (*The Maccabean,* later *The New Palestine*), and who had led the opposition to Brandeis, became president of the Zionist Organization of America. The Lipsky administration remained in office until 1930.

Brandeis's commitment to Zionism did not slacken despite his dissociation from the movement's leadership. He and his group concentrated their efforts on the economic development of Palestine, and inspired the creation of what became the Palestine Economic Corporation which sought to encourage investment in economic projects that could become self-supporting. A Palestine Endowment Fund was also established to administer bequests and trust funds, primarily for projects not expected to yield a financial return.

Felix Frankfurter withdrew from formal participation in the Zionist movement, together with Brandeis. Nonetheless, he too maintained his active interest in the upbuilding of the Jewish national home in Palestine. In 1931, disturbed by the restrictions of Britain, the mandatory power over Palestine, on immigration and the purchase of land by Jews, Frankfurter published a much cited critical article in *Foreign Affairs,* entitled "The Palestine Situation Restated."

HADASSAH

No survey of American Zionism would be complete without special mention of Hadassah, the Women's Zionist Organization of America, for it is the largest Zionist organization in the world, and one of the largest women's organizations in the United States. In 1969 Hadassah had 1,350 chapters and groups, and over 318,000 members.

Hadassah began as one of several Zionist women's study circles organized in scattered regions of the United States at the turn of the 20th century. Henrietta Szold, leader of a Harlem, New York group, toured Palestine in 1909, was appalled by the extensive disease and limited medical facilities there, and organized the Hadassah chapter of the national Daughters of Zion (1912), to promote Jewish institutions and enterprises in Palestine and to foster Jewish ideals. The following year the organization sponsored two visiting nurses in Palestine, and by 1914 seven chapters of Daughters of Zion held their first convention and voted to change their name to Hadassah.

During World War I, the World Zionist Organization called upon Hadassah to organize a medical relief group to deal with the wartime health emergency in Palestine. The American Zionist Medical Unit which sailed for Palestine in the summer of 1918 consisted of 44 physicians, nurses, sanitary engineers, dentists, and administrative staff. It was supported jointly by Hadassah and the American Jewish Joint Distribution Committee. Within a few years the medical unit became known as the Hadassah Medical Organization, a major medical presence in Palestine, offering medical aid to Arabs as well as Jews.

Hadassah founded the first school of nursing in Palestine, a hospital in Jerusalem, and the first medical school in Israel. It also sponsored dispensaries and special child health and welfare programs, many of which were, in the course of time, turned over to Israel's municipalities or to the government. By 1970 the Hadassah-Hebrew University Medical School had graduated 1,218 physicians. The Rothschild-Hadassah University Hospital had grown into a 700-bed teaching hospital with an outpatient department handling 250,000 visits annually.

In addition Hadassah has been a major supporter of Youth Aliyah, an international program for the transfer of young (children and adolescent) refugees to Palestine/Israel and their placement in agricultural settlements. Since 1935 over 135,000 children from 80 lands have

The first Hadassah nurses' unit photographed with the Central Committee of Hadassah, on the eve of sailing for Palestine, June 1918. Henrietta Szold is seated in the front row, far right.

been trained and rehabilitated under these auspices, with 40% of the funds coming from Hadassah contributions.

Hadassah is a nongovernmental organization of the United Nations and an accredited observer attached to the United States Mission. It sponsors a broad educational program in the United States, emphasizing Jewish history and heritage, current developments in the Middle East, and United States policy as it relates to the Middle East; its monthly magazine reaches over one million readers. Hadassah's educational and fundraising activities (in 1971 it raised over 14 million dollars for its projects in Israel) serve as the primary vehicle for the Jewish identification of many American Jewish women.

OPPOSITION TO ZIONISM

In contrast to the general acceptance of Zionist ideology among American Jewry since World War II, Zionism encountered great opposition among certain groups of American Jews in its early years.

Unlike the Conservative and Reconstructionist positions, which were generally supportive of the Zionist cause and viewed Zionist endeavors in Palestine as a means of achieving renaissance in Jewish life in America as well, Orthodox religious circles were divided almost from the outset on the Zionist issue. The small but articulate Agudat Israel group within the ranks of Orthodox Jewry was against Zionism because of its conviction that it was a secularist ideology. Only during World War II did this group abate its anti-Zionist stand; it has accepted the reality of Israel's existence. On the fringe of Orthodoxy, however, extremist opposition to Israel's existence has been maintained by the *Satmarer rebbe* and his followers, who condemn the Zionists for trying to hasten the coming of the Messiah and the final redemption by establishing a "heretical" state.

Within the lay leadership of American Jewry, Zionism at first found its strongest opponent in the American Jewish Committee. However, after the Balfour Declaration (1917) promised the Jews a national homeland in Palestine, the Committee tacitly recognized the ZOA as the representative of those Jews directly concerned with the welfare of Palestine. Nonetheless "Diaspora nationalism" (i.e., Zionism) continued to remain an issue of contention, for the American Jewish Committee leadership viewed it as a threat to its patriotism. Thus it opposed the Biltmore Program of 1942 which urged the creation of a Jewish commonwealth in Palestine. The Committee expressed the hope that the future of Jewry would be secured by universal recognition of human rights to be protected by the United Nations. Its opposition to Zionism continued in various forms until January 1948 when, under the pressure of the pro-Zionist consensus in the United States, the Committee declared its acceptance of the Jewish state recommended by the United Nations Special Committee on Palestine.

Even after Israel's creation, the Committee continued to feel apprehensive about the status of American Jews in the light of that state's existence. In 1950 David Ben-Gurion, then prime minister of Israel, exchanged letters on the subject with the president of the Committee, Jacob Blaustein. Ben-Gurion stated that Israel represented only its own citizens and had no claim to speak in the name of the Jews in the Diaspora. The Jews of the United States, as a community and as individuals, owed political loyalty only to the United States, and the Jews in Israel had no intention of interfering in the affairs of Jewish communities abroad.

Among the staunchest opponents of Zionism, since the turn of the century, have been certain influential Reform rabbis. In 1907 several faculty members of Hebrew Union College resigned (or were forced to resign) their positions because of their Zionist sympathies. Notable exceptions to the anti-Zionism of the Reform rabbinate were Rabbis Stephen S. Wise, Judah L. Magnes, and Abba Hillel Silver. The main body of the Central Conference of American Rabbis (Reform) delivered pronouncements against Zionism until 1920; thereafter the movement followed an unofficial position of non-Zionism which allowed it to cooperate with Zionists in philanthropic enterprises. In 1935 it revised its collective negative stand on Zionism in favor of individual choice, and further conciliation with Zionism occurred after the passage of the Columbus Platform of 1937 (see chapter 4).

A small minority group within Reform, however, continued with its opposition to Zionism, and in November 1942 the American Council for Judaism was formed around a core of Reform rabbis and influential lay leaders. The Central Conference of American Rabbis tried to halt this split within its ranks, but was unsuccessful. The American Council for Judaism became the most articulate and extreme anti-Zionist spokesman among American Jews. It maintained that its members were Jews by religion alone, and that their religion made it incumbent upon them to take only a universalist position, which meant, in practice, a stance opposed to strong ethnic bonds and to Jewish nationalism. The organization claimed that Zionism and the State of Israel worked against the assimilation of the Jews into the general American society, and placed in question their loyalty to the United States.

The Council, which claimed 20,000 members at its peak, has occupied an isolated position in American Jewish life. Although concern over "dual loyalty" was visible in varying degrees during the 1940s and 1950s, American Jews have since generally accepted the position that every individual has many loyalties which exist in some tension with each other. This conclusion stemmed from other tendencies within the American democratic society, and from the shock the Jewish community experienced at the threat to Israel's existence just prior to the Six-Day War in 1967.

The Six-Day War led several of the American Council of Judaism's most prestigious lay supporters to abandon its ranks, and most of the Reform congregations organized under its influence have since denied identification with its viewpoint.

MOBILIZATION OF THE COMMUNITY

With the outbreak of World War II, the ZOA formed the American Zionist Emergency Council, presided over by two rabbis who commanded the respect of the American Jewish community, the Reform leaders Stephen S. Wise (New York City) and Abba Hillel Silver (Cleveland).

Rabbi Wise had been among the early leaders of the American Zionist movement, articulating its ideology and organizing its followers. With Brandeis and Frankfurter he had influenced the formulation of the text of the Balfour Declaration, and had spoken on behalf of Zionist aspirations in Palestine at the Versailles Peace Treaty Conference (where he also pleaded the cause of the Armenian people). Wise sounded the first warnings of the dangers of Nazism to the Jewish and non-Jewish world. As a Zionist leader, president of the American and World Jewish Congresses, and co-chairman of the American Jewish Conference (composed of representatives of all major Jewish groups and delegates from local Jewish communities, see below), he presented the Jewish cause to President Franklin D. Roosevelt and the U.S. State Department, as well as to the nation-at-large.

As a political spokesman for American Zionism, Rabbi Abba Hillel Silver made a name for himself as one of the country's leading orators. His preaching and writing were marked by a fervent loyalty to the concept of Jewish peoplehood, a religious mood of messianism, and a pattern of thinking that was both realistic and logical. For Silver, Judaism and Zionism constituted a natural and harmonious blend. "The upbuilding of a Jewish national home in Palestine is one great, urgent, and historically inescapable task of Jewry. The upbuilding of Jewish religious life in America and elsewhere throughout the world, inclusive of Israel, is another. One is no substitute for the other. One is not opposed to the other."

Silver perceived that the post-war influence of the United States would be decisive in achieving a Jewish state in Palestine, and he set to work to mobilize American public opinion. In 1943 he became head of the influential American Zionist Emergency Council. Its fruitful work under his leadership was evident in the passage by Congress of resolutions favoring the establishment of a Jewish commonwealth, and in commitments from the Republican and Democratic party platforms. (Abba Hillel Silver was one of the few major Jewish figures in the 20th century identified with the Republican Party.)

Washington diplomats sought to exploit the differences in the various approaches of American Jews to the Palestine question, and tried unsuccessfully to dissuade the American Jewish Conference, established in 1943 to deal with the problems of Palestine and the European Holocaust, from demanding the formation of a Jewish commonwealth in Palestine after World War II. However, the Conference, swayed by Rabbi Silver's oratory, rejected a compromise demanding only free Jewish immigration to Palestine, and voted to adopt the Biltmore Program formulated by the Zionist Organization in 1942 (and named after the New York hotel where the conference was held). This program urged that the British mandate over Palestine be replaced by a Jewish commonwealth, so that the Jewish national homeland promised in the Balfour Declaration might be realized.

After the war, as a continuation of the organizational framework created by the American Zionist Emergency Council, an American section of the Jewish Agency Executive (with headquarters in Jerusalem)

Extraordinary Zionist Conference at the Biltmore Hotel, N. Y., May 1942, which recommended an end to the British Mandate and the establishment of a Jewish commonwealth in Palestine. Among those present were: (1) Israel Goldstein, (2) Louis Levinthal, (3) David Wertheim, (4) Louis Lipsky, (5) Meyer Weisgal, (6) Stephen S. Wise, (7) Chaim Weizmann, (8) David Ben-Gurion, (9) Nahum Goldmann, (10) Tamar De Sola Pool, (11) Abba Hillel Silver, (12) Devorah Rothbart, (13) Hirsch Ehrenreich, (14) Isaac Naiditsch.

was established in New York. It was the representative of the various Zionist organizations.

During the years following the war's end in 1945, American Jewish communal life was dominated by the needs of the Jewish refugees in Europe, and by the Jewish struggle in Palestine/Israel. These years marked the acceptance of Zionism by the bulk of the Jewish community in America. Between 1940 and 1948 the Zionist Organization of America grew in membership from 49,000 to 225,000; Hadassah, which num-

Rally opposing U.S. Palestine policy, N.Y., July 1947.

bered 81,000 women in 1940, multiplied more than threefold.

Anti-Zionist sentiment faded as the impact of the Holocaust which destroyed a third of the world Jewish population, and the determination of the remnant to survive, permeated the consciousness and conscience of the American Jewish community. Academicians joined the ranks of Zionist supporters. Kurt Lewin, one of the most original psychologists of his generation, and a pioneer in group dynamics (he organized and directed the research center for group dynamics at Massachusetts Institute of Technology), applied his theories to Jewish psycho-social needs, and came to view Zionism as a sociological necessity. He contended that in order to belong and develop normally within society, Jews must have their own country.

The American Zionist Emergency Council also sought to enlist general public opinion and the backing of the American government for its demands for free Jewish immigration to Palestine and the establishment of Jewish self-government there. Vast public meetings were convened, and some non-Jewish political and religious leaders were won over to the Zionist cause.

On two occasions early in 1944, and late that year and early in 1945, the House of Representatives Foreign Affairs Committee was about to pass resolutions endorsing the Jewish commonwealth in Palestine, with every prospect for early passage in both houses of Congress. On each occasion, however, the War Department, at the request of the State Department, succeeded in having them tabled as "prejudicial" to the war effort.

American Zionist leaders came to exercise a dominant position in world Zionist policy, as the United States assumed a leadership role in international affairs. They contributed decisively to the political ground-work that underlay the establishment of Israel on May 14, 1948, and to the formal recognition granted it by President Truman immediately after its creation.

In addition to their efforts in the political field, American Zionists were among the most active participants in practical aid to the Jewish community in Palestine. Several thousand American Jewish volunteers navigated the "illegal" immigrant ships across the Mediterranean in defiance of Great Britain's "White Paper" limiting Jewish immigration into Palestine. American Zionists also provided large sums of money and secret shipments of arms to the Haganah, the underground Jewish defense organization that sought to protect Jewish settlers against Arab rioters, and was later to form the basis of Israel's Defense Forces. During Israel's War of Independence in 1948, the greatest number of foreign volunteers to its fighting forces (1,500 out of a total of 5,000 volunteers) came from the American Jewish community.

After Israel's creation, the United States explicitly committed itself to support that state's existence and security, but Washington tended to be restrained in its day-to-day attitude toward problems of the Middle East. In part this was due to the influence of the "Arabists"—American diplomats, missionaries, and businessmen who had cultural, religious, and economic interests in the Arab world. Above all, the United States was sensitive to the dynamic Soviet policy in the area, and feared that the region would become polarized, with all the Arab states eventually oriented toward Moscow, and the United States isolated as a kind of protecting power over Israel. Preoccupation with the cold war competition was reflected in the United States's attitude toward many aspects of the Arab-Israel conflict—military aid, boundaries, utilization of water resources, navigation through international waterways, the resettlement of refugees, the Arab boycott, terrorism and retaliation. American diplomacy was often vacillating so as not to offend Arab sensitivities.

The leaders of American Jewry sought to mobilize the community to influence the national decision-makers to remain alert to Israel's interests. Israel's Sinai Campaign of 1956, in particular, resulted in strained relations between that country and the United States, and many American Jewish bodies and individuals made representations in Washington in support of Israel's position.

During the Six-Day War, Arthur Goldberg, then United States permanent representative to the United Nations, successfully argued the American position calling for a cease-fire without Israel's previous withdrawal from occupied territories. He thereby earned the enmity of the Arab nations, which accused him of influencing American foreign policy on behalf of Jewish interests. Goldberg was also said to have had a major hand in the drafting of the November 1967 Security Council resolution which served as a basis for the Jarring Mission to the Middle East.

ECONOMIC ASSISTANCE

In the 1930s the Zionist Organization of America had devoted most of its attention to fundraising, mainly through the United Palestine Appeal. By the 1940s, however, the creation of the United Jewish Appeal had made fundraising for Palestine, and then Israel, an almost universal, non-ideological expression of Jewish identification and communal participation.

In April 1960, the Jewish Agency for Israel, Inc. (an American administrative body, not to be confused with the Jewish Agency in Israel which is the executive and representative of the World Zionist Organization) was formed to budget and allocate funds raised in the United States for immigrant needs in Israel.

Aid to Israel has been channeled through the UJA and other overseas agencies, and through the Israel Bond Organization. In times of crisis for Israel the sums collected reached unprecedented proportions, as evidenced at the time of the Six-Day War. In 1966 the sale of Israel Bonds totalled 11 million dollars; in 1967—75 million dollars! Money from the UJA was used predominantly for social welfare and development purposes; the proceeds of bond sales, which were initiated in 1951, were used for economic development as well as current purchases.

Private investment in Israel has been fostered by groups such as the Palestine Economic Corporation. The Jewish National Fund, a public body formed at the Fifth Zionist Congress in 1901, has served as a fundraising-educational vehicle enabling Jews in the United States and other countries to "invest" in Israel by planting trees and supporting land conservation projects In addition, many of the larger welfare, cultural, educational, and religious agencies in Israel receive support from groups of "American Friends" which provide material assistance to these institutions.

Since the establishment of the State of Israel, proceeds of the United Jewish Appeal and similar campaigns, Israel Bond sales, institutional and personal remittances, as well as short- and long-term loans and investments from the United States, have accounted for a significant proportion of Israel's capital imports. In addition, more than 13 million dollars in foodstuffs were donated to Israel through private American voluntary agencies such as the American Jewish Joint Distribution Committee and Hadassah.

POST-WORLD WAR II EMPHASES

By the 1950s the position of American Jewry relative to the total Jewish world had changed beyond recognition. With the annihilation of most of Central and a great part of East European Jewry, and the emigration of masses of Jews from Europe, the American Jewish community was left by far the largest Jewish community of the Diaspora. Before World War II approximately twice as many Jews lived in Europe as on the American continent. After World War II nearly twice as many lived in the United States alone, as in all of Europe.

REDISCOVERY OF THE JEWISH POLITY

As a result of these demographic changes the organizational aspects of the worldwide Jewish polity have been strengthened. Parhaps paradoxically, at the very moment that the individual Jew has greater freedom of choice than ever before in the matter of his attachment to the Jewish group, and his degree of identity with Jewish ethnicity, there has been a rediscovery of the special character of the Jewish community in the broadest sense, crossing national boundaries and economic and social distinctions.

In the United States, the Jewish community assumed responsibility for the physical welfare and social and cultural rehabilitation of Jewish communities throughout the world. In the post-war period, American Jewish organizations were also involved with problems of anti-Semitism in the Soviet orbit, the Muslim countries, and South America.

Several brand-new Jewish communities in far-flung areas of the world were created as a result of the efforts of American Jews who served in foreign assignments during the post-war period, particularly in the American armed forces in the Far East, or as part of the American "presence" that was established there after World War II. These communities generally developed about military religious facilities provided through the chaplaincy of the American armed forces. American Jewish chaplains and soldiers often mobilized the local Jewish civilian populations wherever any existed and in some cases (Japan, Okinawa, Taiwan) were instrumental in transforming them into permanent Jewish communities. However, the survival of these small groups appears to depend upon the continued presence of the American Jews who live and work in these distant areas as merchants, representatives of international business firms, advisors and consultants to government and industry.

THE STRUGGLE FOR SOVIET JEWRY

Concern for the "silent Jews" of Russia has grown in recent years to become a major cause enlisting the psychological and material support of American Jewry.

The problems of Russian Jewry had exercised world Jewish opinion for many years before the overthrow of czarism. Russian Jews were the subject of relief and resettlement projects, international protests, and interventions. In the first years after the October Revolution of 1917, renewed attention was focused upon the large and vital Jewish community in Soviet Russia which was enmeshed in the civic turmoil engendered by the war and the revolutionary changes in the USSR.

The problem of Soviet Jewry found a place on the agenda of the founding assembly of the World Jewish Congress in 1936, but the contemporary widespread sympathy for the anti-Nazi stance of the Soviet Union, and the belief that the USSR had tried to eradicate anti-Semitism, muted discussion of the question. In 1948, with the first indications of an official policy of anti-Semitism in the USSR, interest in the problem of

Soviet Jewry began to revive, and when the campaign against "rootless cosmopolitans" began to sweep Eastern Europe, culminating in the "Doctors' Plot," a special world Jewish conference on the situation of Soviet Jews was contemplated. (The death of Stalin in March 1953 led to the revocation of the Soviet charges against the doctors.)

Details released about the extent and virulence of Stalin's anti-Jewish campaign of terror made the world realize that the Jewish problem was still acute after almost 40 years of Soviet rule which was to have eliminated anti-Semitism. In New York City, the editors of the Communist paper, *Daily Worker*, criticized the USSR's treatment of its Jewish population, and the Communist Party closed the paper and transformed it into a weekly, called the *Worker*, with a different staff.

During the 1960s the Soviet government's discrimination against its Jewish population in matters of language, education and religion, its dissemination of anti-Jewish literature, its persecution of individual Jews for "economic crimes" or for Jewish communal activity, and its denial to Jews of the right of emigration, particularly to Israel, became major issues in world Jewish discussion. Almost every Jewish organization in the United States raised the problem of Russian Jewry as one of the utmost importance to the Jewish people, second only to the existence and security of Israel.

Jewish and non-Jewish intellectuals held special conferences to investigate the facts and issue appeals to the Soviet government. Of particular significance was the Conference on the Status of Soviet Jews (1963, New York) under the sponsorship of Supreme Court Justice William O. Douglas, Rev. Martin Luther King, Senator Herbert Lehman, Bishop James Pike, labor leader Walter Reuther, socialist ideologist Norman Thomas, and novelist Robert Penn Warren. The Conference issued an "appeal to conscience" and disseminated extensive factual material on the problem.

At the same time the Jewish community in the U.S. established the American Jewish Conference on Soviet Jewry, which encompassed all the major Jewish organizations in the country (including the American Jewish Committee, which generally did not participate in comprehensive Jewish frameworks). This body sponsored mass rallies, press conferences, and meetings with the White House and State Department, and published information on the situation of the Jews in the USSR. In 1967 an Academic Committee on Soviet Jewry was formed, sponsored by leading Jewish academic figures. Jewish student groups supporting the struggle for Soviet Jewry sprang up throughout the United States. The young people staged public demonstrations of sympathy, particularly at Soviet diplomatic missions.

In the late 1960s, too, the Jews of the Soviet Union who had seemingly remained inert under Stalinist persecution, began to assert overtly their Jewishness and their identification with Israel. The underlying factors in their "renaissance" were the classic ones: bitter resentment of the anti-Semitism which still existed in Soviet society and its administration after half a century of Bolshevik rule; and a surprising amount of deep, residual Jewish feelings, and especially of identification with Israel, which persisted despite the absence, for at least a generation, of any Jewish schools or communal organizations. The Six-Day War had been a turning point. The Soviet government had revealed itself to be the chief protector and supplier of Egypt and the other Arab states. Official Soviet propaganda had been violently anti-Israel and anti-Zionist, with strong anti-Semitic overtones.

Vocal elements among the Jews of the USSR proceeded to demand the right to leave and go to Israel. The right of Soviet Jews to emigrate became an international issue of considerable magnitude, and activity on their behalf was widespread throughout the Jewish world. In addition to exercising moral and psychological pressure on the Soviet Union, the campaign on behalf of Russian Jewry served to awaken many American Jews who were otherwise alienated from the Jewish community, to a sense of their own Jewish identity.

IMPLICATIONS OF ISRAEL'S EXISTENCE

The implications of the existence of Israel are just beginning to make themselves felt in the organization, orientation, and content of American Jewish communal life.

Membership in Zionist organizations dropped drastically after the founding of the state, as the development of Israel became a philanthropic, political, and to some extent cultural interest of American Jewry as a whole. In recognition of this fact, the structure of American Zionism was reformed in 1970 to provide for the affiliation of individuals having no particular Zionist party or organizational ties. While Jewish religious, welfare, and community relations institutions in the United States are all officially "non-Zionist," in practice they all support Israel and urge an American policy of friendship and economic aid for the state.

Since the establishment of Israel, controversies have cropped up between Israeli leaders and American Zionists over their interrelationships. The Americans demanded, and were assured of, the separation of the activities of the state from those of the Jewish Agency and the World Zionist Organization. The Israelis wanted Jerusalem to be the center of all Zionist activities throughout the world, and American Zionists fought the imposition of Israel's authority over the Zionist organization. The latter's demands for recognition as the liaison for all activities involving American Jews and Israel was legalized through the passage of the Zionist Organization and Jewish Agency Law in the Knesset (parliament) of Israel, and by the covenant subsequently signed between the Israel government and the Jewish Agency.

Nonetheless, every major American Jewish organization has already begun to feel the effect of the trend toward concentrating in Israel all the decision-making processes for the world Jewish people. This tendency has been particularly noticeable since the Six-Day War, after which the Israel government began to take steps to tie the institutions and organizations of world Jewry closer to Israel. Israel's greater ability to deal with political matters, as a sovereign state, and its great stake in strengthening the worldwide Jewish polity, have led it to assume this central role. This development has also been made possible by the fact that Israel has become the focal point of Jewish identification throughout the world, the one Jewish phenomenon whose crucial importance is accepted by virtually all Jews. At times Israel's desire to mobilize widespread Jewish public opinion has led to some tensions between it and American Jewish organizations, who cherish their independence and voluntaristic nature.

JEWISH EDUCATION

The impact made on the diaspora communities by the State of Israel is hinted at in the extensive ideological debates and in the voluminous literature on the subject. (A variety of Israel institutions also direct extensive periodical literature toward the American Jewish community.)

American Jews have shown themselves more willing to be identified as Jews, to affiliate with Jewish organizations and institutions, and to

U.S. students during their two-year study stint at the Jerusalem branch of the Ḥafetz Ḥayyim Yeshivah of N.Y.

send their children to Jewish schools as a result of their feelings toward Israel. Israel occupies an important place in American synagogue activities, sermons, and various religious celebrations. Israel's Independence Day has been incorporated into the days commemorated in the American Jewish calendar. In many synagogues prayers for the welfare of the State of Israel and world Jewry are recited on Sabbaths and holidays, following the prayer for the welfare of the United States. The Conservative and Reform movements and leading Orthodox institutions have established rabbinical study and youth educational programs in Israel.

Israel's impact on Jewish education in the United States is also reflected in the increased emphasis on the Hebrew language in the Jewish school curriculum. Hebrew songs and Israel folk dances have become part of American Jewish popular culture, and Jewish art, which traditionally concentrated on East European themes, has expanded to include Israel landscapes and symbols.

RELIGIOUS AND IDEOLOGICAL ISSUES

The reality of Israel's existence has had a profound impact on the ideologies of American Jews. Orthodox Jewry in America feels itself intimately involved in the course of religious affairs in Israel, and presses that state to pursue official religious policies in accord with its own religious beliefs. In turn, Israel's rabbis command influence and respect among Orthodox Jewish circles in the United States. The Conservative and Reform movements, on the other hand, are concerned that the legal establishment of religious Orthodoxy in Israel discriminates against non-Orthodox Jews there. Some have demanded the separation of state and religion, and the recognition of non-Orthodox forms of Jewish religious practice, particularly in areas of personal law, such as marriage, divorce, and conversion. The concern expressed by the American religious groups implies that the religious forms practiced in Israel are of direct relevance to them.

A RELATIONSHIP OF INTERDEPENDENCE

The creation of the State of Israel has had a profound effect on the psychological makeup of the American Jew; it has heightened his sense of morale and has deepened his self-image.

The intense reaction of American Jewry to the crisis of 1967—the unprecedented rallying of material and moral support for Israel on the part of many Jews who had long renounced any interest in and concern for things Jewish—highlighted a trend that had been growing for two decades: the interdependence between Israel and American Jewry. While such interdependence had been apparent for some time, it had always seemed that Israel was more dependent upon American Jewry than the reverse. But the events of 1967 demonstrated that American Jewry was highly dependent upon Israel too. While Israel's destruction might not endanger the physical security of the American Jew, the psychological effect could be devastating.

A running controversy between major Israeli figures and the leaders of the American Jewish community has centered about the meaning of the Diaspora and the obligation of Zionists abroad to emigrate and

Israel Prime Minister Golda Meir meeting with U.S. President Nixon at the White House, Washington D.C., September 1969.

settle in Israel. American Zionists have claimed that the United States was not *galut* (exile), because Jews have been secure and not oppressed there; they affirmed the continued existence of Jewish communities throughout the world, simultaneous with their deep emotional commitment to Israel.

Still, the American Jewish community has recognized the central Jewish issues of the modern era as the need for the Jews to survive as a people and the role of Israel in guaranteeing this survival. Thus, one of the cornerstones of American Jewish commitment to Israel is the provision of aid to ensure its physical survival and economic viability. In addition, the American Jewish community increasingly recognizes Israel as the cultural center of the Jewish people which will continue to maintain various communities throughout the Diaspora.

The relationship between Israel and the Diaspora communities is symbiotic. Israel provides the cultural, ethnic, and religious force to keep the Jewish people from cultural disintegration; the Diaspora provides the moral, political and financial assistance needed to ensure Israel's continued survival and growth.

7

MATURITY AND RESTLESSNESS
(THE POST-WAR PERIOD)

POST-WAR PROSPERITY

In common with U.S. citizens generally, Jews enjoyed an era of prolonged prosperity during the post-World War II years. Homecoming soldiers found jobs or attended college en masse under the liberal terms of the "GI Bill of Rights."

Less than a century after the United States housed a distant, little populated outpost of the Jewish people, American Jewry had attained great numbers, prosperity, cultural eminence, and political prestige. Such growth and accomplishment had no precedent in the history of the Jews.

POPULATION STABILIZATION

The number of Jews apparently increased only slightly after World War II. Unfortunately, Jewish population estimates, while comparatively accurate for many cities, were unreliable for the country as a whole. The Jewish population, probably overestimated at 5,000,000 in 1945, stood around 6,060,000 in 1971. In comparison, the U.S. population was 140,000,000 in 1945 and over 200,000,000 in 1971. In 1971 the percentage of Jews in the U.S. had dropped to 2.9%.

The reasons underlying the small Jewish population increase are strongly suggested by the median Jewish household size and the mean number of children born per 1,000 women, both lower than that of other religious or ethnic groups. With no more than about 12% of Jewish families having four or more children, Jewish natural increase was well below that of the U.S. as a whole.

Immigration provided little of the Jewish increase. From 1944 through 1959, 191,693 Jews settled in the United States. The large majority were European survivors, over 63,000 of whom entered under the provisions of the Displaced Persons Act of 1949. Otherwise, the quota system of the Johnson Act and its successor McCarran-Walter Act of 1952 remained intact until new legislation was enacted in 1965.

From 1960 through 1968 about 73,000 Jewish immigrants arrived. Jewish immigrants after 1957 tended to be Israelis (frequently of European birth), Cubans leaving the Castro regime, and Near Easterners. The United Service for New Americans, a descendant of the National Refugee Service and the Hebrew Immigrant Aid Society (HIAS), and local community organizations aided the immigrants. Due to their comparatively small numbers and the stabilization of American Judaism, the influence of post-1945 immigration on Jewish life was small, except in Orthodox circles.

INTERNAL MIGRATION

U.S. Jewry continued to be a metropolitan group. About 40% dwelled in the New York City area, as had been the case since 1900. The sum total of Jews living in Greater New York, northeastern New Jersey, and the nine next largest communities (Los Angeles, Philadelphia, Chicago, Miami, Boston, Washington, Baltimore, Cleveland, Detroit) equalled 75% of U.S. Jewry. Close to 90% of all Jews in the United States lived in ten states which contained somewhat less than one-half of the general population.

The most notable demographic phenomenon within these and other urban centers was Jewish movement to the suburbs, which to some extent merely continued the usual trend to move to better neighborhoods as income and aspirations rose. Seeking greater space, more relaxed living, and a more homogeneous social environment, large numbers of Jews quit the ever more congested and aging cities. By 1958, 85% of Cleveland Jews lived beyond the city boundaries. Virtually the entire Jewish population in Detroit, Newark, and Washington, D.C. similarly left the central city within the next decade. Every large city saw a considerable proportion of its middle class, including Jews, settle in the suburbs, especially as massive Negro immigration precipitated formidable social problems. Jewish neighborhoods tended to become Negro rather quickly, except in New York where the process was a slow one.

Coincidental with the suburban movement, was the migration of large numbers of Jews within the United States. The increase of the Los Angeles Jewish population from 150,000 in 1945 to 535,000 in 1971, and of Miami from 7,500 in 1937 to 40,000 in 1948 and around 187,000 in 1971, was almost wholly the result of internal migration. Much of it came from the Middle West whose Jewish population failed to increase after the 1920s. Boston's Jewish population increased from 137,000 in 1948 to 180,000 in 1971, apparently owing to heavy Jewish participation in that area's scientific and technological growth.

NEW OCCUPATIONAL PATTERN

After 1945 a new occupational pattern of U.S. Jewry became evident. No nationwide survey was conducted, but many studies of individual communities made clear that employment in the professions was rising greatly, and proprietorship and management somewhat less so. Skilled, semi-skilled, and unskilled labor was sharply decreasing, and clerical and sales employment somewhat declining. Forestry, mining, and transportation in all forms hardly employed any Jews, as in the past; the small contingent of Jewish farmers slowly decreased in size.

The rise in number of professionals was a general phenomenon. Thus, in the small, venerable Jewish community of Charleston, to which few immigrants came, professionals more than quadrupled between the mid-1930s and 1948. Charleston's antithesis, Los Angeles, likewise saw its Jewish professionals increase from 11% to 25% of heads of household between 1941 and 1959. In addition to the continuing concentration of Jews as physicians, lawyers, accountants, and (in New York City) teachers, they were prominent as scientific professionals in such new industries as electronics.

Earlier occupational patterns lasted longer in New York City where skilled and unskilled workers comprised about 28% of the Jewish labor force in 1952 and in 1961, and professionals only 17% in both years. In such professions as law, medicine, dentistry, and teaching Jews formed a clear majority of those employed. Industries in which they had provided the major labor force, especially the needle trades, remained Jewish only at the higher levels of skill and entrepreneurship. By 1970 the crucial role of the clothing industry in the lives of American Jews was past. Negro and Puerto Rican workers were increasingly employed in the metropolitan centers; as the ladies' garment industry moved out of urban areas in search of cheaper labor and lower overhead costs, its labor force became more ethnically diverse.

Jews were extensively represented in urban retail trade, construction of homes and shopping centers, and metropolitan real estate. The same could be said of such mass media areas as television, films, and advertising, and of cultural enterprises like book publishing, art dealing, and impresarioship in music and theater. Stockbrokerage and other spheres of finance continued to involve Jewish firms and brokers, but the prominence enjoyed by Jewish financiers during the later 19th and early 20th centuries did not return.

Various local studies showed that around 1960 some 25% of employed Jews were in professional and semi-professional occupations (as were 13.9% of the employed U.S. population), and 30% were proprietors, managers, or self-employed businessmen (as were 10.7% of the employed U.S. population). The proportion in business was especially high in smaller cities, where Jews continued in their old role as leading local merchants.

Local surveys demonstrated also that the proportion of professionals was higher in the younger Jewish strata. This finding, combined with the fact that some 80% of Jewish youth of college age attended college during the 1960s, strongly suggested that the proportion of professionals would continue to rise.

In these vocational trends, U.S. Jews anticipated the general movement of employment away from manual, craft, agricultural, and factory work into clerical, technical, managerial, and professional occupations. Their continued attachment to independent entrepreneurship in a corporate age was unique, however.

Somewhat less complete evidence indicated that Jewish incomes stood appreciably higher than those of any other religious or ethnic group in the United States in the 1960s.

DECLINE IN ANTI-SEMITISM

After 1945 anti-Semitism in the United States did not assume the ideological strength it had achieved in the preceding decades. Direct anti-Jewish agitation after World War II was limited, for the most part, to isolated fringe groups which were declining in number. Among the active exponents of anti-Semitism were such individuals and groups as the Columbians, the minuscule but vociferous American Nazi Party, the National Renaissance Party, and such publications as Gerald L. K. Smith's *The Cross and the Flag* and Conde McGinley's *Common Sense*. Much more threatening from the Jewish viewpoint were the persistence and growth of ultra-conservative groups which officially denied anti-Semitic proclivities but provided a rallying point for many who were anti-Semitically inclined. Significantly, however, the anti-Communist crusade initiated by Senator Joseph McCarthy in the early 1950s, while receiving widespread popular support, never attacked Jews as such.

Studies indicated that whereas 63% of the American public attributed "objectionable traits" to the Jews as a group in 1940, only 22% felt that way in 1962. A 1969 poll found that only 8% of American voters would oppose a candidate because he was a Jew, whereas in 1937 the figure was 46%. Jews played an important and active role in all areas of political, public, and community life, although to a lesser extent outside major population centers.

Yet the chauvinism of an old, established patrician class combined with a nativist-populist tradition continued to perpetuate patterns of social discrimination against Jews in upper-level social institutions and housing, and in some areas of employment, particularly on the executive or management levels. Repeated studies indicated that the Jews continued to be the only white group in the United States for whom social rank was consistently lower than economic status.

Nonetheless, quotas in the universities and in certain professions, and exclusion from the highest posts of political life, had well-nigh ended. In the post-World War II era the Jews of America rose very close to the top of American political, economic, and intellectual life.

COMMUNAL STRENGTH

Economic prosperity, the neutralization of once sharp ideological differences, growing social homogeneity, and the closing of the rift between natives and immigrants resulted in a lengthy period of communal consensus which extended from 1950 to about 1968. The State of Israel became a unifying rather than divisive force. Funds were ample for generally agreed upon communal purposes in the United States and overseas. A benevolent neutrality prevailed among religious groupings, except in some Orthodox circles. Communal interests focused primarily on local matters as Jewish suburbia built its institutions, while in older urban areas communal institutions struggled to survive or relocated.

JEWISH COMMUNITY COUNCILS

Nearly every city, except New York and Chicago, conducted a combined campaign for overseas and domestic needs and had some form of central Jewish community organization. The Jewish community councils, founded during the 1930s, generally merged with the older federations of Jewish philanthropies and were governed by an executive board and a none-too-potent community assembly of representatives of organizations. In some cities, however, contributors to the combined campaign above a minimal level (usually 10 dollars) could cast their vote for a fixed proportion of the delegates to these assemblies. These central Jewish communal bodies supported community relations committees which coordinated the various local efforts of the Jewish defense organizations. They also sponsored the local bureaus of Jewish education, settled intra-communal disputes, in some communities supervised kashrut, and functioned as the recognized Jewish spokesman in the general community. The social service agencies affiliated with these federations enjoyed far-reaching autonomy. The most important community activity, by far, was the annual campaign, whose proceeds were allocated, after negotiations, by carefully devised formulas.

At the national level, ideological groupings and specialization of activities evolved, but no stable central body developed. The defense organizations coordinated their activities in the National Community Relations Advisory Council. The American Zionist Council did likewise for Zionist bodies, especially on political issues, and the Synagogue Council of America, with little power, obtained occasional unity among the denominational federations of synagogues. The Council of Jewish Federations and Welfare Funds provided guidance for its constituent groups in areas of Jewish philanthropic policy, educational and social services. In 1955 the Conference of Presidents of Major American Jewish Organizations was established, to consult informally in matters concerning Israel and overseas Jewish problems. By virtue of its age, size, prestige, and non-partisan Jewish character, B'nai B'rith tended to play a focal role in such central efforts.

RELIGIOUS VITALITY

Jewish religious life expanded considerably after 1945 as Judaism was all but officially recognized as the "third American religion," despite the fact that the number of its adherents was smaller than the other major religious groupings.

Public commissions habitually included a Jewish member alongside Protestants and Catholics, and official ceremonies, including presidential inaugurations, arranged for Jewish as well as Christian clerical participation.

The gradual shift in public consciousness toward viewing the Jewish community as a religious rather than an ethnic group reflected the American insistence upon its component ethnic groups assimilating into the "melting pot." America was much more accepting of the concept of differences based on faith, probably because of its Protestant origins. Thus, the Jewish community's retention of its particular identity was attributed to its specifically religious nature.

The 1950s was a period of unprecedented interest in Jewish religious life and thought, as part of the "revival of religion" in American culture during those years, and the writings of such figures as Martin Buber and Abraham J. Heschel received wide attention. Numerous interfaith

The three chapels on the Brandeis campus, designed by Max Abramovitz, symbolizing the nonsectarian character of the university.

institutes and assemblies were held. Indirectly the climate was created for the Jewish role in the Catholic ecumenical movement of the 1960s.

While it was customary to divide U.S. Judaism into Reform, Conservative, and Orthodox denominations, each with central institutions and recognized leaders, the religious reality more closely resembled a spectrum in which the membership, beliefs, and practices, and even the rabbinate, of one group shaded into the next.

The number of denominationally identified congregations grew rapidly. In 1954 there were 462 Reform congregations, 102 more than in 1948; of the 473 Conservative there were 156 more than in 1948. (Many had been Orthodox and evolved into Conservatism.) There were 720 affiliated Orthodox congregations, but many were inactive leftovers from immigrant days. However, the Synagogue Council of America estimated, in 1957, that there were 4,240 congregations in the United States. This great disparity could be partially explained by the large number of minuscule, unaffiliated, and inactive groups in the latter figure.

The organized American rabbinate in 1955 numbered 1,127 men in the two large Orthodox professional bodies, 677 Reform, and 598 Conservative rabbis.

A 1950 estimate placed total synagogue membership at a maximum of 450,000 families, besides about 250,000 persons who had seats in the synagogue on the High Holy Days. In 1958 there were over 450,000

Sally Priesand, of the Reform H.U.C.-J.I.R., the first woman to receive a rabbinical ordination (1972).

families in Conservative and Reform congregations; the Orthodox could not be properly determined, but a 1965 study suggested 300,000 committed Orthodox individuals. Altogether, the largest institutional and membership growth was found among the Conservative movement, which had 833 congregations affiliated with the United Synagogue in 1970, as compared with some 700 in the Union of American Hebrew Congregations in that year.

A wave of synagogue construction permitted this increase of affiliation, as did the burgeoning of new suburban districts. Between 1945 and 1952 an estimated 50 to 60 million dollars was spent on synagogue building, and the ten-year period which followed may have seen twice that amount expended.

Notwithstanding the high rate of affiliation with the synagogue, there was increasing dissatisfaction with its activities on the congregational level and in the area of Jewish education. Nor did great material growth make Jewish religious life any more intensive. A poll taken in 1945 showed that only 18% of the Jews attended public worship at least once monthly, as against 65% of Protestants and 83% of Catholics. A 1958 poll of weekly attendance again showed 18% of Jews, as against 74% of Catholics and 40% of Protestants. Only small numbers of Jews observed the Sabbath scrupulously, maintained the dietary laws in full, and observed daily prayers.

There was, however, widespread, well-documented interest in Judaism on college campuses, and in numerous instances young people adopted traditional religious life patterns and beliefs. This revitalization of Jewish religious tradition may have been, in part, a search for community; shared rituals and experiences offered a psychic restoration which other young people sought in encounter or sensitivity groups.

The three recognized religious groupings were found in every Jewish community of any size, but some were strong in particular cities. Thus, the centers of Orthodoxy were in Boston, Baltimore, and above all New York City. Philadelphia and Detroit were strongly Conservative, while Cleveland, San Francisco, and Milwaukee were largely Reform.

DENOMINATIONAL ISSUES

The denominations had their struggles over internal issues. The Reform majority, now pro-Zionist, moved toward increased ritual and traditionalism in religious observance, over the opposition of a vigorous "classical Reform" minority. Reform congregations leaned in either direction, but the majority of Reform rabbis attempted to utilize the classic sources of Jewish law in dealing with religious problems.

Within the Conservative movement, internal differences tended to be muffled in loyalty to the central institution, the Jewish Theological Seminary, and its traditionalist faculty. The main issue exercising Conservative rabbis was Jewish law, the extent to which it could be modified within its own categories, through its own methodology, and by whom. In an attempt to demonstrate the reality of the Conservative conception of the flexibility of the *halakhah* (Jewish law), the Rabbinical Assembly considered the classic problem of freeing the deserted wife *(agunah)* from her marital bond. (In Jewish law, only the husband may issue a divorce, and a husband who has disappeared obviously cannot grant a divorce.) In 1954 the Rabbinical Assembly promulgated a supplement to the marriage certificate which obligated the groom in advance to accept the judgment of a religious tribunal established to deal with such cases. In 1968 the Law Committee of the Rabbinical Assembly gave Conservative rabbis the right to annul Jewish religious marriages if the husband refused to cooperate in the traditional procedures for religious divorce. Yet while the Conservative rabbis and scholars debated this and other problems of halakhic change, the lay membership of Conservative congregations proceeded in its own unhalakhic way of life.

Orthodoxy shed its status as the Judaism of immigrants, and the number of acculturated, middle-class congregations with modern American-trained rabbinic leadership sharply increased. There was also a large accretion to Orthodoxy from post-1945 immigration. The Orthodox movement became intellectually active and began to produce works of religious and philosophic content in addition to books of traditional rabbinic scholarship. Jewish publishers found a market for reprintings of the Talmud and nearly the entire corpus of rabbinic classics.

CULTURAL FRAMEWORK

By the end of the 1940s the Jews, as an overwhelmingly native group, extensively college educated and heavily concentrated in the mercantile and professional classes with longstanding cultural interests, began to assume a remarkable degree of prominence in U.S. cultural life. While their previously notable position as physicians, scientists, lawyers, psychoanalysts, and musicians continued, Jews now began to excel in fields once inaccessible to them.

MOVING INTO THE MAINSTREAM

It was only after World War II that the Jewish community felt itself sufficiently rooted in the language and mainstream culture of the United States for Jewish writers in English to begin to leave their imprint upon the general literary scene. Beginning in the 1950s, a considerable number of Jewish writers attained importance and national distinction, and literary critics Lionel Trilling, Leslie Fiedler, Alfred Kazin, and Irving Howe helped mold the intellectual climate of American letters.

Of more unique interest, Jewish subjects came to occupy the forefront of literary interest. Novels and short stories, of extremely varied quality, on themes including the European Holocaust, Israel, and middle-class American Jewish life, sold in the millions of copies to non-Jews as well as to Jews. The regional genre of American literature, which long reflected "Southern" and "Mid-Western" themes, made room for "Jewish" works. Broadway plays with Jewish themes proved to be box-office favorites. Indeed, occasional murmurs were heard regarding the alleged domination of American culture by a New York Jewish circle. Whether this was largely literary politics, or legitimate literary judgment, there was no doubt that Jews were the principal marketers of cultural products in the United States.

WITHIN THE WALLS OF ACADEME

Restrictive admissions practices at universities began to yield to public criticism after World War II, and the doors of the universities opened to Jewish students. Many veterans who were returning to the campus under the GI Bill which paid for their education vigorously objected to discriminatory practices in civilian life as incompatible with the mandates of democracy for which the war had been fought. Moreover, educational institutions increasingly found themselves unable to obtain the government funds available for expansion while maintaining a practice of discrimination in admission practices. In New York City, for example, Rabbi Stephen S. Wise mounted an attack on Columbia University in 1946, charging it with practicing unofficial discrimination against Jews, and petitioning the City Council to withdraw its tax exemption from the institution. Columbia reacted by removing the long-standing question of religious identification from its application forms.

Federal agencies and educational associations also criticized restrictive policies. In 1947 President Truman's Commission on Higher Education charged that quota systems and policies of exclusion had prevented young people of many religious and racial groups, but particularly Jews and Negroes, from obtaining a higher education and professional training. A 1949 study by the American Council on Education showed that the average Jewish applicant for college admission had considerably less chance of acceptance than a Catholic or Protestant of comparable scholastic ability. In that same year, application forms of 518 colleges and of 88 schools of medicine and dentistry were still found to contain at least one and usually several potentially discriminatory questions.

In reaction to public criticism, several states outlawed discriminatory practices in education, and scholastic merit gradually became the major criterion for admission to private institutions of learning, although other factors—geographical distribution of the student body, preferential treatment of children of alumni, desire for a balanced student body—remained operative. As a result, Jewish enrollment at private colleges rose substantially. In 1968, Jews comprised 20% of the student bodies at the prestigious Ivy League colleges which had long maintained covert anti-Jewish admissions policies.

The growth in Jewish enrollment on college campuses paralleled the general boom in the American college population, which zoomed from two million students in 1946, to a population of seven and a half million students enrolled in over two thousand institutions of higher learning in 1968. During this period of educational explosion, the Jewish college population grew from just under 105,000 in 1953, to 275,000 in 1963, and then to 375,000 in 1968. Due to the even more rapid pace at which the overall growth of college enrollment moved, however, the Jewish percentage among the general college population dropped from 9.3% in 1953 to 5% in 1968. In the latter year, less than 40% of the U.S. college-age population was in school, but among Jews of that age group nearly 80% attended college.

Studies carried out in the mid-60s indicated that 23.6% of the Jewish students in colleges and universities were in the field of business administration, 18.9% in education, 17.6% in engineering, 8.2% in law, 7.6% in medicine, and 5.2% in pharmacology. The last three fields showed a much higher percentage of Jewish students than the national enrollment. Other professional fields in which Jewish students were highly represented were dentistry, optometry, psychology, and philosophy.

More than half of all Jewish students (51.3%) attended public institutions, and New York City, with its large Jewish population and its tuition-free city colleges, continued to have the largest number and proportion of Jewish college students in the world. Nevertheless, New York City began to decline as a center of higher education for Jewish students (in 1935, 53% of all Jewish collegians in the United States studied in New York City institutions; this percentage dropped to 27.6% in 1963) as the growing affluence of the community enabled more parents to send their children out of town for a college education. The growth of the State University of New York opened additional opportunities for a relatively inexpensive college education outside the metropolitan area, and private colleges liberalized their admissions' policies.

At the same time, however, many state universities began to restrict their enrollment of out-of-state students. In 1969, 73 (more than one-half) restricted the admission of nonresidents. Inasmuch as New York and New Jersey constituted a major Jewish population center of the United States and both states consistently "exported" large numbers of students because their own college systems could not accommodate all applicants, the restriction hit hard at Jewish students. Although sympathetic to the demands for the admission of more Negro students to American universities, especially to tax-supported institutions, the Jewish community was also increasingly concerned that such redistribution would cut down Jewish admissions.

College faculties were forced to expand rapidly to meet the demands of the burgeoning post-war student enrollment. Federal and state legislation which prohibited discriminatory employment practices virtually eliminated ethnic restrictions in faculty appointments, and Jews were named to university posts in increasing numbers.

Prior to World War II, only a few hundred Jews had held academic posts, mainly in the municipal colleges of New York City. But at the close of the 1960s a survey indicated that some 10% of all college faculty members had been reared as Jews. (Only 6.7% still gave their present religion as Jewish at the time of the survey; this reflected a similar drop in religious identification found among non-Jewish faculty members. The percentages for past and present identification among Protestant faculty members were 64% and 45.3%; and Catholics, 15.4% and 11.8%.) At the same time, some leading universities—California, Chicago, Columbia, Harvard, Michigan, Pennsylvania, Princeton, the City University of New York—were estimated to have up to 20% or more Jewish faculty members.

Other than in the City University of New York, however, relatively few Jews gained admittance to the ranks of educational administrators (college presidents and deans).

In the late '60s an undercurrent of resentment and envy at the marked presence of Jews in the academic world and the professions was becoming manifest among Negro and Spanish-American ethnic groups, as they began to seek more status and a larger share in America's economic pie.

JEWISH STUDENT GROUPS

The large number of Jewish students on college campuses in the postwar years was reflected in the growth of Jewish student groups.

The oldest Jewish student organization on a North American campus, Zeta Beta Tau (ZBT) fraternity, had been founded in New York City in 1898 to encourage the study of Jewish life and culture among Jewish students. Soon afterward, however, it was converted into a Greek-letter society. Jewish social and professional fraternities grew in number to provide a framework for Jewish students who were generally excluded from the Greek-letter fraternities and sororities. In 1941 Jewish fraternities and sororities had 540 local chapters and a membership of 85,000—and very little Jewish content. After World War II, however, in response to changing university policies and the growing public demand for the elimination of discriminatory restrictions, most Greek-letter societies began to accept members regardless of their social, racial, or religious background. Thus deprived of one of their major reasons for existence, most Jewish groups experienced a significant drop in membership by the late 1960s.

Additional Jewish student clubs emerged on major campuses in the early years of the 20th century, and were affiliated with the Intercollegiate

Menorah Association, which had 50 chapters in 1930. Zionist societies sprang up at several major universities and merged into various inter-collegiate associations. In 1946 the Intercollegiate Zionist Federation of America was formed and during the period immediately preceding the founding of the State of Israel its membership rose to 10,000. The organization was dissolved in 1953, but it spawned a succession of smaller student Zionist groups.

There were also 252 Hillel groups on campus in 1969. These were maintained by B'nai B'rith, which had provided professional direction and programming for Jewish collegiate activities since 1923. In addition, independent or religiously affiliated Jewish student groups existed at many colleges.

The 1960s also introduced the phenomena of the kosher dining club on campus, the Jewish student house, and the *havurah* (fellowship) which sought to create a "total Jewish environment" for living and studying on campus. In 1970 such groups, with membership ranging from 10 to 50 in each unit, were operating on some 80 campuses.

As a result of the growing anti-Israel stance of the New Left (see below), and of the rejection of whites by the increasingly militant Black civil rights movement, Jewish students began to turn to the Jewish community to provide an arena for acting out their moral and social convictions. They sought to stimulate Jewish community projects for social justice and peace, and to counter the anti-Israel activities of the New Left and of the Arab students on campus. An increasing number of Jewish students began to turn to classic Jewish sources in search of answers to the social and moral problems of contemporary life. Some helped create "Free Jewish Universities" on campus, to provide programs involving students and faculty in the study of Jewish thought and life, and in political action on behalf of Israel and Soviet Jewry. Student lobbying also stimulated the growth of accredited Jewish studies programs on American campuses.

JEWISH STUDIES ON CAMPUS

Jewish studies, defined as the systematic study of Judaism and Jewish life and experience through the ages, began to emerge in the American university curriculum to a significant degree only in the late 1930s. The Old Testament and Hebrew had long been taught, but only insofar as a knowledge of the Hebrew Bible was considered necessary for an under-standing of Christianity and the training of Christian clergymen.

The first courses in post-biblical Judaism were introduced into the curriculum of American universities toward the end of the 19th century, but the number of institutions offering such courses remained small. In 1945, full-time teaching staff in Judaica could be found only at Berkeley, Chicago, Columbia, Harvard, Iowa, Johns Hopkins, Missouri, New York University, Pennsylvania, and several New York City colleges. The number began to increase rapidly in the 1950s, and by 1969 nearly 80 Jewish scholars were teaching full-time in American universities; courses in Judaica—Bible, Talmud, Hebrew language and literature, philosophy, history, and folklore—were taught part-time at nearly 200 additional institutions in the country.

A variety of factors contributed to the growth of Judaic studies, among them the articulation of a growing demand for such studies arising from increased Jewish self-awareness generated by the impact of the Holocaust and the creation of the State of Israel; the democratization of academic policies and admission practices which led to substantial increases in Jewish enrollment; the climate of greater acceptance of Jews and Judaism by the general and academic communities; the growing recognition of Hebrew as a living language and of Judaism as an es-sential component in the fabric of Western civilization; and the post-war growth of specialized area studies and of religious studies.

A major innovation in the area of Jewish studies was the foundation, in 1946, of Brandeis University, the first non-sectarian Jewish-sponsored liberal arts college in the United States. Its students, faculty, and staff are multi-religious and multi-racial; its broad curriculum includes departments in advanced Jewish studies, East European Jewish affairs, and Jewish education.

YIDDISH AND HEBREW EDUCATION

After 1950 Hebrew literary creativity in the United States nearly vanished as writers focused their talents upon Israel's Hebrew-speaking popula-tion. Despite the small Yiddish-speaking immigration following World

War II, Yiddish letters continued their decline, largely because of the linguistic assimilation of American Jews. Significant Yiddish writers continued to publish, however, in the few New York City Yiddish dailies, and in various periodicals. Isaac Bashevis Singer became a literary celebrity during the 1960s—in English translation. Several popular books in English brought the richness of the Yiddish language to the attention of the general public.

Jewish cultural activity in English increased, through the media of the Anglo-Jewish press, Jewish institutional lecture platforms, synagogue study groups, and various Jewish monthlies and quarterlies, some of which were of the highest standard.

It was no longer unusual to find information about Jewish affairs in the general press and magazines, and on television. University presses and commercial publishers issued serious works on Jewish subjects, in addition to best-selling novels of varying quality.

Jewish scholarship, while still concentrated in seminaries and *yeshivot,* slowly began to find a place in universities with the establishment of academic chairs in Jewish studies. To the generation of mature, European-trained scholars was added a new one educated in the United States, and frequently in Israel as well.

As the American Jewish community began to assume the scholarly mantle that had been the pride of the European Jewish community before its decimation in the 1930s and 1940s, it also developed a series of outstanding libraries providing the necessary scholarly resources.

The library of the Jewish Theological Seminary of America (New York City) had the most important collection of Hebraica and Judaica, in both manuscripts and printed books, outside of Israel. In 1966 a disastrous fire destroyed a large section of the library, but much of it was reconstituted. Other important libraries were attached to Hebrew Union College-Jewish Institute of Religion (Cincinnati and New York), Dropsie University (Philadelphia), and to particular organizations, such as the American Jewish Historical Society (Waltham, Mass.), the Zionist Archives and Library (New York City), and the YIVO Institute for Jewish Research (New York City).

Additional important Jewish collections were housed in the New York Public Library, the Boston Public Library, the Library of Congress in Washington, D.C., and various university libraries.

BASIC JEWISH EDUCATION

The Jewish community's new, respectful attitude toward Jewish scholarship was accompanied by a growing interest in basic Jewish education. The European Holocaust and the establishment of Israel had created a new climate receptive to group belonging and the quest for Jewish knowledge. Enrollment in Jewish schools increased, owing particularly to the post-1945 "baby boom." The total Jewish school enrollment which numbered about 200,000 in 1936–37 reached 589,000 in 1962. It was estimated that in the 1950s more than 80% of Jewish children of elementary school age attended some Jewish educational institution.

Judged by standards of pupil enrollment, parental interest, and communal financial support—subsidies to Jewish education from Federations and Welfare Funds rose from half a million dollars in 1936 to six million dollars in 1967—Jewish education made considerable progress. But measured by total hours of instruction and scholastic attainments, the schools did not meet desirable educational standards, and the Jewish educational level of American Jewry remained superficial. Over half of the Jewish children receiving a Jewish education went to Sunday schools (generally attached to Reform congregations); perhaps one-third attended weekday congregational schools (usually at Conservative synagogues). A 1967 survey showed that 42% of the afternoon schools met only one day a week. Moreover, the largest percentage of pupils was in the first three to four grades, indicating that the average child received only three to four years of systematic schooling. Jewish education was also severely handicapped by a shortage of qualified teachers.

In the 1960s some interest was evidenced in an intensified educational program, with additional hours of instruction, revised curricula, high school departments, and summer camping and other informal educational programs. In 1969 Jewish educational camps of various ideologies—Hebrew or Yiddish speaking, under Orthodox, Conservative, or Reform sponsorship, or of general Jewish content—cared for almost 12,000 campers in closed environments which sought to create a total Jewish milieu of esthetic group-living experiences. Increased efforts have been made by almost every American Jewish body toward intensifying Jewish education and strengthening the connection between American Jews and Israel.

The Jewish day-schools which combined a regular public school

A class at Camp Morasha, operated by the community service division of the Rabbi Isaac Elchanan Theological Seminary.

curriculum with an intensive Jewish program increased strikingly in number. In 1935 there were 17 day-schools with an enrollment of 4,600. In 1948 the number had risen to 128 schools with over 18,000 pupils, and in 1970 approximately 80,000 children were enrolled in well over 200 day-schools, most of them under Orthodox auspices. There was a smaller expansion of yeshivah high schools and of schools for full-time study of Talmud.

As a concomitant of United States foreign policy in the 1950s and 1960s, Jewish chaplains in the armed forces assumed a growing responsibility for the education of children of Jewish servicemen stationed with their families far from civilian synagogues and Jewish schools.

CHURCH-STATE RELATIONS

The Jewish community continued to feel concern in the post-World War II era over problems of church-state relationships, especially in the field of education. It maintained its historic opposition to religious observances in governmental functions and particularly in the schools. This stand was put to the test over Catholic demands for government aid to their parochial school system. A series of Supreme Court decisions which permitted private schools to receive federal funds for school buses, lunches, and textbooks was generally regretted by the Jewish community, while decisions which barred school prayers and outside sectarian religious instruction within the schoolday framework (released time) as unconstitutional were widely applauded by Jews. This, in turn, aroused some anti-Semitic reactions. The passage of federal and state legislation in 1964 and 1965, providing limited aid for private schools, tended to quiet the issue. Orthodox Jewry which had relatively few of its children in the public schools opposed rigorous church-state separation in education, partly in hopes of securing public funds for its own hard-pressed day schools.

Since the ethnic and religious groups within the United States were to a large extent economically distinctive, and generally resided in well-defined neighborhoods, contact between them was quite limited, and was generally confined to such areas as trade unionism, popular entertainment, and sports.

Local disputes erupted between Jews and non-Jews from time to time, typically in predominantly older Christian suburbs to which a substantial number of Jews had moved. This was generally due to Jewish opposition to long-established Christmas observances in the public schools, and it frequently brought latent local group tensions to a head. While the American Jewish Congress took the most rigorous separationist position, the American Jewish Committee and other Jewish organizations adopted a policy of tacit acceptance of these observances while trying to prevent them from becoming too pronouncedly sectarian. In addition, several Jewish theologians wished to modify the traditional Jewish insistence on a strict separationist policy because of their conviction that the public school tended to inculcate secularism as a quasi-religion. Combined Christmas-Hanukkah observances were frequently a syncretistic "compromise." Most Jews in suburban towns preferred this tactic, particularly because they had to oppose Protestants as well as Catholics on this issue.

CATHOLIC-JEWISH DIALOGUE

The Nazi atrocities against the Jewish people had evoked widespread sympathy among leaders of the Catholic Church in the United States, and stimulated interest in specifically Catholic-Jewish interchanges. After World War II, however, the issue of the Catholic response to the Nazi Holocaust became a source of friction between the two religious groups. Jewish opinion was divided on the issue. Some emphasized Christian "indifference" to the annihilation of the Jews, and others focused on the considerable assistance extended to Jewish victims of the

Nazis by Catholic clerics and laymen in numerous countries. (A world spotlight was focused on the issues in the 1960s, by a German play accusing Pope Pius XII of "silence" in the face of Jewish annihilation.) The opposition of the Holy See to Israel's control over Jerusalem, and its call for the internationalization of the Holy City in 1947, as well as the Vatican's reluctance to recognize the State of Israel, did not improve relations between American Jews and Catholics.

Radical changes in Catholic-Jewish relations took place in the late 1950s and 1960s as a result of the accession of Pope John XXIII in 1958, and the Vatican II Ecumenical Council which he convened. The sweeping changes in the Roman Catholic Church inaugurated by the Council destroyed a powerful barrier to Catholic-Jewish rapprochement. These included a major attempt to rectify the ancient anti-Jewish attitude of the Church through excision of objectionable references from the Good Friday liturgy, and a denial of the collective responsibility of Jews in all ages for the crucifixion. For the first time in the history of conciliar declarations, Rome also expressly named and attacked anti-Semitism, and attempted to meet belated worldwide criticism of the passive or aloof attitude of Pope Pius XII during the European Holocaust.

The movement within the church to "exonerate" the Jews from the charge of "Deicide" and to formally recognize the theological legitimacy of Judaism was highly active in the United States, and stirred considerable Jewish participation and enthusiasm, particularly on the part

Abraham Joshua Heschel
with Cardinal Bea at
American Jewish Com-
mittee headquarters in
N.Y., April 1963.

of Jewish human-relations agencies. A period of Catholic-Jewish theological conversation and "dialogue" commenced, in which Roman Cardinal Bea and U.S. prelates were leaders. The most prominent Jewish spokesman was Rabbi Abraham J. Heschel, professor of Jewish ethics and mysticism at the Jewish Theological Seminary of America, and one of the most influential modern philosophers of religion in the United States.

However, the final document issued by Vatican II in 1965 was disappointing and Catholic (as well as Protestant) silence during the Arab military preparations against Israel in May 1967 was very disillusioning to American Jewry. Catholic-Jewish dialogue continued, but in a subdued key. Among the cooperative efforts between Jews and Catholics (and Protestants) is the attempt to remove anti-Semitic elements from church textbooks.

PROTESTANT-JEWISH DIALOGUE

In the aftermath of World War II, Protestantism was at great pains to condemn anti-Semitism and to express contrition for not having acted more strongly during the Nazi era. It was this mood of repentance that created substantial Protestant support in the late 1940s for Zionist efforts toward the creation of the State of Israel. Nonetheless, Protestants retained serious philosophical problems concerning the theological need to convert Jews, and the theological understanding of the right of the Jews to the Holy Land.

Protestant-Jewish bonds were strengthened by joint involvement in the civil rights movement and in the Vietnam debate in the 1950s and 1960s. Ties were forged between rabbis and ministers of all denominations; among the leading voices of American Protestantism, Paul Tillich and Reinhold Niebuhr evinced an abiding respect for Judaism.

Since 1950 there has been a growing tendency among the promoters of interfaith contacts to change the character of their interreligious relationships, and to translate such expressions as "good will" and "brotherhood" into an honest and fruitful dialogue adjusted to the requirements of a pluralistic society. Upon the initiative of interested Jews and Christians, interfaith dialogues have been held in academic and theological institutions, with important religious and intellectual personalities of both faiths taking part. A number of Jewish organizations, including the World Jewish Congress, the Anti-Defamation League of B'nai B'rith, and the American Jewish Committee, have created special departments for the advancement of interfaith activities. As a result of these numerous encounters, there has emerged a ramified literature on the question of dialogues in general, and on Jewish-Protestant relations in particular.

Within Orthodox Judaism, there are many reservations concerning the interfaith movement, which is considered unacceptable on principle. Other Jewish circles have also expressed their suspicions of these dialogues. Moreover, despite the extensive activity carried on by the promoters of the dialogues, the interfaith movement has succeeded in winning over to its cause only a limited elite among Protestants. This was no doubt one of the reasons for the crisis in Jewish-Protestant relations after the Six-Day War in 1967. The silence of the churches which preceded the war, and the subsequent unfriendly, even hostile, declarations of the Protestant leadership concerning Israel and her post-war policies was disillusioning, and indicated the limitations of the dialogue, as conducted previously. Protestant churches have shown evidence of an increasing hospitality to Arab anti-Israel propaganda, much of which has emanated from the Christian churches of the Arab world. Such material has often been careful to make a distinction between anti-Semitism, which is ruled out, and anti-Zionism and opposition to Israel, which is affirmed. Nonetheless, this distinction is not always maintained. In place of the old stereotype of the Jew as a weak and cringing figure, cursed by God for rejecting or killing Jesus, a new stereotype became prevalent in some Protestant circles, of the Jew as the arrogant and ruthless victor over the Arab.

There is a new awareness among American Jews that the significance of the "ecumenical age" can be overestimated. Recent Christian ecumenism did not do away with anti-Semitism. The increased friendship and understanding between Jews and Christians has involved the most modern and intellectual elements of the Western world; yet large parts of the Christian community have remained unaffected by these contacts.

It has also become evident that many Christians who participated in the interfaith dialogues, due to their ignorance of the true essence of Judaism as a synthesis of a people and a religion bound to the Land of Israel and to the city of Jerusalem, had no understanding of the way in which Diaspora Jews identified themselves with Israel. Those Jews and

Christians who, despite all these setbacks, have insisted on continuing the dialogue, have come to the conclusion that future dialogues must include a rethinking on the part of Christians of many theological doctrines, including the profound historical, religious, and liturgical meaning of the Land of Israel and of Jerusalem to the Jewish people.

NEGRO-JEWISH RELATIONS

The late 1960s was a period of major social tension in the United States as relations between American Negroes and the white population deteriorated progressively in the major northern urban centers. On a variety of levels, the American dream of peaceful integration of ethnic and religious groups was replaced by confrontation in the name of group identity and group interests. Since the American Jewish community, despite its increasing mobility, still remained essentially urban in nature, it found itself involved in these tensions that were not of its own making.

THE STRUGGLE FOR CIVIL RIGHTS

The acquisition of equal rights by American Negroes had long been a goal of legal and political action, as well as philanthropic endeavor, by Jews. Not only were such Jewish organizations as the American Jewish Committee and the American Jewish Congress early supporters of legislation and litigants in court to secure Negro rights, but individual Jews had long provided a large proportion of the activist manpower and funds for this struggle. Julius Rosenwald (1862–1932), the son of German Jewish immigrants who rose from clerk in a clothing store to president of Sears, Roebuck and Company and was active in general civic affairs as well as Jewish philanthropy, contributed substantially to the cause of the American Negro community. He underwrote the construction of YMCA buildings for Negroes in 25 cities, served for 20 years as a trustee of Tuskegee Institute, and gave several millions of dollars for the construction of rural schools and model urban housing for Negroes.

Louis Marshall, president of the American Jewish Committee and the foremost leader of the American Jewish community in the early decades of the 20th century, was a consistent champion of the Negro community and fought major legal battles on their behalf in addition to being active in the National Association for the Advancement of Colored People. (The N.A.A.C.P. had two Jewish presidents: Joel Elias Spingarn [1930–39], and his brother Arthur B. Spingarn [1940–66].)

BLACK MILITANCY

Soon after the 1954 Supreme Court decisions regarding the unconstitutionality of segregated school facilities, the objectives of the blacks in the United States altered significantly, and the vocal demand for equality became a more active effort to obtain social, economic, and political parity. This new thrust, which had its roots in the changed attitudes of the Korean War veterans who had served in the recently desegregated U.S. armed forces, became particularly significant for the Jewish community when, in the early 1960s, black students began an activist civil rights movement.

The civil rights movement attracted many young Jewish college students to its ranks. During the "civil rights summers" of the mid-1960s young Jews constituted, by some reports, as high as 50% of all the white student youths who went to the South to assist Negroes in their battle for voting privileges and equal treatment in public places. They worked with the Student Nonviolent Coordinating Committee (SNCC), the Congress of Racial Equality (CORE), and Martin Luther King's Southern Christian Leadership Conference (which also had a respectable

Civil rights march from Selma to Montgomery, Alabama, March 22–26, 1965. Abraham Joshua Heschel (with beard) is in the front row. To his right are Ralph Bunche, Martin Luther King, and Ralph D. Abernathy.

component of rabbis among its supporters). The passage of the Civil Rights Acts of 1964 and 1965, prohibiting racial segregation in all forms, was viewed by Jews with deep satisfaction. During this period, Jewish student involvement in the civil rights movement spread to the black ghettos in the northern states.

Jewish legal involvement in the cause of Negro civil liberties was particularly marked during the 1960s. Jack Greenberg of the Legal Defense Fund of the N.A.A.C.P., William Kunstler of the National Lawyers Guild, Carl Rachlin of the Congress of Racial Equality, and other individual Jewish lawyers participated heavily in helping the civil rights movement to handle its huge case load. Jewish legal involvement in the defense of Negro rights continued to play a significant role as a bond between the black and Jewish communities even as the relationship between them worsened in other areas.

After these victories, the break in the long-established Negro-Jewish alliance in the late 1960s came as a bitter shock to the Jewish community. The widening rift in relationships between the two groups was the result of developments in the inner dynamics of Negro life. Young Negroes were experiencing deep-rooted disenchantment with the white establishment. The civil rights legislation which had aroused hopes in the black community failed to receive the necessary funds in the U.S. Congress. The legislation remained more theoretical than of practical value and its passage had swept away the momentum of the civil rights movement. It was, in effect, a hollow victory.

The disillusioned black militants became more strident in their rhetoric and more alienated from white society. With the growth of Negro self-identity ("Black is beautiful"), some elements within the black community came to feel that Jewish figures were too prominent in what they preferred to regard as their own revolution. Black separatism intensified and Jews became increasingly unwelcome as front-line participants in the black civil rights organization.

Demographic patterns in many of the large cities created another source of friction between Negroes and Jews. In these urban areas the Negro community frequently moved into older Jewish sections of the inner city as the economic status of Jews enabled the latter to move to the suburbs. There was, however, a "holdover" of the older population in the form of storekeepers and landlords. These Jews (plus Jewish school teachers and social workers) were often the most visible white men and women in the life of blacks in the North. The wave of riots which swept northern Negro districts between 1964 and 1968 impelled the departure of most of the white (Jewish and non-Jewish) businessmen in the neighborhoods, and violently shook the delicate balance of urban peace.

ETHNIC BALANCE AND MERITOCRACY

The growing sense of black power expressed itself in proposals for new social policies that would provide opportunities for Negroes within the American society consonant with their proportion—about 10%—in the total population. Within the framework of an official policy of "affirmative action," minority groups—Negroes, Mexican-Americans, American Indians, and women—were to be afforded increased opportunities in civil service employment, in university teaching posts, and in acceptance to schools of higher learning. These proposals, while expressed as goals rather than as "positive quotas," stirred deep fears among American Jews that the economic and social gains of Negroes were to be made at Jewish expense, and that Jewish opportunities in higher education and professional employment would be reduced to make room for blacks. As the Jews were only 3% of the population, they would be seriously harmed if a system of proportional representation were applied in any field to which they had been disproportionately attracted. Elements in the Jewish community expressed the view that they had achieved their position in these areas through "meritocracy," rather than by pulling their ethnic weight.

These fears were given public expression in 1968, when New York City public school teachers, most of them Jews, went out on strike against the proposal of "school decentralization," which they interpreted as a move to ease them out or reduce their opportunities for promotion in order to advance Negroes and Puerto Ricans in the school system. Serious eruptions of anti-Semitism accompanied the strike; the Jewish community was disturbed when these expressions elicited no reaction from the Mayor, the Board of Education, or the white intellectuals and upper classes.

It would appear that, since Israel's victory in the Six-Day War, the taboo on expressing hostility to Jews has been weakened. There have probably been more unfriendly references to Jews in print and in public statements since 1967 than during the previous twenty years.

Although surveys indicated that anti-Semitism among the masses of American Negroes was no greater, and might be less, than that which existed among white Americans; and although moderate Negro leaders such as Bayard Rustin, A. Philip Randolph, and Roy Wilkins condemned and rejected black anti-Semitism, Jewish attitudes toward the blacks changed perceptibly. The possibility of continued group conflict posed a serious new problem to American Jewry. While the Jewish community recognized that the American political system has always acted as a brake on anti-Semitism, and that the civil position of Jews in the United States has never been fundamentally endangered, they also were aware that latent anti-Jewish stereotypes persisted among some groups in the United States. They recalled the lesson of Jewish history; that latent prejudice is translated into open discrimination whenever social conflict and tensions are severe, and they feared that in a time of social ferment, the American society might consider Jews to be expendable

JEWISH DEFENSE LEAGUE

The appearance of the Jewish Defense League was a visible manifestation of the fears of Jews who remained in the embattled urban areas of the North. Established in 1968 in Brooklyn, New York by a group of militant, mostly Orthodox youths, the J.D.L. initially served as a semi-vigilante unit seeking to protect neighborhood Jews from physical attacks. The J.D.L. derived its membership mainly from the urban work-

DAILY NEWS
NEW YORK'S PICTURE NEWSPAPER ®

Rabbi Meir Kahane: "I knew I had to take my stand."

Critics say the Jewish Defense League is a bunch of 'goons' and 'vigilantes.' JDL's founder, Rabbi Meir Kahane, says the group is only fighting anti-Semitism and trying to destroy the image of Jews as 'patsies.' He claims to speak for the grass-roots Jew with the battle cry...

'Never again!'

By MICHAEL POUSNER

Rabbi Meir Kahane of the Jewish Defense League at a protest rally for Soviet Jewry, 1971.

ing and lower-middle classes who felt that the established Jewish organizations with their prosperous suburban supporters were unconcerned about their plight and heedless of the rising anti-Semitism.

Later, the group grew into a quasi-political movement, using the slogan "Never again" (with reference to the Holocaust) to symbolize its philosophy of physical defense. In the contemporary style of "confrontation" and "direct action," it adopted a policy of "defense" of Soviet Jewry, Israel, and Jews in Arab countries, by forceful means and public demonstrations in various American cities. Its declared aim was to disrupt commercial and cultural exchanges and tourism between the United States and the U.S.S.R.

The Jewish Defense League achieved a high degree of publicity and also entered into sharp controversy with the organized American Jewish community. Its leader, Rabbi Meir Kahane, settled in Israel in 1970, where he sought to institute a program for the defense of Soviet Jews, and of disadvantaged sections of the Jewish community in Israel.

EXPANDING JEWISH CONCERNS

Toward the end of the 1960s the American Jewish community seemed stable. Population held to predictable rates; immigration was minimal and readily absorbed; demographic and occupational trends continued as they had from approximately 1950; Israel attracted warm political and financial support; and the institutions of the Jewish community were generally well financed and seemed capable of dealing with most of the problems on their agendas. Late in the 1960s, however, quite unanticipated matters and issues arose which stirred unusual interest and anxiety.

ISRAEL'S SIX-DAY WAR

The Middle East crisis of May 1967, which threatened Israel's existence, brought American Jewish concern for Israel to a peak. Some young volunteers left for Israel before war broke out on June 5, 1967; they staffed hospitals and assumed other civilian tasks that had been left untended by the total callup of Israel's manpower. However, American Jewish concern found its main outlet in unparalleled monetary contributions: 232 million dollars donated to the United Jewish Appeal, and 75 million dollars purchased in Israel bonds.

The Zionist movement, which had been dormant for almost 20 years, revived somewhat after 1967. Tourism and Jewish business investments in Israel both increased.

Commitment to the Zionist ideal was also evidenced through increasing American immigration to Israel. In the first $3\frac{1}{2}$ years of Israel's existence, out of a total of almost 700,000 immigrants, only 1,909 had been Americans. Until 1961 immigration from the United States had been less than 1.1% of the total number of new arrivals in Israel. Immediately following the Six-Day War, however, this figure rose dramatically; approximately 17,000 American Jews settled in Israel between July 1967 and the end of 1970. Estimates of future American Jewish migration to Israel were set at an average 10,000 a year.

Some of this migration to Israel reflected a growing disillusionment with the "American dream," a feeling that was also evident in circles other than the Jewish community. But Jews were particularly susceptible to this disillusionment, just because they were concentrated in the educational and occupational groups where it was felt most keenly.

The growing pessimism about the future of American-Jewish life was sometimes expressed in terms of the difficulties of raising children with Jewish commitments within a non-Jewish environment. Sometimes, the pessimism was focused on the fear that America was on the decline as a nation, and that it was also on the decline as a place where Jews would have a secure future.

Jews have had a deep and grateful feeling about America, but the new pessimism made inroads into this feeling. For a person to emigrate from America to some less problematic, more satisfying place was now thinkable. The problem of "dual loyalty" which had troubled the former generation of Jews in America, their need to prove that it was not anti-American to care about Israel or even to want to go and live there, was no longer of consequence. An element of reaction to growing anti-Semitism was also evident in the American Jewish community, although there was no major fear for the future of Jews in the United States.

On the whole, however, migration of American Jews from the United States to Israel was propelled less by the "push" of disappointment in some aspects of American life—the urban problems which weighed heavily on an overwhelmingly urban community; the surge of anti-Semitism and anti-Israelism; the well-publicized glorification of violence by some black militant demagogues and white followers; the sense of the impotence of efforts devoted to liberal causes—than by the "pull" of Israel, as a place where Jews could realize their Jewish identity in every aspect of their lives, and as a pioneering country which still retains the sense of purpose and cohesion that America seemed to have lost.

THE NEW LEFT

Hardly had the euphoria of Israel's victory over the serious Arab challenge to its existence subsided, when the "New Left," in shaky combination with black militant elements, vigorously espoused the Arab cause. Like the Soviet Union and Poland, the New Left often used the term "Zionist" as a synonym for Jew, in attempting to obscure the anti-Semitic character of its propaganda. The challenge of the New Left was more disturbing to the Jewish community because of the disproportionate participation of young Jews in the leadership of the movement.

This wave of left-wing radicalism which attracted many students in the United States (and in Western Europe), and achieved considerable prominence in the late 1960s, embraced various ideologies, from the Maoist interpretation of Marxism to outright anarchism. Until about 1966 the distinguishing characteristics of the New Left were skepticism toward the dogmas and ideology of the "Old Left" (e.g., classical Marxism), rejection of centralized control and emphasis on participatory democracy, and rejection of the central role of the working class in the drama of history. Instead, the deprived class was defined as students, the urban poor, and minorities—Blacks, Mexican-Americans, Puerto Ricans, American Indians, but not Jews.

The first phase of New Left history emphasized organizing deprived whites and blacks in Northern urban communities. The second phase concentrated on massive participation of students in the civil rights movement in the South, particularly in the summer of 1964, when two of the three volunteers civil rights workers who were killed in Mississippi were Jewish youths. The third phase, beginning in Berkeley University in the autumn of 1964, stressed rebellion on the campus, with particular emphasis on issues related to the Vietnam War. By the late 1960s the original characteristics of the New Left were quite blurred. Maoist rhetoric became strong, and violence was celebrated by many New Left elements.

In keeping with their tradition of participation in radical movements in the United States, Jews were active in the New Left, not among the founders, but in later phases of its history. Mark Rudd, Jerry Rubin, Abby Hoffman, and others achieved national reputation. Accurate statistics are not available, but several studies estimate that in the late 1960s one-third to one-half of the committed, identifiable radicals on the most activist campuses were Jewish. (But probably not more than 10 to 15% of all Jewish youth of college age was involved either in the "radical" or "hippie" counter-culture, although even this made them markedly visible within the groups.)

These young questioners and activists were found to come largely from families which were urban, well-educated, professional, and affluent, with a high degree of permissiveness, and which stressed democratic interpersonal relations, and values other than achievement—dominant characteristics of the urban, middle-class Jewish group.

Various theories have been suggested in explanation of this phenomenon. Since Jewish students in the 1960s were generally not deprived, and since anti-Semitism was then negligible, Jewish attraction to this radical movement could not be explained in these negative terms. One prominent theory pointed to the psychological and social characteristics of the Jewish middle-class family—rationalistic, child-centered, psychologically understanding—and argued that this produced children intolerant of rules and restrictions, and insistent on the rapid achievement of an ideal society.

As against many other radical movements in the past, the New Left did not (at least as far as the Jewish participants were concerned) involve any generation gap or break with parental values. It simply pushed these values further! This can be noted in the surprising fact that books by Jewish members of the New Left, Paul Cowan, *Making of an Un-American* (1970), and Michael Myerson, *These Are the Good Old Days* (1970), were dedicated to their parents.

After the Six-Day War in 1967, a crisis developed for many Jewish members of the New Left. The black militants, with whom they were allied on domestic issues, supported the Arabs and indulged in excessive rhetoric in denunciation of the Israelis. (The Black Panthers called Israelis "pigs," denounced "kosher nationalism" as "imperialism," etc.) In addition, the United States, which New Leftists opposed as the symbol of world capitalism and imperialism, provided arms to Israel and was itself the hated enemy of the Arabs, who allied themselves with the Third World and received the support of the Russian and Maoist branches of the Communist movement.

This crisis led some Jewish members of the New Left to dissociate themselves from some of its manifestations. The separation began as early as September 1967 when, at the Conference for a New Politics, organized by New Left elements in Chicago, blacks insisted on the passage of a resolution denouncing the "imperialist Zionist war" in the Middle East. Many Jewish leftists were angered by this resolution since it ran counter to both their Jewish emotions and the facts. Others, however, became virulent enemies of "Zionist imperialism."

JEWISH STUDENT ACTIVISM

Within such an atmosphere, many young Jews were pushed toward identification with the specific interests of the Jewish community and its own peculiar destiny. Some of the Jewish New Leftists who had a more positive attitude toward Judaism and the Jewish community began to organize small, distinctively Jewish, New Left organizations. Independent radical campus groups (e.g. the Radical Zionist Alliance) emerged throughout the United States to counter the New Left pro-Arab ideology from a Jewish point of view.

During the late 1960s, too, an autonomous "radical" Jewish student press emerged on campuses and in metropolitan areas in the United

Mastheads of contemporary
U.S. student organs.

States, with a common editorial philosophy that was critical of the established American Jewish community, politically leftist, yet pro-Israel. Its prime concerns were the establishment of a just and equitable peace in the Middle East, the plight of Soviet Jewry, and general problems of students and of society.

Increasingly, radical Jewish youth groups put pressure on established Jewish organizations to change their priorities, with particular emphasis on more money for Jewish education and a larger role for youth in the activities of the organized Jewish community.

CONCERN FOR SOVIET JEWRY

A major cause for agitation and protest among American Jews at the end of the 1960s was the anti-Semitic discrimination and the near-suppression of Jewish life in the Soviet Union, together with the Soviet regime's refusal to permit Jewish emigration.

The American Jewish Conference on Soviet Jewry, the Academic Com-

N.Y. demonstration against
Soviet exit fees for Jews,
October 1972.

mittee on Soviet Jewry, and the Student Struggle for Soviet Jewry organized the Jewish community in a series of public demonstrations
and mass meetings. Direct appeals to the President, and pressure exerted
by Jewish Congressmen and Senators, kept the problem of Soviet
Jewry in the forefront of United States international policy. During
the late 1960s and early '70s, the problem of the Soviet Jews was a frequent element in meetings held on the highest level between the leaders
of the American and Soviet peoples. In 1972 the imposition of a heavy
education tax on Jews wishing to emigrate from Russia aroused strong
negative reactions within the American Jewish community. Pressure
was brought to bear on Congress not to ratify a U.S.-U.S.S.R. trade
agreement unless this "ransom" demand was dropped.

SURVIVAL OR ASSIMILATION?

What do demographic projections foretell for the future of the American
Jewish community?

Numbering over six million in 1972, the Jewish population of the
United States is likely to continue to increase but slowly. This is a result
of a low birthrate which hovers close to the minimum needed for re-
placement; a rising deathrate reflecting the rise in the average age of the
Jewish population (in 1970, six years older on the average than the
general population); and possible larger losses from intermarriage. As
a result, the Jewish population will constitute an increasingly smaller
proportion of the total population.

Jews will become more dispersed throughout the country as higher
education, changing occupations, lower levels of self-employment, and

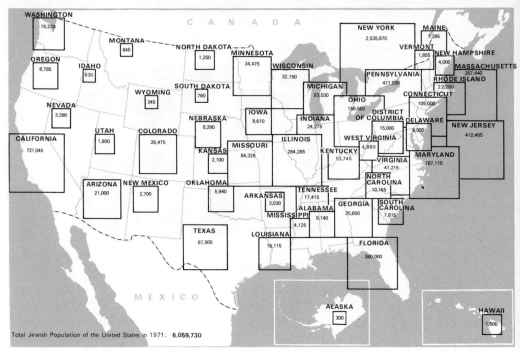

Jewish population of the U.S., 1971.

reduced discrimination outside the urban areas lead to greater geographic mobility. Nonetheless, it is likely that distinct areas of Jewish residential concentration will remain, due to survivalist motivations.

Increasing acculturation will continue, as a function of greater geographic dispersion, of the high percentage of third- and fourth-generation Jews, and of the narrowing of socio-economic differentials as the educational, occupational, and income levels of the general population rise to meet those of the Jews. All this will lead to increasing similarity between Jews and non-Jews on the behavioral level.

Nonetheless, there will probably be little *conscious* assimilation, as there has been none since World War II. As American society became more open to Jews than any country had ever been throughout the entire history of the diaspora, the need for a willed assimilation was removed. American Jews were able to relax in their Jewishness. It was neither necessary to play down the fact of one's Jewishness, nor to make the defensive choice of highlighting it, because the open society was making no assimilatory demands in the name of an American ideology.

However, in the face of the evaporation of specifically Jewish patterns of living, and the increased acceptance of marrying outside the Jewish group, pointing to a watering down of the sense of Jewish identity, some Jewish community leaders have expressed their fears for the survival of American Jewry as a community.

On the other hand, the horror of the Holocaust and the creation of the State of Israel have given many Jews new self-awareness and led them to reaffirm their Jewish identity. Counter tendencies to the pattern of ethnic attrition have been apparent in the educational-survivalist emphasis of the organized community, and in the living patterns of several small groups within American Jewry. Some of the Orthodox Jews, and the ḥasidic elements which settled in the United States after World War II, have been ghettoizing themselves both geographically and psychologically, and appear to be successful in maintaining their religious loyalties and practices, and in increasing their numbers through a high birthrate.

A larger group of American Jews have become more "ethnic" in recent years as a result of a sense of insecurity which derived from increasing urban/racial conflicts, a declining faith in the old assumptions about assimilation into the American society, and continuing concern for Israel's security. They have stressed day school education, emotional ties with Israel, and the cultural aspects of Jewish religious practices.

As noted above, the question of assimilation vs. survival was also posed in an ideological fashion by the new tensions between Jews and Negroes, and by the increasing influence of the New Left. Young Jews saw their inherited Jewish tradition challenged as being bourgeois and oppressively colonial; many of them have found it difficult to accept this position and have been forced to analyze their Jewish identity and loyalties more actively.

Finally, just as Negro emphasis on black identity has had a "fall-out" among other ethnic groups within the United States, it has resulted in Jews emphasizing and appreciating the positive aspects of belonging to a distinctive sub-group within the larger society in which the dominant, conformist, Christian tradition is under attack. In recent years, the American pluralistic society has been emphasizing the value of individual group identity. As a result, young Jews express less of the defensiveness or apologetics regarding their unique loyalty to the Jewish community in the United States and throughout the world than did their parents who were uneasy about their status as an immigrant group.

Within the broad perspective of the history of Jewish assimilation, however, it is far from certain, even with the revived energy for Jewish particularist living in the United States, that the current process of unwitting assimilation can be seriously checked. The basic factor affecting assimilation continues to be the family's length of residence in a non-ghetto, middle class, Western-educated milieu within a relatively open society. Any prolonged period of living within such a relatively open society has produced substantial numbers of almost completely assimilated Jews.

The immediate result of these opposing trends is an increasing polarization within the Jewish community. Ultimately some Jews will quietly disappear into various forms of secularism; others will more consciously affirm their Jewish character through increasing identification with an Orthodox religious tradition and/or increasing association with Israel. The large majority of American Jews, however, have not yet found an answer to the problem of how to continue to live permanently both within the mainstream of American life, and within a Jewish community of their own. Their Jewish identity is strong in times of crisis, but slowly evaporates when not challenged by repeated reappearances of anti-Semitism or anti-Israel actions. Thus the question of survival or assimilation may be posed in the broadest terms: how long can a value system survive which is not embodied in an institution or institutions devoted *exclusively* to the perpetuation of these values?

BIBLIOGRAPHY

BIBLIOGRAPHIES: A. S. W. Rosenbach, *An American Jewish Bibliography . . . until 1850* (1926: American Jewish Historical Society Publications, 30), supp. by (American Jewish Archives) *Jewish Americana* (1954).

M. Rischin, *Inventory of American Jewish History* (1954).

GENERAL WORKS: O. Handlin, *Adventure in Freedom* (1954).

T. Friedman and R. Gordis (eds.), *Jewish Life in America* (1955).

R. Learsi, *The Jews in America* (1954).

A. J. Karp (ed.), *The Jewish Experience in America,* 5 vols. (1969).

H. U. Ribalow, *Autobiographies of American Jews* (1965).

S. W. Baron, *Steeled by Adversity; Essays and Addresses on American Jewish Life* (1971).

M. Davis and I. S. Meyer (eds.), *The Writing of American Jewish History* (1957).

N. Glazer, *American Judaism* (1957).

N. Glazer and D. P. Moynihan, *Beyond the Melting Pot* (1963).

M. U. Schappes, *A Documentary History of the Jews in the United States 1654–1875* (rev. ed., 1952); idem, *A Pictorial History of the Jews in the U.S.* (1958).

UNTIL 1865: J. R. Marcus, *Colonial American Jew,* 3 vols. (1971); idem, *Memoirs of American Jews 1775–1865,* 3 vols. (1955–56).

S. F. Chyet, *Aaron Lopez* (1971); idem, *Lopez of Newport* (1970).

S. W. Baron and J. L. Blau, *The Jews of the United States 1790–1840: A Documentary History,* 3 vols. (1963).

P. S. Foner, *Jews in American History 1654–1865* (1945).

L. M. Friedman, *Early American Jews* (1934).

A. L. Lebeson, *Jewish Pioneers in America, 1492–1848* (1931).

B. W. Korn, *American Jewry and the Civil War* (1951).

B. A. Elzas, *Jews of South Carolina* (1905).

A. V. Goodman, *American Overture: Jewish Rights in Colonial Times* (1947).

H. B. Grinstein, *Rise of the Jewish Community of New York 1654–1860* (1945).

E. Wolf and M. Whiteman, *History of the Jews of Philadelphia from Colonial Times to the Age of Jackson* (1957).

B. W. Korn, *Early Jews of New Orleans* (1969).

SERIAL PUBLICATIONS: *The American Jewish Year Book* (1899–   ; index to 1899–1949 vols. by E. Solis-Cohen, 1967).
The standard periodicals are the *Publications of the American Jewish Historical Society* and the *American Jewish Archives* (1948–   ).

IMMIGRATION AND HISTORY FROM 1865: M. Wischnitzer, *To Dwell in Safety: The Story of Jewish Migration since 1880* (1949).
S. Joseph, *Jewish Immigration to the United States 1881–1910* (1914).
G. Kisch, *In Search of Freedom: American Jews from Czechoslovakia* (1949).
C. S. Bernheimer (ed.), *The Russian Jew in the United States* (1905 = E. J. James (ed.), *The Immigrant Jew in America*).
J. L. Teller, *Strangers and Natives* (1967).
D. F. Fleming and B. Bailyn, *The Intellectual Migration: Europe and America 1930–1960* (1968).
J. Brandes, *Immigrants to Freedom* (1971).
L. Fermi, *Illustrious Immigrants: The Intellectual Migration from Europe, 1930–41* (1968).

SOCIOLOGY: I. Graeber and S. H. Britt (eds.), *Jews in a Gentile World* (1942).
M. Sklare (ed.), *The Jews: Social Patterns of an American Group* (1958); idem et al., *The Lakeville Studies: A Study of Group Survival in the Open Society,* 2 vols. (1967); idem, *America's Jews* (1971).
A. I. Gordon, *Jews in Suburbia* (1959); idem, *Intermarriage; Interfaith, Interracial, Interethnic* (1964).
B. Sherman, *The Jew Within American Society* (1960).
O. I. Janowsky, *The American Jew: A Composite Portrait* (1942); idem, *The American Jew: A Reappraisal* (1964).
L. A. Berman, *Jews and Intermarriage* (1968).
J. Zeitlin, *Disciples of the Wise: the Religious and Social Opinions of American Rabbis* (1947).
L. Wirth, *The Ghetto* (1956²).
W. Herberg, *Protestant-Catholic-Jew* (1960).
M. S. Chertoff (ed.), *The New Left and the Jews* (1971).
C. H. Stember et al., *Jews in the Mind of America* (1966).
C. S. Liebman, *The Ambivalent American Jew* (1973).
J. N. Porter and P. Dreier (eds.), *Jewish Radicalism: A Selected Anthology* (1973).

POLITICS, DIPLOMACY AND ZIONISM: F. E. Manuel, *The Realities of American-Palestine Relations* (1949).
J. C. Hurewitz, *The Struggle for Palestine* (1950); idem, *Middle East Dilem-*

mas—*The Background of United States Policy* (1953); idem, *Diplomacy in the Near and Middle East—A Documentary Record* (1956).

N. Safran, *The United States and Israel* (1969).

J. B. Schechtman, *The United States and the Jewish State Movement . . .* (1960).

H. Finer, *Dulles over Suez . . .* (1964).

I. S. Meyer, (ed.), *Early History of Zionism in America* (1958).

S. Halperin, *The Political World of American Zionism* (1961).

C. Adler and A. M. Margalith, *With Firmness in the Right: American Diplomatic Action Affecting Jews 1840–1945* (1946).

H. L. Feingold, *The Politics of Rescue* (1970).

L. H. Fuchs, *Political Behaviour of American Jews* (1956).

M. Feinstein, *American Zionism 1884–1908* (1965).

A Friesel, *Ha-Tenu'ah ha-Ziyyonit be-Arzot ha-Berit ba-Shanim 1897–1914* (1970), includes a comprehensive bibliography.

S. Udin (ed.), *Fifty Years of American Zionism 1897–1947; A Documentary Record* (1947).

Y. Shapiro, *Leadership of the American Zionist Organization 1897–1930* (1971).

S. S. Wise, *Challenging Years* (1949).

C. Reznikoff (ed.), *Louis Marshall, Champion of Liberty,* 2 vols. (1957).

M. Rosenstock, *Louis Marshall, Defender of Jewish Rights* (1965).

B. Halpern, *The American Jew, Zionist Analysis* (1956).

GROUP RELATIONS AND ANTI-SEMITISM: R. Glanz, *The Jew in the Old American Folklore* (1961); idem, *Jew and Mormon* (1963); idem, *Jew and Irish* (1966).

O. Handlin, *Danger in Discord: Origins of Anti-Semitism in the U.S.* (1964).

H. Broun and G. Britt, *Christians Only* (1931).

B. R. Epstein and A. Forster, *"Some of My Best Friends . . . "* (1962).

C. Y. Glock and R. Stark, *Christian Beliefs and Anti-Semitism* (1966).

C. McWilliams, *A Mask for Privilege: Anti-Semitism in America* (1948).

G. J. Selznick and S. Steinberg, *The Tenacity of Prejudice: Anti-Semitism in Contemporary America* (1969).

C. H. Stember, *Jews in the Mind of America* (1966).

D. S. Strong, *Organized Anti-Semitism in America: The Rise of Group Prejudice during the Decade 1930–40* (1941).

M. Tumin, *Inventory and Appraisal of Research on American Anti-Semitism* (1961).

E. Lipman and A. Vorspan, *A Tale of Ten Cities* (1962).

L. Dinnerstein (ed.), *Antisemitism in the United States* (1971).

J. E. Mayer, *Jewish-Gentile Courtships* (1961).

B. Ringer, *The Edge of Friendliness: A Study of Jewish-Gentile Relations* (1967).

L. Harris and B. E. Swanson, *Black-Jewish Relations in New York City* (1970).

B. Halpern, *Jews and Blacks* (1971).

ECONOMIC ACTIVITY AND LABOR MOVEMENT: M. Epstein, *Jewish Labor in the U.S.A.* (1950).

I. Knox, *Jewish Labor Movements in America* (1958).

E. Tcherikower et al., *Geshikhte fun der Yidisher Arbeter Bavegung in der Fareynikte Shtatn,* 2 vols. (1943); idem and A. Antonovsky, *The Early Jewish Labor Movement in the United States* (1961).

J. S. Hertz, *Di Yidishe Sotsyalistishe Bavegung in Amerike* (1954).

EDUCATION: J. Pilch et al., *History of Jewish Education in America* (1966).

L. P. Gartner, *Jewish Education in the United States* (1969).

A. M. Dushkin and U. Z. Engelman, *Jewish Education in the U.S.* (1969).

A. I. Schiff, *The Jewish Day School of America* (1966).

PHILANTHROPY: R. Morris and I. Freund, *Trends and Issues in Jewish Social Welfare in the United States 1899–1952* (1966).

H. L. Lurie, *A Heritage Affirmed: The Jewish Federation Movement in America* (1961).

B. D. Bogen, *Jewish Philanthropy* (1917).

O. Janowsky, *The JWB Survey* (1948).

The Golden Heritage (1969).

R. Morris and M. Freund (eds.), *Trends and Issues in Jewish Social Welfare in the United States, 1899–1952* (1966).

RELIGION AND INSTITUTIONAL HISTORY: M. Davis, *The Emergence of Conservative Judaism* (1943).

M. Sklare, *Conservative Judaism* (1955).

A. Rothkoff, *Bernard Revel; Builder of American Jewish Orthodoxy* (1972).

M. Waxman (ed.), *Tradition and Change: the Development of Conservative Judaism* (1958).

D. Philipson, *Reform Movement in Judaism* (1967³).

N. W. Cohen, *Not Free to Desist: A History of the American Jewish Committee 1906–1966* (1972).

E. E. Grusd, *B'nai B'rith* (1966).

M. M. Kaplan, *The Future of the American Jew* (1948); idem, *Judaism as a Civilization* (1934).

J. Neusner, *American Judaism* (1972).

B. M. Edidin, *Jewish Community Life in America* (1947).

M. J. Karpf, *Jewish Community Organization in the United States* (1938).

CULTURE: R. Glanz, *Jews in Relation to the Cultural Milieu of the Germans in Americana* (1971).

L. W. Schwartz (ed.), *The Menorah Treasury* (1964).

J. Kabakoff, *Pioneers of American Hebrew Literature* (Hebrew, 1966).

M. Davis, *Beit Yisrael ba-Amerikah* (1970).

The Jewish People Past and Present, 2 and 4 (1946, 1955).

J. A. Fishman, *Yiddish in America* (1965).

R. Wischnitzer, *Synagogue Architecture in the United States* (1955).

A. Kampf, *Contemporary Synagogue Art, Developments in the United States, 1945–65* (1966).

LITERATURE: R. Alter, *After the Tradition* (1969).

S. Liptzin, *Jew in American Literature* (1966).

I. Malin, *Jews and Americans* (1965); idem and I. Stark, *Breakthrough . . .*(1964).

L. A. Fiedler, *Jew in the American Novel* (1959).

M. Hindus, *The Old East Side* (1969).

PRESS: M. Soltes, *Yiddish Press—An Americanizing Agency* (1950).

J. Shatzky (ed.), *Zaml-Bukh tsu der Geshikhte fun der Yidisher Prese in Amerike* (1934), esp. 13–21.

MILITARY SERVICE: J. Fredman and L. Falk, *Jews in American Wars* (1963).
A. L. Lebeson, *Pilgrim People* (1950).

MEDICINE: S. R. Kagan, *The Jewish Contribution to Medicine in America* (1934); idem, *American Jewish Physicians of Note* (1942).

NEW YORK CITY: *1654–1870.* D. and T. de Sola Pool, *An Old Faith in the New World* (1955).

D. de Sola Pool, *Portraits Etched in Stone* (1953).

L. Hershkowitz, *Wills of Early New York Jews 1704–1799* (1967); idem and I. S. Meyer, *Lee Max Friedman Collection of American Jewish Colonial Correspondence: Letters of the Franks Family 1733–1748* (1968).

H. B. Grinstein, *Rise of the Jewish Community of New York 1654–1860* (1945).

J. R. Marcus, *The Jews of N.Y., New England and Canada, 1649–1794* (1951).

R. Ernst, *Immigrant Life in New York City 1825–1863* (1949).

1870–1920. M. Rischin, *The Promised City: New York's Jews 1870–1914* (1962).

A. A. Goren, *New York Jews and the Quest for Community: The Kehillah Experiment, 1908–1922* (1970).

H. Hapgood, *The Spirit of the Ghetto: Studies of the Jewish Quarter of N.Y.* (1902).

A. Cahan, *Bleter fun Mayn Lebn,* 5 vols. (1926–31; partial trans. by L. Stein, Eng. 1970).

R. Sanders, *The Downtown Jews: Portraits of an Immigrant Generation* (1969); idem, *The Grandees* (1971).

M. Dubofsky, *When Workers Organize: New York City in the Progressive Era* (1968).

N. H. Winter, *Jewish Education in a Pluralistic Society: Samson Benderly and Jewish Education in the United States* (1966).

T. Levitan, *Islands of Compassion: A History of the Jewish Hospitals of New York* (1964).

A. Schoener (ed.), *Portal to America: The Lower East Side 1879–1925* (1967).

1920–1970. A. Nevins, *Herbert H. Lehman and His Era* (1963).

A. F. Landesman, *Brownsville: The Birth, Development, and Passing of a Jewish Community in New York* (1969).

P. S. Foner, *The Fur and Leather Workers Union: A Story of Dramatic Struggles and Achievements* (1950).

S. Poll, *The Hasidic Community of Williamsburg; A Study of Sociology of Religion* (1962).

S. P. Abelow, *History of Brooklyn Jewry* (1937).

OTHER AREAS: M. Axelrod, et al., *Community Survey for Long Range Planning, A Study of the Jewish Population of Greater Boston* (1967).

A. Ehrenfield, *Chronicle of Boston Jewry from the Colonial Settlement to 1900* (1963).

A. Mann (ed.), *Growth and Achievement: Temple Israel, 1854–1954* (1954).

B. M. Solomon, *Pioneers in Service* (1956).

A. A. Wieder, *Early Jewish Community of Boston's North End* (1962).

B. A. Elzas, *The Jews of South Carolina . . .* (1905).

I. M. Fein, *The Making of an American Jewish Community: The History of Baltimore Jewry from 1773 to 1920* (1971).

E. Wolf and M. Whiteman, *History of the Jews of Philadelphia* (1957).

S. Adler and T. E. Connolly, *From Ararat to Suburbia: The History of the Jewish Community of Buffalo* (1960).

P. P. Bregstone, *Chicago and Its Jews* (1933).

S. Rawidowicz (ed.), *Chicago Pinkas* (1952).

M. A. Gutstein, *A Priceless Heritage: the Epic Growth of Nineteenth Century Chicago Jewry* (1953).

M. Vorspan and L. P. Gartner, *History of the Jews of Los Angeles* (1970).

F. Massarik, *Report on the Jewish Population of Los Angeles* (1953).

R. Glantz, *Jews of California from the Discovery of Gold until 1880* (1960).

N. B. Stern, *California Jewish History; a Descriptive Bibliography* (1967).

L. J. Swichkow and L. P. Gartner, *The History of the Jews of Milwaukee* (1963).

W. G. Plaut, *The Jews in Minnesota* (1959).

I. Lehrman and J. Rappaport, *Jewish Community of Miami Beach* (1956).

B. Postal and L. Koppman, *Jewish Tourist's Guide to the U.S.* (1954).

INDEX

293